Leisure, Recreation and Events in Hospitality and Tourism

Leisure, Recreation and Events in Hospitality and Tourism

Dr. Pralay Ganguly
Principal
GNIHM – JIS Group

TECHSAR™
NEW DELHI

Published and Printed by
Techsar Pvt. Ltd.
4435-36/7, Ansari Road, Daryaganj
New Delhi-110 002 (India)
E-mail: tech_info@techsarworld.com
Website: www.techsarworld.com

ISBN: 978-81-968876-2-9

Reprint 2025

Preface

Hospitality over the years has cropped up to be a revolutionizing occurrence and it is emerging as a catalyst of the developmental process due to economic benefits and employment generation as well as to ensure several socio-cultural advancements.

Hospitality and tourism industry is delivering various services to its stakeholders with new concepts considering the leisure, luxury and comfort of guests by which organizations' manipulate their resources to deliver such programmes, facilities and services to stakeholders and the general community. Again, in broader context, hospitality all over the world is expanding day by day and there is perfect mélange on traditional and modern concept, all luxuries nowadays become necessity as per the leisure, recreation and relaxation is concerned. This book touches all the modern concepts adopted by world hospitality in terms of managing leisure, recreation and events.

In India, since the inception of hospitality and tourism education some of the aspects of leisure and events were taught at the undergraduate level in the initial years but in recent years it is a subject in hospitality and tourism management, both in UG & PG level programmes with some changes in order to keep up with recent developments in the field of leisure, recreation and event management.

Various wings of hospitality industry offering guests wide ranges of recreational facilities in and around for the comfort and pleasure. Festivals, conferences, ceremonies, weddings, formal parties, concerts, or conventions are large-scale events which involve studying the brand, identifying its target audience, devising the event concept, and coordinating the technical aspects before launching the event. In modern era the development of technology and considering the sustainability aspects the event management is more challenging for hospitality professionals and the same has been elaborated well for hospitality professionals in this book.

Leisure and recreation is part of the hospitality and tourism study where various forms of active and passive recreations in which tourists are engaged with during their leisure time or during travel. There are not many comprehensive Indian texts available on leisure, recreation, and events, so I decided to develop one book which will meet the needs of the students pursuing hospitality and tourism programmes both degree and diploma. Not only for students, this book will also be helpful for all stakeholders related to hospitality and for common people for their pleasure, recreation, stress-free life and healthy and comfortable living.

Pralay Ganguly

Contents

Chapter **1**

Leisure & Recreation

Objectives

After going through this chapter the reader will be able to:

- Understand the idea of leisure and recreation.
- Look on historical perspectives and sociology in leisure and sports.
- Develop idea on recreation and community involvement.
- Understand some emerging trends in leisure and recreation.

1.1 INTRODUCTION

Recreation is a leisure activity that is essential for human biology and psychology. It is done for enjoyment, amusement, or pleasure. Leisure is all about how a person spends time during free time, may engage in some recreational activities also. Ethnic leisure services require direct contact with the host. Various games are one of the important activities and have many physical and psychological advantages. There are various types of active and passive recreational activities where people involve themselves as per their preference. There are various indoor and outdoor sports/recreational activities where people engage themselves during their leisure time.

1.2 LEISURE AND RECREATION

Leisure

During the days of ancient Greece, leisure served chiefly to identify the upper classes in society, since it was regarded as their unique possession. Economists and sociologists have defined leisure simply as non-work time.

It is not directed to work, work responsibility, or burden. It is all about freedom and meeting one's personal needs. The unobligated time view of leisure sees it essentially as time that is free from work or travel, study or social involvement based on work.

Recreation

"The process of giving new life to something," is known as recreation. The recreation process leads to happiness. Pleasure or relaxing activity to restore or refresh or to get energy for work, etc. all about restoration for health. Recreation is morally sound and mentally/physically upbuilding. Recreation is not a matter of motion but rather emotions.

Recreation provides personal well-being. There are various kinds of indoor and outdoor recreational activities like gardens, open spaces, playgrounds (outdoor), and art, music, dance, etc. (indoor).

Generally, government agencies, voluntary organizations, and private organizations provide recreation services.

The objectives of recreation are:

- To enhance social development.
- To improve fitness and health.
- To reduce stress.

Some factors like time, age, gender, marital status, education, etc., affect the choice of recreation. Some everyday recreational activities are:

- Shopping
- Gaming
- Water sports
- Adventure sports
- Health and wellness
- Timeshare
- Theatre
- Various forms of entertainment

Social media plays an important role these days for leisure and recreation branding and recreation marketing is a form of service.

Meaning of Recreation

- Process of giving new life to something.
- Lifestyle and development of a positive attitude.
- Allows people to have fun and rejuvenate.

Active recreation and passive recreation

Recreational activities which do not involve much physical activities are known as passive recreation, for, example, reading books, watching motives, etc., but in active recreation physical activities are involved like cycling, running, climbing, etc.

Meaning of Leisure

Leisure is all about relaxation and recreational activities during unobligated time and is basically stress-free in nature.

- A time free from work.
- It can be used as rest or recreation.
- It can involve extensive activity or no activity.

Fig. 1.1 Leisure and recreation

Stakeholders in leisure management are community, guests, and local service providers. Leisure staffs who work for no pay are known as volunteer staff.

Fig. 1.2 Active and passive recreation

1.3 GOVERNMENT AND PRIVATE SPONSORED RECREATION

The involvement of people in public and private sponsored recreational activities are increasing day by day where the motto of the organizations is to make sure a meaningful and stress-free engagement.

National Parks

- Park used for conservation purposes.
- Parks having natural beauty.
- Animal watch.
- Spending leisure time.

Commercial Recreation

Theme parks (immerse visitors in another time and place with themed architectures, landscaping, personnel, and rides.

Private clubs are organizations that people join for social, recreational, professional, or fraternal reasons. Club members typically pay an initiation fee to join the club. There are types of clubs, such as:

Country clubs are located outside the city (horseback riding, golf, pool, hotel, restaurant)

City clubs are located within the city catering to business people.

Professional clubs have profeeionals as members such as doctors, dentists, lawyers, etc.

Military clubs have uniformed officers

Yacht club are for sailing and other aquatic activities

Athletic club have people engaged in sports

University club have alumni

Fraternal club are for camaraderie, charitable causes, etc.

Non-commercial Recreation

- Voluntary organization (boy scouts, YMCA).
- Campus recreation (sports competition, leisure-oriented activities).
- Employee recreation (gym, team building, company outing).

1.4 OUTDOOR RECREATION

Outdoor activity refers to recreation engaged outdoors, most commonly in natural settings. The activities themselves—such as fishing, hunting, backpacking, and horseback riding—characteristically determine where they are practised.

They are pursued variously for enjoyment, exercise, challenge, camaraderie, spiritual renewal, and an opportunity to be in nature. Though the activities are inherently lean to sports they nonetheless do not all demand that a participant be an athlete, and competition generally is less stressed than in individual or team sports organized into opposing squads in pursuit of a trophy or championship. When the activity involves exceptional excitement, physical challenge, or risk, it is sometimes referred to as "adventure recreation" or "adventure training", rather than an extreme sport.

Other traditional examples of outdoor recreational activities include hiking, camping, mountaineering, cycling, canoeing, caving, kayaking, rafting, rock climbing, running, sailing, skiing, sky diving and surfing. As new pursuits, often hybrids of prior ones, emerge, they gain their own identities, such as coasteering, canyoning, fast packing, and blogging.

Outdoor recreation

Outdoor								
Mountain	**Forest**	**Beach and sea**	**Freshwater**	**Air**	**Desert**	**Family**	**Cultural and historical**	**Exercise**
Trekking	Wildlife safari	Snorkelling	Angling/fly fishing	Gliding	Safari	Amusement park	Indigenous culture	Outdoor fitness
Rock climbing	Camping	Scuba diving	Canyoning	Ballooning	Safari park			Outdoor gym
Mountain biking	Birdwatching	Parasailing	Whitewater rafting	Flying	Sandboarding	Off-leash dog park	Metal detecting	Fitness trail
Motorbike expedition	Elephant safari	Sport fishing	Water sports	Paramotoring		Bungee jumping	Benchmarking (geolocating)	Plogging
Skiing	Tree climbing	Windsurfing	Kayaking	Skydiving		Picnicking	Sightseeing	
Snowboarding	Adventure park	Water sports	Canoeing	Paragliding		Corn maze		
Snowshoeing	Mushroom hunting	Clam digging	Waterskiing	Wingsuit flying		Plogging		
Ice climbing	Orienteering	Running	Jet Skiing			Ziplining		
Mountain climbing	ATV riding	Swimming	Stand Up Paddleboarding					
Canyoning	Paintball	Plogging	Raft building					
Skyrunning	Hunting	Coasteering						
Abseiling	Horseback riding							
Backpacking	Plogging							
Plogging	Caving (Potholing)							
Mountaineering	Airsoft							
Caving (Potholing)								

1.5 NATURE AND SCOPE OF LEISURE AND RECREATION (GLOBAL/LOCAL CONTEXT)

Recreation refers to all those activities that people choose to do to refresh their bodies and minds and make their leisure time more interesting and enjoyable. Examples of recreation activities are walking, swimming, meditation, reading, playing games and dancing. RV refers as recreational vehicle.

Leisure refers to the free time that people can spend away from their everyday responsibilities (e.g., work, and domestic tasks) to rest, relax and enjoy life. It is during leisure time that people participate in recreation and sporting activities.

Sport refers to any type of organized physical activity, e.g., soccer, rugby, football, basketball, and athletics.

1.6 RECREATION, LEISURE IN THE COMMUNITY

In many low-income countries where people work every day just to survive, the concept of leisure time is not always well understood and nor is it a priority. Indeed, many activities that are considered recreational in high-income countries are considered a means of livelihood in low-income countries, e.g., fishing and handicrafts.

In most communities the type of recreational and sporting activities people participate in are determined by age, gender, local context (e.g. rural vs. urban) and socioeconomic status. For example, children in poor communities are likely to play games using natural materials, such as sticks or stones or using discarded manufactured items like tyres and rope. Leisure time is also likely to be based around cultural activities, such as traditional dances, storytelling, religious festivals, and events, and visiting entertainment troupes.

Ensuring that local community stakeholders are supportive of the recreational event is important becauseit helps to attract local participants. In many poor and rural communities there are no designated places for people to spend their leisure time, such as community centres and sports stadiums, so it is common for people to gather in places of worship, tea shops, houses, and open spaces.

Communities in low-income countries often have pressing priorities and limited budgets. As a result, the development of formal recreation and sports activities/programmes is usually dependent on donors. It is important that external funding is carefully managed to ensure that the programmes/activities are appropriate to the local context.

1.6.1 Benefits of Participation

Participation in recreation and sports activities can have many benefits for both the individual and community. These include:

- **Health promotion and disease prevention:** Recreation and sports activities are an enjoyable and effective way to improve health and well-being; they can relieve stress, increase fitness, improve physical and mental health, and prevent the development of chronic diseases, such as heart disease.

- **Skills development:** Physical and social skills are some of the many skills that can be developed through participation in recreation and sports activities.
- **Awareness raising, reduction of stigma and social inclusion:** Recreation and sports activities are a powerful, low-cost means to foster greater inclusion of people with disabilities; they bring people of all ages and abilities together for enjoyment, and provide people with disabilities the opportunity to demonstrate their strengths and abilities, and promote a positive image of disability.
- **International peace and development:** Sport is a universal language that can be used as a powerful tool to promote peace, tolerance and understanding by bringing people together across boundaries, cultures, and religions.
- **Empowerment:** Recreation and sports empower people with disabilities by positively influencing their self-confidence and self-esteem.

1.7 GEOGRAPHY LEISURE AND RECREATION IN ASIAN PERSPECTIVE

The history of recreation begins with the Greeks. The region known as Southeast Asia is a World War II era political construction, an 'externally imposed geographic convenience' (Reid, 1993) broadly understood (both geographically and culturally) as the area between China and India. Currently consisting of 11 countries that span 4.5 million km^2, Southeast Asia is conventionally divided into maritime Southeast Asia (Brunei, Indonesia, Philippines, Singapore, Timor-Leste) and mainland Southeast Asia (Cambodia, Laos, Malaysia, Myanmar, Thailand, Vietnam).

The method of studying the past should be in the continuity of present. Complementarity means places differ from each other. And the way refers to the medium of travel used by transport modes. While there is a tremendous amount of ethnic, religious, and linguistic diversity within the region, countries in Southeast Asia share several indigenous cultural practices and pre-colonial trade relationships, as well as (except for Thailand) the common experience of European colonization. The region also shares common post-independence struggles, nation-building efforts, and similar aspirations to 'develop' and 'modernize'. Finally, ramai (Indonesian word meaning 'crowded, noisy, fun') aesthetics in music, visual arts, and even food are shared throughout the region, and sufficient other resemblances and continuities exist for contemporary scholars to argue for the utility of viewing the entire region as a single area.

Leisure practices in pre-colonial Southeast Asia were often intertwined with religious and spiritual beliefs, which were syncretic blends of several religions and shaped by local beliefs and practices. Festivals and important dates on religious calendars were important ways in which religion and leisure came together through games, performances, markets, and the creation and consumption of seasonal delicacies. Centuries after the populations of Indonesia and Malaysia had converted to Islam, the great Hindu epics continue to feature prominently in music, performing arts, and material arts.

Straddling the equator, Southeast Asia is a tropical region, with exceptions in highland areas. Approximately 70% of Southeast Asians live leisure activities in Southeast Asia, from pre-colonial period along the coast, and the sea is an important venue for leisure activities for many. Swimming, free diving for shellfish, and fishing are common leisure pursuits. Sailboat races are common throughout coastal Southeast Asia and are linked to a variety of related leisure activities, including boat building, boat decoration, and sailing. Such maritime leisure pursuits are linked to food production but are considered enjoyable, in much the same way that hunters enjoy the thrill of the hunt, while contributing to the family kitchen.

Many male leisure activities in Southeast Asia developed from the skill set of a warrior or soldier. While in parts of Southeast Asia royal figures in the pre-colonial era funded extravagant spectacles of war elephants fighting for the entertainment of their subjects and to show off their resources to stage such displays, many war-inspired leisure activities were not directed or funded by the state. The arts of sword fighting, archery, and other forms of combat were popular male pastimes. Various types of martial arts developed in Southeast Asia over the centuries, with varying levels of influence from China and India.

East Malaysian state of Sabah, men spend hours together at the general store, talking and playing cards and snooker. Women and children come to the store (the only store in the village), but they make purchases and then leave. In some leisure activities such as dance, puppet show, and music performances and some games, men and women would mix as members of the audience, but many activities, as discussed above, were dominated by men. In their more limited leisure time, women engaged in pragmatic activities in the domestic sphere, including embroidery, batik, and other handicrafts. For example, the Hmong women from the mountains of Vietnam sew 'story quilts', colourful embroidery on black fabric showing images from daily life like farming and gathering water.

These activities were also high-class dependent, as the elite had different social expectations and norms for how women would spend their time than the lower classes. Various leisure activities have emerged in Southeast Asia that challenge conventional gender norms. For example, while cockfighting (and its attendant gambling) is considered an archetypal male hobby in the region, many men engage in more gentle leisure activities involving birds, including bird breeding, pigeon racing, and birdcage decorating. In Thailand, Malaysia, Singapore, Indonesia, and Brunei, the folk sport dove-cooing contests have experienced resurgence among men.

Colonial policy and, more recently, industrialization had significant impacts on leisure activities in urban Southeast Asia, shifting leisure times from a seasonal structure based on agriculture to one based around industrial, 'modern' production schedules. As such, the impact on leisure has been far more pronounced for urbanites than for rural, agriculture-dominated societies. In the late colonial era, formal and standardized leisure activities became more common as European team sports were introduced more widely, including soccer, badminton, volleyball, basketball, and others, as part of 'muscular Christianity' and the 'Western civilizing mission'. The Japanese occupation (1942–45) of parts of Southeast Asia also introduced new activities and a higher degree of standardization, including group calisthenics and civilian marching troops.

The Japanese occupiers also attempted to standardize some Southeast Asian leisure activities that were maintained after independence, including pencak silat, an indigenous martial art, as a way to instill a sense of Asian pride and foster a sense of solidarity with the Japanese. This politicization of leisure activities continued after independence and became an important strategy for nation-building in the former colonies.

1.8 EXPLORING A CAREER IN RECREATION ADMINISTRATION

A focus on promoting exercise, leisure, and healthy living in an enjoyable setting suggests a major in 'recreation administration'. This field entails overseeing the daily operations of recreational facilities, programme creation, and administrative tasks. Students receive instructions in diverse areas like business, finance, marketing, management, indoor/outdoor recreation, and specialized tracks such as 'golf course operation' and 'grounds management'. Organizational, interpersonal, and communication skills are essential, given the multifaceted responsibilities, while hands-on experience through internships prepares graduates for fulfilling roles.

Positive Impacts of Recreation Facilities

Recreation facilities play a pivotal role in enhancing the quality of life and community health. Thoughtful planning, guided by data and outcomes, shapes the development of these facilities, catering to diverse needs. Benefits span personal, communal, and economic realms, ranging from improved well-being and reduced crime to enhanced cultural understanding and economic growth. The symbiotic relationship between recreation and thriving communities is evident, enriching the social fabric and economic prosperity.

1.9 RECREATION SERVICES

1.9.1 Recreational Activities can be Classified into Several Categories

1. Physical activities including games, sports, exercises, and gymnastics.
2. Mental and intellectual activities involving discussions, debates, reading, writing, and arts.
3. Self-defence and self-discipline activities, such as NCC, NSS, and scouting.
4. Cultural and social activities encompassing drama, music, dancing, community service, and festivals.
5. Art and craft activities including painting, carpentry, tailoring, and embroidery.
6. Outdoor activities such as outings, camping, and mountaineering.
7. Hobbies like stamp collecting, photography, and picnics.

1.9.2 Recreation should Possess Key Characteristics for Optimal Benefits

1. Leisure time engaged during free time, separate from working hours.
2. Enjoyable activities should be enjoyable, not tedious.

3. Satisfaction should offer immediate satisfaction.
4. Voluntary choice of activity should be personal, devoid of compulsion.
5. Constructive activities should contribute positively to physical, mental, and emotional well-being.
6. Socially scceptable recreation should align with societal norms and individual well-being.

Understanding the classification and characteristics provides insight into the multifaceted world of recreation services and their significance in individual and community well-being.

1.10 LEISURE TRENDS: LEISURE AND RECREATION

Indoor recreation facilities are provided by several providers in the region including municipalities, school districts, community associations and the private sector.

Some common indoor facilities

Arenas, fieldhouses, indoor fitness, community halls/banquet rooms, meeting rooms, gymnasiums, indoor pools, indoor playgrounds, curling ice, indoor sports, facilities in school, indoor recreation/ social engagement.

The one constant is change. For any leisure business this applies to the evolution of technology and games, as well as the changing expectations and interests of your guests.

Seven important leisure trends are as follows.

1. Sustainable and educational activities and attractions

Innovation, sustainability, and education are important. More and more venues choose to switch to a greener business model. Sustainable leisure and recreation can be anything from zero emission e-karting to taking advantage of the popularity of vegetarian dishes.

Educational activities are also becoming more popular. For example, escape rooms can be used and regardedas educational activities because they challenge a guests' problem-solving skills.

Since it is a thrilling game, it will not even feel like you are learning something. The educational aspect adds extra depth to your activity and transforms it into a total involvement. This is exactly what guests are looking at present.

2. Personalized experiences through mass customization

In every area of life, people expect to have a choice. In what they buy, how they decorate their house, the design of their shoes, and also in what they engaged.

Instead of 1 standard experience for the many, the leisure world now shifts to many customized experiences for many different individuals.

Acknowledging that different people enjoy different itineraries, leisure businesses are now focusing on creating personalized experiences through scheduling and smart booking systems, like Briq's booking software.

When guests can customize their own experience in a leisure venue's web shop, they are more likely to book more activities and spend more time (and money) at a venue than when they can only select single activity.

3. Staycations are a lasting leisure industry trend

A staycation is all about a complete experience of an entire day of fun without travelling for too long. It is a popular option for those who want to get away without having to consider travel restrictions or quarantine rules.

To meet this demand, venues are starting to offer custom activities packages that last the whole day. These packages include different activities as well as food and beverages.

4. AI in support of leisure to enable contactless payments and social distancing

Many leisure centres quickly switched to contactless payments instead of cash, they also had to look for ways to ensure social distancing through Artificial Intelligence (AI) solutions that ensure capacity management.

AI has become an integral part of the guest experiences of many activity and attraction parks. From digital stop lines to soft marketing promotion and machine operated scheduling andcapacity control management, the leisure world will only continue to expand its use of AI to support frictionless fun in the present times.

5. Technological ecosystem through integration partnerships

The times that one big system covered all a leisure centre's tech needs most definitely belong to the past. Nowadays, to deliver the best products and services possible, software companies specialize in one particular area and team up with other specialists to offer the best overall solutions.

That is why it isa key to choose software providers that offer many combinations to set up the best tech stack possible for your leisure venue. For example, Briq Bookings takes care of online booking and scheduling, and teams up with many other software providers that are experts in their fields.

6. Machine learning and data insights are key to better experiences

With all that tech comes data. And with data the leisure industry no longer guess what is best for their guests. With machine learning and all accumulated data combined guest experiences can now perfectly be tailored to required needs of demography and wishes.

What data you need to gather and how you can turn that data into tangible results for your leisure venue. With booking systems like Briq's, that is integrated with specific data gathering tools such as search engine, Google Analytics, you automatically gain all the insights you need to create better deals and to better promote your experience.

7. Gamification, augmented reality, and immersive experiences

Gamification is the addition of video game elements to (physical) activities. The goal is to create a playful and, in most cases, even an immersive experience, in which the guest is pulled into another world. This is definitely the case for activities and attractions that are (fully) digital such as virtual reality games.

For example, race enterimpressive offers professional moving 4D race simulators with which you experience what it is like to race in your favourite supercar. Speed lovers from all over the country come to try the exclusive racing experience. And, of course, to improve their racing skills. Gamification does not have to be fully digital. Many traditional leisure activities are also being gamified.

PROGRESS CHECK

1. What is the difference between leisure and recreation?
2. How did leisure serve as a distinguishing factor in ancient Greek society?
3. How is recreation beneficial for personal well-being?
4. What are some examples of outdoor recreational activities?
5. How do government agencies, voluntary organizations, and private organizations contribute to recreation services?
6. What is the main objective of engaging in recreational activities?
7. How is recreation different from work in terms of its focus?
8. What are passive recreational activities?

MULTIPLE-CHOICE QUESTIONS

1. The method of studying the past should be
   (a) In the continuity of present (b) In isolation of past
   (c) In relation of future (d) In the light of legends
2. Recreation is engaged upon during
   (a) Work time (b) Leisure time (c) Committed time (d) Sleep time
3. ____________ tourism is the time when an individual can do what he likes to refresh
   (a) International tourism (b) Leisure tourism
   (c) Recreational tourism (d) None
4. ____________ leisure services require direct contact with the host
   (a) Rural (b) Ethnic (c) Environmental (d) None
5. Stakeholders in leisure management is considered as
   (a) Community (b) Guest
   (c) Local service provider (d) All the above
6. Leisure staff who work for no pay are called
   (a) Casual staff (b) volunteer staff (c) Part-time staff (d) Leisure staff
7. Ensuring that local community stakeholders are supportive of the recreational event is important because
   (a) It helps the smooth running of the event
   (b) It is a legal requirement
   (c) It helps to attract local participants
   (d) It discourages participants from outside of the community
8. Which of the following should be developed first
   (a) The leisure and recreation marketing strategy
   (b) Sponsorship proposals for the event

(c) Leisure and recreation plan

(d) A work breakdown structure

9. Which of the following plays an important role these days for leisure and recreation branding

(a) Community (b) Social media (c) Visual styling (d) Return gifts

10. Recreation marketing is

(a) A product (b) Tangible (c) A service (d) A good

11. Complementarity means

(a) Places differ from each other (b) Places are the same as each other

(c) Places are an exact distance apart (d) Places on the same line of latitude

12. The way refers to

(a) The medium of travel used by transport modes

(b) The carrying unit

(c) Motive power

(d) The terminal

13. An RV is a

(a) Recreational vehicle (b) Road vehicle

(c) Recreational van (d) Recreational vesper

14. Disneyland only European theme park is in which country?

(a) France (b) Spain (c) Portugal (d) Italy

15. All the followings are the example of active recreational activities, except

(a) Hiking (b) Cross country skiing

(c) Ping pong (d) Canoeing

16. Which of the following is true?

(a) Jogging, swimming, and cycling are primarily anaerobic in nature

(b) Aerobic activity must be done continuously to obtain health benefits

(c) Lifestyle physical activity is usually aerobic

(d) Jogging is just as safe as walking

17. Which sport would promote the most cardiovascular fitness?

(a) Football (b) Wrestling (c) Baseball (d) Soccer

18. Recreation is defined as:

(a) "The process of giving new life to something."

(b) Bonding with Mother Nature

(c) Any process that is non-work related

(d) Socializing with two or more people

19. The recreation process leads to

(a) Having fun (b) Happiness (c) Saving money (d) Socializing

20. Which of the following includes commercial recreation?

(a) Clubs (b) Attractions (c) Theme parks (d) All of these

21. The executive workout includes a
    (a) Jacuzzi (b) Massage (c) Nap (d) All of these
22. Which of the following is not a trend in recreation and leisure?
    (a) A decrease in travel and tourism
    (b) Increase in fitness activities
    (c) Learning opportunities for the elderly
    (d) Increase in personal leisure time
23. Duties of leisure management staffs is considered a
    (a) Job specification (b) Job description (c) Job responsibility (d) None of these
24. An example of special leisure activity is
    (a) Sports event (b) Cultural event (c) Pleasure event (d) Yoga
25. The objective of recreation includes
    (a) To improve health (b) To enhance social development
    (c) To reduce stress (d) All of the above
26. Camping is related with
    (a) Mountain recreation (b) Forest recreation
    (c) Freshwater recreation (d) Desert recreation
27. Trekking is an example of
    (a) Forest recreation (b) Mountain recreation
    (c) Desert recreation (d) Cultural recreation
28. The ________ view of leisure sees it essentially as time that is free from work or travel, study or social involvement based on work
    (a) Activity (b) Unobligated time
    (c) State of freedom (d) Spiritual expression
29. The history of recreation begins with the
    (a) Greeks (b) Romans
    (c) Native Americans (d) Paleolithic/Neolithic periods

Answers to Multiple-Choice Questions

1. (a)	2. (b)	3. (b)	4. (b)	5. (d)	6. (b)	7. (c)	8. (c)
9. (b)	10. (c)	11. (a)	12. (a)	13. (a)	14. (a)	15. (c)	16. (c)
17. (d)	18. (a)	19. (b)	20. (d)	21. (d)	22. (a)	23. (b)	24. (d)
25. (d)	26. (b)	27. (b)	28. (b)	29. (a)			

Chapter 2

Play-sports and Leisure

Objectives

After going through this chapter the reader will be able to:
- Understand the idea of leisure and recreation.
- Look on historical perspectives and sociology in leisure and sports.
- Develop idea on various theories, forms of sports and leisure.
- Understand importance and benefits of sports.

2.1 INTRODUCTION

Leisure management is how organizations manipulate their resources to deliver leisure programmes, facilities and services to stakeholders and the general community. A leisure study is a social science that studies leisure activities. It includes sport and recreation, tourism, and other activities such as yoga, the arts, and nature conservation.

The Sport Studies minor provides students with a broad cultural perspective on sport, leisure, and recreation, cultivating the necessary skills, knowledge, and attitudes for effective leadership in the field. The programme studies sport as a phenomenon of the human condition. Sport has long been a major part of our culture and many others, and remains a significant part of society - and students will get to study its place within these realms. They will also explore the significance of sport and its relationship to other social institutions such as the media, economy, family, education, and politics.

2.2 HISTORICAL PERSPECTIVES

In ancient Greece, play was considered an essential part of childhood education. It was seen to develop positive character traits such as honour, loyalty, and beauty. Play was also thought to teach children the values of Greek society.

However, as the Catholic Church gained dominance in Western Europe, play came to be seen as a social threat. The body was thought to detract from more spiritual or work-oriented values, and so every effort was made to curb the pleasurable forms of play that had been popular in the Greek and Roman eras.

Gradually, however, educators and philosophers such as Froebel, Rousseau, and Schiller came to the defence of play as an important aspect of childhood education. For example, Froebel wrote of play as the highest expression of human development in childhood.

Bodily movement that is produced by the contraction of skeletal muscle and that substantially increases energy expenditure is known as physical activity. Lifestyle activities are the base of physical activity pyramid. Walking considered a real lifetime activity. Play is the purest, most spiritual activity of man at this stage. A child who plays thoroughly with self-active determination, perseveringly until physical fatigue forbids, will surely be a thorough, determined man, capable of self-sacrifice for the promotion of the welfare of himself and others.

2.3 SOCIOLOGY OF SPORTS

Sociology of sport is a sub-discipline of sociology that focuses on sports as social phenomena. It is an area of study concerned with the relationship between sociology and sports, and also various socio-cultural structures, patterns, and organizations or groups involved in sports. This area of study discusses the positive impact sports have on individual people and society economically, financially, and socially. Sociology of sport attempts to view the actions and behaviour of sports teams and their players through the eyes of a sociologist.

The emergence of the sociology of sport (though not the name itself) dates from the end of the 19th century, when first social psychological experiments dealing with group effects of competition and pace-making took place.

There are many perspectives through which sports can be viewed. Therefore, very often some binary divisions are stressed, and many sports sociologists have shown that those divisions can create constructs within the ideologies of gender and affect the relationships between genders, as well as advocate or challenge social and racial class structures. Some of these binary divisions include: professional vs. amateur, mass vs. top-level, active vs. passive/spectator, men vs. women, and sports vs. play.

Sports need to involve sociology for several reasons. Problems such as injuries in the world of sports are inevitable. When there are recurring problems within a sports team or individual, you need to understand how to manage and deal with it in the safest, and most efficient way possible. Sociology can help explain reasons for which the problem occurred, which can be highly beneficial. In this way it can function as a constructively critical friend, rather than you being in the shadows. In most pre-modern societies, the gender role for females and males in sports was enforced at a young age. The sociology that formed surrounding sports enforced the idea that sports were too masculine for women and were encouraged to play non-competitive games while men competed. One of the initial purposes of sports and games was to prepare young children for adulthood. Another purpose of organized sports and games is to teach life values and good morals through practice, teamwork, discipline, and much more. The separation between the roles of men and women in a society of sports is expressed through media and gender identity.

Today, most sports sociologists adhere to at least one of the four fundamental theories that define the relationship between sports and society: structural functionalism, social conflict, feminism, and symbolic interactionism. Theories attempt to explain why groups of people elect to perform certain actions and how societies, or teams, react or change in a certain way. Structural functionalism views society, or the world of sports, as a complex, but interconnected system, where each part works together as a functional whole.

2.4 THEORIES OF PLAY

Theories of play are frameworks or perspectives that aim to explain the significance, functions, and developmental aspects of play in human life. Play is a complex and multifaceted behaviour that occurs across cultures, age groups, and species. It serves various purposes, including cognitive, social, emotional, and physical development. Over the years, researchers and scholars have proposed different theories to better understand the nature and importance of play. Here are some of the prominent theories of play.

1. **Surplus energy theory:** This early theory, proposed by Herbert Spencer, suggests that play is a way to discharge excess energy in individuals. According to this perspective, play serves to release pent-up energy and helps maintain physical and mental balance.
2. **Instinct theory:** Building upon Spencer's theory, the instinct theory posits that play is a manifestation of instinctual behaviours in animals and humans. Play activities are believed to be connected to survival instincts, practice for future life roles, and the development of necessary skills.
3. **Psychoanalytic theory:** Sigmund Freud introduced the concept of play as a means for children to work through their unconscious conflicts and desires. Play, especially in children, serves as a safe space where they can express and process their emotions, fears, and wishes.
4. **Cognitive development theories:** Jean Piaget and Lev Vygotsky are notable figures in this category. Piaget's theory suggests that play is integral to children's cognitive development, helping them learn about the world and develop problem-solving skills through exploration and interaction. Vygotsky's sociocultural theory emphasizes the role of play in social and cognitive development, with an emphasis on the importance of social interactions and collaborative play.
5. **Functional play theory:** This theory, proposed by Mildred Parten, categorizes play into different types based on the child's developmental stage and the functions of play. These categories include solitary play, parallel play, associative play, and cooperative play. Each stage serves a distinct purpose in a child's social development.
6. **Psycho-social play theory:** Erik Erikson, known for his stages of psychosocial development, suggested that play is an essential medium for children to explore and resolve conflicts related to their identity, social roles, and relationships.
7. **Evolutionary play theory:** This the orysuggests that play acts to practise and learn behaviours needed for survival. This theory looks at play from an evolutionary perspective, proposing that play behaviours have evolved as adaptive strategies to

enhance survival skills, social bonding, and the development of cognitive and physical abilities.

8. **Neuroscientific theories:** Recent advancements in neuroscience have led to the exploration of the neurological underpinnings of play. Researchers are studying how play affects brain development, neural plasticity, and the formation of connections between brain regions.
9. **Cultural play theory:** This theory recognizes the influence of cultural and societal factors on the types and functions of play. Different cultures have distinct play patterns that reflect their values, beliefs, and traditions.
10. **Flow theory:** Proposed by Mihaly Csikszentmihalyi, this theory emphasizes the concept of "flow", where individuals engage in activities, including play, that are intrinsically rewarding and immersive. Play can lead to a state of flow, where people are fully engaged and derive joy from the activity itself.

These theories provide various perspectives for understanding the complexities of play. It is important to note that no single theory can comprehensively explain all aspects of play, as play is a multifaceted phenomenon with influences from biological, psychological, social, and cultural factors.

2.4.1 Early Classical Theories of Play

Early classical theories of play have laid the foundation for understanding the significance and purpose of play in human development and society. These theories emerged in the late 19th and early 20th centuries and have influenced our understanding of play's role in learning, socialization, and psychological well-being. Some notable early classical theories of play include:

1. **Surplus energy theory (Herbert Spencer):** Herbert Spencer proposed the surplus energy theory, suggesting that play was a result of excess energy that needed to be expended. According to this theory, play allowed individuals to release pent-up energy and maintain physical and mental balance. This theory focused primarily on the physiological aspects of play and its role in maintaining equilibrium.
2. **Pre-exercise theory (Karl Groos):** Karl Groos believed that play served as a form of practice for survival skills needed in adulthood. He proposed the pre-exercise theory, which posited that play provided young animals, including humans, with an opportunity to develop and refine essential skills, such as hunting, gathering, and social interactions. This theory emphasized the adaptive and evolutionary aspects of play.
3. **Recapitulation theory (G. Stanley Hall):** G. Stanley Hall's recapitulation theory drew parallels between the development of the individual and the evolutionary history of the species. He suggested that play allowed children to relive and practise activities that were crucial for human survival in ancient times. Hall believed that play reenacted ancestral behaviours, helping children to adapt to their environment and acquire necessary skills.
4. **Catharsis theory (Sigmund Freud):** Sigmund Freud introduced the catharsis theory, which proposed that play provided an outlet for children to express their unconscious

desires and emotions in a safe and symbolic manner. Through play, children could work through unresolved conflicts and anxieties. This theory laid the groundwork for understanding the therapeutic aspects of play in psychological development.

5. **Sociocultural theory (Lev Vygotsky):** Lev Vygotsky's socio-cultural theory emphasized the role of social interactions and cultural context in shaping cognitive development. He believed that play was a crucial zone of proximal development, where children could engage in activities that were slightly beyond their current level of competence with the guidance of more knowledgeable individuals. Play, according to Vygotsky, served as a means of learning and internalizing cultural norms and values.

These early classical theories collectively contributed to our understanding of play as a complex phenomenon with multifaceted roles in human development. While some of these theories have evolved and been refined over time, they continue to influence contemporary research on play and its impact on various aspects of human life.

2.4.2 Current Theories of Play

As of my last knowledge update in September 2021, there were several prominent theories of play that have been discussed and studied by researchers in the fields of psychology, education, and child development. Keep in mind that there might have been further developments or newer theories introduced since then. Here are a few of the well-known theories of play:

1. **Piaget's cognitive development theory:** Jean Piaget, a Swiss psychologist, proposed that play is a crucial part of a child's cognitive development. Play is important for memorization of facts. He identified different stages of play, such as sensorimotor play (infancy), symbolic play (early childhood), and games with rules (middle childhood). According to Piaget, play helps children to learn and explore their environment, experiment with ideas, and develop cognitive skills.
2. **Vygotsky's sociocultural theory:** Lev Vygotsky emphasized the role of social interaction in cognitive development. This theory is all about social interaction and cultural context. He believed that play is a zone where children can advance their cognitive abilities by interacting with more knowledgeable individuals (peers or adults) and increase imaginative thinking. Play, in this context, serves as a means through which children internalize cultural values, practices, and knowledge.
3. **Erikson's psychosocial theory:** Erik Erikson proposed that play contributes to the development of a sense of identity and a person's psychosocial well-being. Play provides children with opportunities to explore different roles, solve conflicts, and develop a sense of competence, identity, and self-esteem.
4. **Parten's stages of play:** Mildred Parten, a researcher in child development, categorized play into different stages based on the level of social interaction involved. These stages include solitary play (playing alone), parallel play (playing alongside others but not interacting), associative play (informal interaction with peers), and cooperative play (organized play with shared goals).

5. **Sutton-Smith's play theory:** Brian Sutton-Smith proposed a comprehensive theory of play that viewed play as a multifaceted activity that encompasses various forms, including competitive, imaginative, and exploratory play. His theory highlights the complexity of play and its connection to human evolution, culture, and development.
6. **Neuroscientific perspectives:** More recent theories incorporate neuroscientific insights to understand the neurological underpinnings of play. These theories explore how play affects brain development, emotional regulation, and social bonding. Flow of play introduced by Mihaly Csikszentmihalyi.
7. **Functional play theories:** Some theories focus on the functional aspects of play, suggesting that play serves essential functions such as skill development, stress reduction, social bonding, and preparation for adult roles. As per Friedrich Froebel play helps to develop fine motor skills. As per Sigmund Freud play helps to develop emotion.

Remember that theories are subject to evolution as new research emerges and our understanding of human development deepens.

2.4.3 Stages of Children's Development

Children's development can be broadly categorized into several stages, each characterized by distinct physical, cognitive, emotional, and social changes. While the specifics can vary among individuals, here are three commonly recognized stages of children's development:

1. **Early childhood (infancy and toddlerhood):**
   - **Infancy (0-2 years):** During this stage, infants experience rapid physical growth and development. They learn to control their body movements, develop their senses, and start forming attachments to caregivers. Motor skills, like rolling over, crawling, and eventually walking, are milestones achieved during this period. Language development begins with cooing, babbling, and eventually saying their first words.
   - **Toddlerhood (2-3 years):** Toddlers become more independent and assertive during this stage. They develop greater control over their motor skills, enabling them to explore their environment more actively. Language acquisition expands rapidly, and they begin to form more complex sentences. Emotional outbursts and the beginning of social interactions with peers are characteristic of this stage.
2. **Middle childhood (preschool and elementary years)**
   - **Preschool (3-6 years):** This period is marked by continued language development, imaginative play, and increased social interaction. Children develop greater self-control and the ability to follow rules. Cognitive skills, such as counting, recognizing shapes, and understanding basic concepts, develop rapidly. They also start developing friendships and learn about sharing and cooperation.
   - **Elementary school age (6-12 years):** Cognitive and academic development become more prominent during this stage. Children refine their motor skills,

engage in more structured learning, and develop a better understanding of cause-and-effect relationships. They become more aware of social norms, rules, and the feelings of others, leading to more complex social interactions and friendships.

3. **Adolescence**
   - **Early adolescence (11-14 years):** This stage is characterized by rapid physical growth and changes associated with puberty. Cognitive abilities, such as abstract thinking, develop further. Adolescents begin to explore their identity, establish a sense of self, and form deeper relationships outside the family. Emotional intensity and mood swings are common as they navigate the challenges of transitioning from childhood to adulthood.
   - **Late adolescence (15-18 years):** Adolescents continue to develop emotionally, socially, and cognitively. They gain a greater understanding of their strengths and interests, leading to more defined goals for the future. Critical thinking, problem-solving, and decision-making skills improve. Peer relationships and social activities play a significant role in shaping their identity.

These stages are general guidelines and can overlap or vary depending on the individual child's experiences and environment. It is important to remember that every child is unique, and their development may not adhere precisely to these stages.

2.4.4 Parten's Classification of Play

Parten's classification of play is a well-known framework in developmental psychology that categorizes different types of play based on the social interaction and participation of children. It was proposed by Mildred Parten in the 1930s and has since become a foundational concept in the study of child development. The classification scheme outlines various stages of play, each representing a different level of social engagement and complexity.

Mildred Parten's classification of play is a theoretical framework that provides insights into the evolving nature of children's play as they grow and develop. This classification categorizes play into six distinct stages, progressing from solitary play to more complex and cooperative forms of interaction.

1. **Unoccupied play:** The first stage, unoccupied play, involves seemingly random movements or actions without a specific goal. Children may engage in activities like pacing, twirling their hair, or fiddling with objects. This type of play is often observed in infants and toddlers who are exploring their surroundings and developing motor skills. Unoccupied play does not involve interactions with other children and is more about individual exploration.
2. **Solitary play:** Solitary play involves a child engaging in activities independently, without interaction or cooperation with peers. During this stage, a child might play with toys, engage in imaginative play, or focus on a task without seeking input or engagement from others. Solitary play is common among young children who are still developing social skills and may be content playing alone.

3. **Onlooker play:** In onlooker play, a child observes and watches other children play, but does not actively participate in the activities. This type of play allows the child to learn by observing and imitating others, contributing to the development of social understanding and skills. Onlooker play can be a transitional stage as children begin to show interest in the play of their peers but are not yet fully engaged in interactive play.
4. **Parallel play:** Parallel play is characterized by children playing side by side with similar toys or engaging in similar activities, but without significant interaction or collaboration. Children at this stage are more aware of their peers and may occasionally imitate each other, but their primary focus remains on their own play. Parallel play is often seen in toddlers and young pre-schoolers who are exploring their environment while still developing the ability to share and cooperate.
5. **Associative play:** Associative play involves more interaction and sharing of materials between children. Although each child may engage in their own activity, there is a level of verbal communication and sharing of ideas. Children may exchange toys, comment on each other's activities, and engage in casual conversations. This stage marks a significant shift towards cooperative interactions and the development of basic social skills.
6. **Cooperative play:** Cooperative play is the most advanced stage in Parten's classification. It involves children collaborating and working together in organized activities with shared goals. This type of play requires negotiation, communication, and division of roles. Children engage in complex games, role-playing scenarios, and team-based activities. Cooperative play fosters the development of advanced social skills, problem-solving abilities, and a deeper understanding of group dynamics.

Parten's classification of play provides a valuable framework for understanding the social development of children through their play activities. The classification starts from solitary, non-social play and progresses to complex cooperative interactions. It highlights the importance of play in children's cognitive, emotional, and social growth, and it has been widely influential in both research and educational settings.

2.5 RECENT DESCRIPTIONS OF SPORTS AND LEISURE

Recent descriptions of leisure commonly include references to the presence of choice or, alternatively, the absence of compulsion; the presence of intrinsic rather than extrinsic motivations, and the absence of internal or external constraints on carrying individual preferences into action. These elements are, in turn, often bundled together under the broad and therefore imprecise label of freedom. Most research of this sort in the U.S. has, however, concentrated on individual choices and preferences, and has thus neglected important historical, socio-cultural influences affecting the structure and content of individual action, not least during leisure. These issues will recur throughout the following survey, which begins with a look at two individuals whose theories of leisure are most widely recognized.

Play is a vital part of human development and has been studied by psychologists and educators since the early 20th century. Play can be seen as a form of self-expression, a social necessity, and a way to learn and develop skills. Play helps children to develop their imagination, creativity, and problem-solving skills. It also helps them to learn how to interact with others and to develop social skills. Roger Caillois identified four major types of play: agon (competition), alea (chance), mimicry (imitation), and ilinx (vertigo).

- Agon is competitive play, such as sports or games.
- Alea is chance-based play, such as gambling or lottery.
- Mimicry is imitative play, such as pretending to be a superhero or an animal.
- Ilinx is dizzying or vertiginous play, such as spinning around or riding a roller coaster.

All four types of play are important for human development. Agon helps children to learn how to compete and deal with winning and losing. Alea helps children to learn about chance and probability. Mimicry helps children to learn about different roles and identities. Ilinx helps children to experience the thrill of risk-taking and excitement.

Alea includes games of chance—those games or contests over whose outcome the contestant has no control; winning is the result of fate rather than the skill of the player. Games of dice, roulette, and baccarat, as well as lotteries, are examples of alea.

Ilinx is a kind of play, described by sociologist Roger Caillois, a major figure in game studies. Ilinx creates a temporary disruption of perception, as with vertigo, dizziness, or disorienting changes in direction of movement. Mimicry is based on the acceptance of illusions or imaginary universes. Children engage in mimicry through pretend play. This category includes games in which players make believe, or make others believe, that they are other than themselves.

2.6 AMATEUR SPORTS: A HISTORICAL PERSPECTIVE

The concept of amateur sports, where participants engage without remuneration, has undergone significant evolution. Once a cherished ideal, the boundary between amateur and professional sports blurred with the rise of monetized sports. While some organizations still uphold amateurism, the distinction has waned. Professionals stand out due to honed habits and routines, allowing them to excel consistently. This mindset shift underscores the changing landscape of modern sports.

In the ever-changing landscape of disruptive technologies, Recreation administration careers, and the dynamic realm of amateur sports, the thread that ties them together is the constant evolution shaping industries and shaping human engagement.

Here are 5 key distinctions between amateurs and professionals

1. **Inspiration vs. schedule:** Amateurs wait for inspiration before acting, while professionals adhere to a disciplined schedule regardless of motivation.
2. **Goals vs. habits:** Amateurs fixate on goals and instant results, often leading to procrastination. Professionals prioritize building habits that naturally lead to goal achievement.
3. **Achievement vs. improvement:** Amateurs focus on achieving specific milestones, often stagnating after success. Professionals view achievements as signs of improvement, continuously seeking growth.

4. **Stalling vs. growth after failure:** Amateurs shy away from failure and give up in the face of challenges. Professionals embrace failure as a stepping stone to growth, using feedback to refine their skills.
5. **Opinions vs. truth:** Amateurs seek validation from others and conform to common practices. Professionals question norms, challenge assumptions, and seek the truth in their field.

2.7 IMPORTANCE OF PLAY

Theories of play are fundamental frameworks that attempt to explain the significance, nature, and functions of play in human development, learning, and culture. These theories provide insights into why play is an essential and universal aspect of human behaviour, helping us understand its psychological, cognitive, social, and emotional implications. Theories of play contribute to various fields, including psychology, education, anthropology, sociology, and more. Here are some reasons why theories of play are important.

1. **Child development and learning:** Theories of play offer insights into how children develop physically, cognitively, socially, and emotionally through play. They help educators, parents, and caregivers design effective learning environments and activities that support children's growth and learning.
2. **Cognitive development:** Play is closely linked to cognitive development. Theories of play, such as Jean Piaget's stages of cognitive development, highlight how play contributes to children's intellectual growth by allowing them to explore, experiment, and problem-solve in a safe and imaginative context.
3. **Imagination and creativity:** Play encourages the development of imagination and creativity. Theories like Lev Vygotsky's socio-cultural theory emphasize how imaginative play helps children develop symbolic thought and internalize cultural practices.
4. **Social development:** Play provides opportunities for social interaction and learning. Theories like the social learning theory emphasize how play allows children to practise social roles, negotiate rules, and develop social skills like cooperation and communication.
5. **Emotional regulation:** Play offers a space where children can express and regulate their emotions. Theories like the affective play theory focus on how play helps children cope with stress, anxiety, and other emotions.
6. **Cultural and societal norms:** Different cultures and societies have unique play practices that reflect their values, traditions, and norms. Theories of play help researchers and anthropologists understand the role of play in cultural transmission and identity formation.
7. **Therapeutic applications:** Play therapy is used as a therapeutic tool to help individuals, especially children, express their feelings and work through emotional challenges. Theories of play contribute to the development of effective therapeutic techniques.

vation and problem-solving: Play encourages experimentation and risk-taking, ring innovation and problem-solving skills. Theories of play shed light on how -based approaches can stimulate creative thinking in various fields.

ult play and leisure: Play is not limited to childhood; adults also engage in play d leisure activities that contribute to stress relief, relaxation, and overall well-being. neories of play help us understand the lifelong importance of play.

olicy and education: Theories of play influence educational policies and practices. Understanding the importance of play can lead to the development of curriculum that integrates playful learning experiences, enhancing educational outcomes.

. **Balancing work and life:** In a world driven by productivity and achievement, play and recreation offer a necessary counterbalance. Integrating leisure activities into one's routine promotes a healthier work-life balance, preventing burnout and enhancing overall satisfaction. Taking breaks to engage in enjoyable pastimes rejuvenates the mind, allowing individuals to return to their responsibilities with renewed focus and energy. Play and recreation are not mere frivolities but essential components of a fulfilling and balanced life. They contribute to physical health, emotional well-being, social interactions, cognitive development, and cultural enrichment. Embracing play and recreational activities enhances the overall quality of life, fostering happiness, creativity, and a deeper connection with oneself and others. It is important for individuals to recognize the value of play and prioritize it alongside their other responsibilities.

Theories of play provide a framework for understanding the multifaceted nature of play and its implications across different domains of human life. They help us appreciate play as a complex and vital aspect of human existence that contributes to learning, development, socialization, and overall well-being.

2.8 ROLES OF PLAY IN RECREATION AND LEISURE

Sports' role in leisure

Exercise contributes to the prevention of degradation and biological degeneration and increases the body's ability to counteract some tensions. The influence of exercise on the body can be felt, for not only the organs and functions currently required for effort. Cumulatively, through repetition, it helps the body achieve morphogenetic and physiological gains, with tonic effects on vigour and health. An important aim of 'physical education and sports' is to contribute to individual personality development. Team sports games represent a means of operational achievement of the objectives of physical education and sports. The regular practice of physical activities and generally of any form of physical exercise (walking, running, aerobics, stretching, etc.), sustained by a healthy diet and by the absence of behaviours that are potentially detrimental to human health (addiction to alcohol, smoking, etc.), has an important role in the prevention of chronic diseases. One of the main motivations for sport analyzed and discovered by specialists, is to create a healthy lifestyle through practising physical exercises.

In the process of their development, human beings tend to improve their physical, intellectual, and moral characteristics to become a socially useful people. Therefore, they are always concerned about their health, and their capacity to work, and in this context, they understand the need to get more exercise and practise sports on a regular basis . The dynamics of modern society require special skills from individuals, both psychological (ability to adapt to constant changes, high-stress resistance, etc.) and biological (functional and motor potential). Specialists found a growing interest of young people for sports activities and underlined the consequences of lack of physical activity with adverse effects on human life (obesity, body-mass index increased, deformation of the spine, heart problems, etc.) also practising motor activities can improve socialization, communication, and intergroup relationships.

The influence of exercise on the locomotor, respiratory, cardiovascular, and other systems and its influence on digestion, nutrition, excretion, but especially on the nervous system and on mental activity is stimulating, exercise being essential for life and for balance and harmony in human life. The competition, the meeting of physical training and the sport leisure activities, are each a means of fostering the social relations of modelling personality and strengthening its characteristics, but also a repression of mental stress accumulated. Building up and maintaining a healthy lifestyle is an objective that is particularly important in our day-to-day existence. Family and school play an important part in raising awareness among young people (pupils, students) about the need to practice physical activities as a prerequisite for achieving that objective. Appropriately developed exercise programmes can help people under stress use up excess energy, release frustration, they can contribute to reducing anxiety, depression, distrust, loneliness, and the lack of interest in everything around.

Some common benefits of play:

1. Maintain health
2. Socialization
3. Movement
4. Self-improvement
5. Challenge
6. Competition
7. Affiliation
8. Communication
9. Satisfaction
10. Disconnection necessities

Play serves as a multifaceted tool that promotes physical, mental, emotional, and social well-being in the context of recreation and leisure. Its diverse benefits make it a vital component of a balanced and healthy lifestyle.

PROGRESS CHECK

1. What is the role of play in leisure and recreation?
2. Briefly explain the relationship between sociology and sports.
3. How does recreation contribute to mental and emotional well-being?

4. Distinguish between amateurs and professionals.
5. Briefly explain early classical theories of play.
6. Write a short note on current theories of play.

MULTIPLE-CHOICE QUESTIONS

1. According to Jean Piaget's theory, play is important for
   (a) Physical exercise (b) Social interaction
   (c) Memorization of facts (d) Following rules
2. Which theorist introduced the concept of 'flow' in play?
   (a) Erik Erikson (b) Lev Vygotsky
   (c) Jean Piaget (d) Mihaly Csikszentmihalyi
3. Vygotsky's zone of proximal development suggests that play can
   (a) Hinder cognitive development (b) Promote imaginative thinking
   (c) Only involve solitary activities (d) Impede social skills
4. The 'Surplus Energy Theory' suggests that play is a way to
   (a) Conserve energy (b) Expend excess energy
   (c) Develop logical thinking (d) Imitate adults
5. Erik Erikson's theory emphasizes that play helps children
   (a) Compete with their peers (b) Develop a sense of identity
   (c) Isolate themselves from others (d) Avoid risks and challenges
6. The 'Recapitulation Theory' suggests that play
   (a) Encourages conformity (b) Resembles ancestral behaviours
   (c) Is irrelevant for learning (d) Focuses solely on creativity
7. According to Friedrich Froebel, play materials such as blocks and puzzles
   (a) Should be avoided to prevent distraction (b) Help develop fine motor skills
   (c) Limit imaginative thinking (d) Are only suitable for older children
8. Which theorist proposed that play serves as a method of releasing pent-up emotions?
   (a) Sigmund Freud (b) B.F. Skinner (c) Abraham Maslow (d) Albert Bandura
9. The 'Competence-Reflectance' theory suggests that play contributes to a child's
   (a) Fear of failure (b) Sense of competence and mastery
   (c) Inability to collaborate (d) Isolation from others
10. Which theory suggests that play acts as practice and learn behaviours needed for survival?
    (a) Psychosocial Theory (b) Play Therapy Theory
    (c) Evolutionary Play Theory (d) Constructivist Play Theory
11. The 'Sociocultural Theory of play, proposed by Lev Vygotsky, emphasizes the role of
    (a) Instinctual behaviours (b) Solitary play
    (c) Cultural context and social interaction (d) Repetitive activities
12. Sports considered as ____________ phenomena
    (a) Social (b) Economic (c) Cultural (d) Administrative

13. Surplus energy theory of leisure is a part of
    (a) Classic theory (b) Modern theory (c) Ancient theory (d) None of these
14. Mimicry is an example of
    (a) Agon (b) Alea (c) Ilinx (d) None of these
15. Cathartic theory of recreation deals with
    (a) Painful emotion (b) Recapitulation (c) Compensation (d) Relaxation
16. The benefits of participation in recreation & sports
    (a) Health promotion (b) Skill development (c) Empowerment (d) All of these
17. In disruptive technology:
    (a) Product & services change the marketplace
    (b) Technology changes the marketplace
    (c) The rule of facilitator changes the marketplace
    (d) None of the above
18. Amateur sports are sports in which participants engage
    (a) With remuneration (b) Without remuneration
    (c) Contractual engagement (d) None of the above
19. When an individual plays soccer to recharge his/her energy, what play theory is he/she subscribing to?
    (a) Relaxation theory (b) Surplus energy theory
    (c) Catharsis theory (d) Self-expression theory
20. What is the definition of physical activity?
    (a) A set of attributes that people have or achieve relating to their ability to perform physical activity
    (b) Only activities that involve sports
    (c) Bodily movement that is produced by the contraction of skeletal muscle and that substantially increases energy expenditure
    (d) None of these
21 Which of the following is the base of the Physical Activity Pyramid?
    (a) Agility (b) Active sports and recreational activities
    (c) Active aerobics (d) Lifestyle activities
22. Which of the following is considered the real lifetime activity?
    (a) Walking (b) Push-ups (c) Skipping (d) Jogging
23. Play is usually associated for better or worse with
    (a) Purposeful outcomes (b) Productive outcomes
    (c) Non-purposeful outcomes (d) Non-productive outcomes

Answers to Multiple-Choice Questions

1. (c)	2. (d)	3. (b)	4. (b)	5. (b)	6. (b)	7. (b)	8. (a)
9. (a)	10. (c)	11. (c)	12. (a)	13. (a)	14. (c)	15. (a)	16. (d)
17. (a)	18. (b)	19. (a)	20. (c)	21. (d)	22. (a)	23. (c)	

Chapter 3

Contemporary Issues on Leisure and Recreation

Objectives

After going through this chapter the reader will be able to:

- Understand the public and private role in leisure and recreation.
- Develop ideas on commercial recreation and its impact on stakeholders.
- Examine environmental aspects of leisure and recreation.
- Develop ideas on contemporary issues on leisure and recreation.

3.1 INTRODUCTION

In our rapidly evolving world, leisure and recreation have transcended their traditional roles, emerging as vital forces shaping societies, economies, and governance. This chapter delves into the intricate interplay of these facets. Leisure activities are catalysts for social cohesion, bridging gaps and forging connections. Virtual platforms and shared interests redefine social interaction, fostering belonging and collective identity. Leisure's economic footprint is extensive, spanning tourism, entertainment, and sports. We dissect how it drives job creation, stimulates markets, and nurtures innovation, becoming a powerful economic engine. Effective management requires astute policies, ensuring access, safety, and resource preservation. We explore the governance intricacies, regulatory frameworks, and collaborative approaches that underpin leisure and recreation.Join in this exploration, uncovering the profound and transformative dimensions of leisure and recreation. As we navigate their societal, economic, and administrative tapestry, we gain insight into their far-reaching influence and potential for positive changes.

3.2 PLANNING/ADMINISTRATIVE ROLE

The government's role in advancing commercial recreation are described below.

3.2.1 Complementary Collaborations

Recognizing its limitations in meeting the diverse recreational needs of all citizens, the government plays a vital role in complementing private enterprises to ensure optimal recreation opportunities. This collaborative approach involves various actions:

1. **Infrastructural support:** Government's involvement extends to maintaining, regulating, or facilitating infrastructure like roads and utilities, which are essential for sustaining commercial recreation and tourism.
2. **Promotion and development:** Governments actively promote tourism and commercial growth, contributing to economic vitality while enhancing recreational options.
3. **Public facilities access:** Residents benefit from public facilities where they can use recreation equipment purchased privately, amplifying leisure accessibility.
4. **Affordable programmes:** Inclusivity is achieved through government-provided low-cost introductory programmes, enabling broader participation.
5. **Guidance and referral:** By referring individuals to commercial recreation opportunities, governments bridge the gap between citizens and private offerings.

3.2.2 Cooperative Endeavours

Government and private enterprises collaborate directly to establish recreation initiatives, as evident in these cooperative arrangements:

1. **Public programmes at commercial venues:** Public agencies conduct programmes within commercial facilities, enriching the diversity of offerings.
2. **Private programme operations:** Private enterprises may be contracted to manage certain programmes within public agency facilities, leveraging their expertise.
3. **Co-sponsored events:** Collaborative event hosting between public and private entities fosters memorable experiences.
4. **Resource sharing:** Equipment, supplies, and staff knowledge are shared, optimizing efficiency.
5. **Concessions and amenities:** Concession leasing for food, beverages, or other services enhances the visitor experience.
6. **Facility development:** Joint efforts lead to shared facility development, maximizing available resources.
7. **Financial support:** Governments offer financial assistance, including low-cost loans or property tax abatements, promoting sustainable growth.
8. **Land leasing for development:** Public land is leased for commercial recreation, exemplified by partnerships like USFS and ski areas or Coconino County Parks and Recreation Department and Flagstaff Extreme Adventure Course.

3.2.3 Collaborative Planning

Effective long-term recreation and tourism planning necessitates a harmonious partnership between government and private enterprise, with considerations as given below.

1. **Public involvement:** Commercial recreation and tourism representatives actively participate in public hearings related to recreation and natural resources, ensuring diverse perspectives.
2. **Community engagement:** Commercial representatives serve on advisory boards and planning commissions, fostering a holistic approach to development.
3. **Comprehensive planning:** Local and state comprehensive plans incorporate insights from commercial owners and managers, promoting a well-rounded strategy.
4. **National policy influence:** Industry input informs national policy decisions, ensuring a balanced approach to industry regulation.
5. **Local and state regulation:** Commercial representatives contribute insights into local and state regulatory decisions, enhancing effective governance.

In this integrated approach, government and commercial recreation stakeholders collaborate synergistically, fostering a diverse, vibrant, and sustainable leisure landscape for all.

3.3 EMERGENCE OF DISRUPTIVE TECHNOLOGIES

Disruptive technologies, defined as transformative innovations reshaping markets, often challenge established norms and replace industry leaders. These innovations tend to evolve from modest beginnings, altering business practices significantly. Notable examples include Airbnb and Uber, currently reshaping the hospitality and tourism sectors. Predicting the course of disruptive forces remains challenging, demanding vigilance from managers as opportunities for change within commercial recreation abound.

3.4 DEFINING COMMERCIAL RECREATION

1. **Commercial recreation:** Private enterprises offer fee-based recreation products or services with long-term profit goals.
2. **Commercialized public recreation:** Government or nonprofit organizations offer fee-based recreation services, resembling commercial ventures.
3. **Entrepreneurial recreation:** Organizations exploit environmental changes by innovatively managing resources.
4. **Tourism:** Travelling and staying outside usual environments for leisure, business, or other purposes.
5. **Intrapreneur:** Someone within an organization driving innovation and change.

These distinctions and definitions shed light on the mindset, actions, and industries that shape our approach to work, recreation, and innovation.

3.4.1 Public-private Recreation Continuum

Within the realm of recreation, a spectrum emerges that underscores the diverse interplay between the public and private sectors. This continuum reflects the intricate relationships between these entities, shaping the multifaceted landscape of leisure and entertainment. This understanding is crucial for comprehending the intricate dynamics of this complex industry.

3.4.2 Four Categories of Commercial Recreation

An array of commercial recreation categories exists, forming a comprehensive framework that reveals their interconnectedness. This taxonomy elucidates the diverse nature of these sectors, shedding light on their distinct yet interwoven functions.

1. **Travel industry:** Focused on facilitating movement and offering travel-related services for individuals, encompassing various facets of the journey.
2. **Hospitality industry:** Centred on providing accommodations, dining, and related amenities, creating a holistic experience for travellers.
3. **Local commercial recreation industry:** Primarily concentrates on furnishing retail products, entertainment, and recreational programmes within local communities.
4. **Facilitators:** These entities serve as support systems for the core industries, contributing to the seamless operation and enhancement of services.

The multifaceted tapestry of commercial recreation thrives on collaboration and mutual reinforcement across these categories, resulting in a vibrant and ever-evolving sector.

3.4.3 Commercial Recreation and Tourism

Commercial recreation refers to the profitable provision of leisure activities, facilities, and programmes to meet public demand during free time. Despite its negative connotation in the field, commercial recreation and tourism have expanded with the growing interest in travel and entertainment. This industry, now both profitable and vital, encompasses various aspects explored in this introduction, including its scope, characteristics, and trends.

1. **Commercial recreation:** Providing profitable leisure experiences and services. Private enterprises are the primary focus.
2. **Tourism:** Travelling to new places outside the usual setting to engage in activities, driven by factors like excess time, money, and access. It encompasses a broad range of motivations and Leiper tourism system is made up of three components like tourist, geographical features, and tourism industry. Social tourism is assisted tourism for disadvantaged.

The combination of these terms leads to the umbrella concept of "commercial recreation and tourism". The industry has evolved historically, with recent innovations making global travel more accessible. Consumerism has also fuelled the expansion of leisure experiences.

The industry encompasses a variety of businesses, from movie theatres to hotels, contributing to its multifaceted nature. Specific categories include:

- **Hospitality:** Accommodations, beverages, meals, and amenities, like hotels and resorts.
- **Travel:** Transportation services for travellers, such as airlines, rental cars, trains, and cruise ships.
- **Local recreation:** Community-based offerings, including fitness centres, water parks, and events like concerts.

3.5 SPORTS ORGANIZATIONS AND ACTIVITIES

A mosaic of sports-related organizations and activities underpin the global pursuit of athletic excellence and personal growth. These entities span various niches, catering to both amateur enthusiasts and professionals. From grassroots initiatives to international bodies, they collectively contribute to the development, empowerment, and transformation of individuals through sports and physical activities. Their diverse missions encompass coaching, ethics, anti-doping efforts, community engagement, and more, uniting people worldwide in the pursuit of physical achievement and personal betterment.

3.6 RECREATION FORMS IN THE CONTEXT OF INTERNATIONAL TOURISM

Recreation, involving leisure activities during one's spare time, encompasses a wide spectrum from golfing to rock climbing. Defining recreation within tourism, however, proves more intricate. Exploring common terms used in the tourism sector helps shed light. "Outdoor recreation" refers to activities in natural settings, while "adventure tourism" involves physical activity, the natural environment, and cultural immersion, such as river rafting and rock climbing. These activities may be categorized as "soft" or "hard" adventures based on experience, fitness, and risk. "Nature-based tourism" connects closely to the natural environment, spanning activities like whale watching, birding, hiking, and kayaking. The classification of these activities into outdoor recreation, adventure tourism, or nature-based tourism depends on factors like engagement style, distance travelled, and the environment.

Exploring land-based and water-based recreation and tourism

Land-based recreation and tourism encompass activities like golfing, mountain resorts, skiing, backcountry adventures, cycling, and camping. Water-based pursuits include scuba diving, sport fishing, paddle sports, and more. These categories highlight the diverse ways individuals engage with nature and their surroundings.

3.7 RECREATIONAL SERVICES AND PROFESSIONAL CAREER PATHS

A recreation worker plays a pivotal role in designing and leading leisure activities within volunteer agencies and recreation facilities, spanning playgrounds, parks, camps, and senior centres. These professionals curate engaging pursuits in areas like arts, sports, music, and camping. The role encompasses various designations such as Activities Aide, Activities Coordinator, Camp Advisor, and more. Additionally, recreation workers undertake responsibilities including enforcing rules, managing facility operations, providing first aid, organizing, and promoting activities, supervising personnel, resolving complaints, and fostering participant development.

3.8 LAND USE, ENVIRONMENTAL ASPECTS, AND RISK MANAGEMENT IN COMMERCIAL RECREATION

Access to wilderness zones for tourism operations present an ongoing challenge, often necessitating extensive permitting processes with activity restrictions. While provincial and national parks reserve areas for recreation, conducting commercial operations there may encounter barriers. Non-motorized limitations and competition with resource extraction hinder growth, impacting the sector's sustainability. Golden triangle tour circuit links Delhi, Agra and Jaipur and trekking tourism is popular in south Asian country like Nepal. Traditional beach tourism with added attractions is known as beach plus.

Climate change, deforestation, and resource extraction amplify environmental concerns, potentially affecting the tourism economy. Localized resource competition threatens pristine wilderness access, influencing operators' viability. Risk management and litigation further pose challenges, with adventure tourism lawsuits garnering media attention, leading to increased insurance rates, regulatory constraints, certification requisites, and permitting complexities.

The surge in backcountry users underscores the importance of proper training and education, mitigating potential dangers associated with wilderness exploration.

This synthesis introduces the realm of recreational services, shedding light on its multifaceted nature, career paths, and the intricate interplay between environmental considerations and risk management.

3.9 MODERN ERA: LEISURE AND RECREATION

Recreation movement in India was started by G.D Sondhi. The most important factor in organization of recreation is facilities. In modern era this recreation marketing is a service. Participation in park activities like walking, hiking, or skiing correlates with improved health indicators such as lower office visits, body fat percentages, blood pressure, and cholesterol levels. Recreational activities help manage stress and contribute to mental wellness. Recreation plays a pivotal role in human happiness, contributing to emotional, physical, and mental well-being. It fosters community solidarity, bridging gaps and promoting unity among diverse groups. Adequate provision of recreation spaces also contributes to public safety and democratizes opportunities for personal growth and development.

3.9.1 Recreation and Education, Economy, and Democracy

While education and recreation share objectives and activities, they serve distinct purposes. Recreation offers immediate satisfaction and the use of acquired skills, while education aims for long-term growth. Nonetheless, recreational experiences contribute to educational development. Recreation plays an increasing role in both formal education and extracurricular programmes, fostering educated judgment about leisure activities. In the realm of the economy, business leaders recognize the impact of employees' leisure activities on job performance. Investment in recreational facilities yields tangible and intangible returns, benefiting both individuals and communities.Urbanization on the availability of city recreation more recreation opportunity in the city.

In summary, the realm of commercial recreation and tourism is a dynamic industry that encompasses a wide range of activities and services, contributing to human well-being, community cohesion, economic growth, and personal development.

3.9.2 Understanding of Contemporary Issues in Leisure Services

Leisure management involves the effective delivery of leisure services, encompassing a comprehensive grasp of leisure concepts, organizational dynamics, leadership, finance, community engagement, partnerships, diversity, quality, and performance. Essential to this role is understanding what needs to be delivered and who it caters to.

The 'what' of leisure management involves a profound comprehension of fundamental concepts such as leisure, play, sport, recreation, tourism, and events. Furthermore, proficiency in organizational functioning, resource utilization, and outcome measurement is crucial. Amid an evolving industry, planning, organizing, leading, financing, and assessing leisure services demand increased sophistication.

Leisure services often extend beyond efficiency to create positive societal impacts, targeting diverse segments of the community. Managing public funds requires leisure managers to enhance the quality of life for marginalized groups. Understanding the recipients, or 'who' of leisure services, is paramount. The Tree Model of Marketing Delivery emphasizes this, as the success of services hinges on identifying target markets and market segments.

Recreation movement means recreation offered by and organized by social agencies with the intent to determine outcomes. Amenity migration sheds light on the planning process when community dynamics shift due to influxes of part-time residents, impacting local features that initially attracted migrants. Recognizing community connections aids in tailoring programmes to specific needs. For instance, an examination of adult recreational tennis players revealed that the sense of community significantly influenced programme success.

Moreover, a framework for youth programme design, rooted in psychology, contributes to effective programme delivery. Incorporating individual youth needs enhances the quality of leisure services. Leisure planning involves a multi-step process, including policy formulation, assessment of demand, resource evaluation, and an action plan, ultimately monitored and evaluated for effectiveness.

3.10 LEISURE PROSPECTS AND FUTURE

Recent years have witnessed rapid changes in quality of life and leisure habits. Key trends include wealth distribution, time utilization, social interests, leisure at home, and demographic shifts. These trends impact participation in various leisure activities, prompting the need for strategic planning and management based on accurate trend analysis. Sustainability is another concern where leaving a destination in a better condition than you found it is known as'enhancive sustainability'.

3.10.1 Human Service Agencies in a Changing Environment

Human service agencies confront a complex and uncertain landscape marked by increased competition and demand. Managers grapple with dilemmas such as evidence-based practice, collaboration, market principles, and ethical considerations. Organizations strive to balance these factors while prioritizing the long-term well-being of stakeholders and communities.

Human services agencies

Human services workers operate in diverse environments, such as group homes, mental health centres, correctional facilities, and family services agencies. Qualities and skills for human services professionals include active listening, emotional intelligence, organization, critical thinking, and empathy. Social trends of leisure depend upon lifestyle, education, and household.

Professional competence and development

Maintaining professional competence is crucial for growth. Professional development involves activities like continuing education, participation in professional organizations, research, and improving job performance. Approaches include skill-based training, job assignments, networking, and mentoring programmes.

3.10.2 Aging and Leisure Development: Theoretical and Practical Aspects

Leisure activities significantly impact adults, particularly those under 55. However, fewer leisure activities affect older adults. Cultural activities, reading, and hobbies hold the most influence on those aged 55 and above. Retirement can prompt increased participation in moderate-intensity physical activity, enhancing health outcomes.

For seniors, ideal leisure activities include browsing the Internet, joining book clubs, walking, attending movies, gardening, and musical events. Older individuals often have fewer social contacts, yet report higher satisfaction and connectedness. Engaging in active leisure fosters social integration more effectively than passive pursuits.

Understanding serious leisure, a structured pursuit of substantial leisure activities, reveals the potential to enhance social integration among seniors. Senior citizens involved in grey tourism. Facilitating connections through hobbies and community programmes can improve the quality of life for older adults. Successful interventions involve selecting, training, and supporting facilitators to stimulate social interaction.

3.10.3 Leisure Delivery and Facilitation for Adults

Effective facilitation for adult leisure requires careful preparation, adaptability, and active listening. Inclusivity, clear guidelines, and efficient time management contribute to successful leisure experiences. The facilitator's role extends to fostering an inclusive environment, adapting to different circumstances, gauging energy levels, and being flexible to meet diverse needs. Whether a neutral facilitator or one with an agenda, the focus remains on creating meaningful and enjoyable leisure experiences.

3.11 CONCEPT OF PROFESSION AND PROFESSIONAL ORGANIZATIONS

A profession is a specialized occupation grounded in formal education, offering unbiased guidance and services to others in exchange for direct compensation, independent of other business interests.

Professional organizations also referred to as professional bodies or societies, aim to advance a specific profession, advocate for professionals within that field, and serve the public interest. These associations ensure proper practice and may control oversight of the profession.

A professional organization requires a defined structure, policy framework, and organizational culture. Elements like authority, responsibility, and accountability are integral components of any organization. Different types of organizational structures include Line, Functional, and Line and Staff.

Recruitment, selection, job descriptions, job specifications, and work cards are vital aspects of effective manpower planning within any organization.

An example of a professional organization related to leisure is the National Recreation and Park Association (NRPA), which advocates for public parks, recreation, and conservation. NRPA collaborates with similar entities, including federal agencies and nonprofits, and promotes research, education, and policy initiatives to enrich communities.

3.12 RESPONSIBILITY OF LEISURE PROFESSIONALS

Leisure professionals carries various responsibilities to ensure the smooth operation of recreational facilities and the safety of participants.

These include:

1. Enforcing rules and regulations to maintain discipline and safety.
2. Organizing, leading, and promoting recreational activities.
3. Managing daily operations of facilities.
4. Providing first-aid and emergency assistance when needed.
5. Assessing group interests and adapting activities to participant needs.
6. Welcoming and orienting new participants to activities.
7. Explaining principles, techniques, and safety procedures to participants.
8. Evaluating the effectiveness of recreation areas and services.
9. Monitoring staff performance and addressing complaints.
10. Collaborating with community organizations and professionals to plan programmes.
11. Overseeing maintenance and facility use.

3.13 MEN'S AND WOMEN'S LEISURE AND RECREATION

Research indicates that men and women engage in different types of leisure activities. Men tend to participate in outdoor and team sports, while women often lean toward cultural pursuits. Gender influences participation rates, attitudes, and outcomes. Factors such as personality attributes, social groups, and lifestyle contribute to these differences.

PROGRESS CHECK

1. What is the primary purpose of a professional organization in the context of leisure and recreation?
2. Describe the role of the National Recreation and Park Association (NRPA) in promoting public parks and recreation.
3. How do social factors, such as gender and family obligations, influence leisure participation patterns?
4. What is the significance of professional competence in the leisure and recreation field?
5. How can professionals in leisure and recreation ensure continuous growth and improvement?
6. Discuss the concept of gender differences in leisure and recreation experiences.
7. What are the main social impacts of leisure and recreation on communities?

MULTIPLE-CHOICE QUESTIONS

1. The age group is participating in less leisure activities
   (a) 10-25 (b) 25-40 (c) 40-55 (d) 55 & above
2. Social trends of leisure depend upon
   (a) Lifestyle (b) Education (c) Households (d) All the above
3. Leisure trend related with
   (a) The use of time (b) Social interest
   (c) Wealth and poverty (d) All of the above
4. Play is usually associated for better or worse with
   (a) Purposeful outcomes (b) Productive outcomes
   (c) Non-purposeful outcomes (d) Non-productive outcomes
5. NRPA stands for
   (a) National radio and play association (b) National rail preservation association
   (c) National real park alliance (d) National recreation and park association
6. Leisure has been studied by which of the following, except
   (a) Anthropologists (b) Entomologists
   (c) Economists (d) Psychologists
7. Play is a form of
   (a) Game (b) Behaviour
   (c) Spectator sport (d) Play can occur during work
8. What is the effect of urbanization on the availability of city recreation
   (a) More recreation opportunity in the city
   (b) Less recreation opportunity in the city

(c) More recreation opportunity in the suburbs
(d) Less recreation opportunity in the suburbs

9. The term recreation movement means
(a) Recreation offered for free
(b) Recreation offered by private and commercial companies
(c) Recreation without the concern for outcomes
(d) Recreation offered by and organized by social agencies with the intent to determine outcomes.

10. The first step of leisure budget preparation is
(a) To search income (b) Estimate expenditure
(c) Planning (d) Facilities and personnel

11. The most important factor in organization of recreation is
(a) Materials (b) Leadership (c) Facilities (d) Planning

12. Geographical and climatic conditions should be considered when planning
(a) Indoor activities (b) Outdoor activities
(c) Child activities (d) Old people activities

13. Recreation movement in India was started by
(a) De Mellow (b) G.D. Sondhi (c) H.C. Buck (d) Vaidya P.R.

14. Cultural values are to be preserved
(a) For enjoying and playing (b) For life to have human meaning
(c) For enjoying material life (d) For following spiritual life

15. Wilson has just opened a small sports bar in a busy downtown area. He decides to promote his business with social media marketing. Which of the following platforms is most suitable for Wilson's business?
(a) Facebook (b) Twitter (c) Instagram (d) YouTube

16. Notifying local residents and businesses of traffic plans improves
(a) Advertising (b) Community relations
(c) Selling (d) Sales promotion

17. Recreation marketing is
(a) A product (b) Tangible (c) A service (d) A good

18. Leiper tourism system is made up of _________ components
(a) 3 (b) 1 (c) 2 (d) 4

19. Social tourism is
(a) Assisted tourism for the disadvantaged (b) Visiting friends and relatives
(c) Elite tourism (d) Niche tourism

20. The Golden Triangle tour circuit links Delhi, Agra and
(a) Jaipur (b) Kashmir (c) Mumbai (d) Kolkata

21. Trekking tourism is popular in which South Asian country?
(a) Nepal (b) China (c) Iraq (d) Sri Lanka

22. Grey tourism is tourism by
    (a) Senior citizens (b) Snow birds (c) Ecotourists (d) Cultural tourists
23. Traditional beach tourism with added attractions is known as
    (a) Beach plus (b) Added beach (c) Plus beach (d) Beach added
24. Leaving a destination in a better condition than you found it is known as
    (a) Enhancive sustainability (b) Sustainable tourism
    (c) Ecotourism (d) Clean-up tourism

Answers to Multiple-Choice Questions

1. (d)	2. (d)	3. (d)	4. (c)	5. (d)	6. (b)	7. (b)	8. (a)
9. (d)	10. (c)	11. (c)	12. (b)	13. (b)	14. (b)	15. (a)	16. (b)
17. (c)	18. (a)	19. (a)	20. (a)	21. (a)	22. (a)	23. (a)	24. (a)

Chapter 4

Event Management

Objectives

After going through this chapter the reader will be able to:

- Understand the idea of event management and its evolution.
- Take a look at the extraordinary kinds of activities.
- Examine the function of creativity in event management manner.
- Look at about the numerous forms of event control shape.

4.1 INTRODUCTION

Events create possibilities for people to connect to an area, spend time collectively, rejoice and revel in the variety of cultures and foster creativity and innovation. They allow a community to come back alive and offer a possibility for a destination to showcase its tourism enjoy and boom financial interest. Events make contributions notably to community constructing, lifestyle and enjoyment enhancement, cultural improvement, tourism promotion and extended visitation, volunteer participation, fundraising and economic improvement. Most importantly, events create an experience of amusing and vibrancy, resulting in a robust experience of network connectivity, pride, and a feel of location.

4.2 DEFINITION OF EVENTS

There is no single universally regularly occurring definition of event. Many authors have discussed the definition of events and the diverse phrases used to describe them. However, there is most effective restricted settlement on standardized terms across the numerous researches.

The popular practices trade enterprise word list of phrases (APEX, 2005) defines an event as, a prepared event inclusive of a meeting, conference, exhibition, special event, gala dinner, and so on. An event is often composed of several specific but related functions.

Goldblatt (2005) specializes in special activities as a unique moment in time, celebrated with rite and formality to meet particular needs. Getz (2008) notes that activities are spatial-phenomena and that every is precise due to interactions many of the placing, people, and control structures, inclusive of layout factors and the programme. He highlights the fact that the largest enchantment of activities is that they are in no way the identical, and that the guest has to be therell so that it will revel in the experience completely. He indicates definitions, from the attitude of the event organizers, in addition to the visitors.

1. A unique event is a one-time or eventually taking place event out of doors everyday programmes or sports of the sponsoring or organizing body.
2. To the consumer or visitor, a special event is a possibility for leisure, social or cultural experience out of doors the everyday range of alternatives or past normal experience.

Bowdin (2006) noticed that the term, event has been utilized, to portray explicit customs, introductions, exhibitions, or festivities that are deliberately arranged and made to check exceptional events or potentially to accomplish specific social, social, or corporate objectives and objectives. Jago and Shaw (1998) propose six highlights of extraordinary events. They believe that special events ought to: They define a special event as: "Being of limited duration", "Being one-off", "Being of infrequent occurrence", "Rising the awareness, image, or profile of a region", "Offering a social experience", and "Being out of the ordinary", "a once-in-a-lifetime or infrequently occurring event of limited duration that provides the consumer with an opportunity for leisure and social interaction beyond what they are used to". Events of this kind, whether they are a party, a class, or a promotion, have always served to connect people and communities, even if they do not currently attract tourists or have the potential to do so.

The way people plan and hold events is changing as technology does. The then and now of event planning are contrasted in this brief history of event management.

4.3 EVOLUTION OF EVENT MANAGEMENT

The earliest events and social affairs advanced harmony and fellowship among clans and tribes. The principal known event organizer was Cleopatra. She facilitated extravagant over the top gatherings in quest for sweethearts. To impress Mark Anthony, Cleopatra rode a boat filled with candles and perfume down the Nile River. Correspondence was exceptionally restricted. Messages were hand conveyed and it could require weeks on the off chance that not months to convey them.

The Medieval French Royalty continued to host elaborate parties and events. Rich noble ladies were accountable for even the executives. The most well-known was Madame Pompadour, who was the mistress of Marie Antoinette and King Louis XV of France. Costumes and popular music from the time served as themes for the parties.

Meetings and events needed to grow and become more than just parties for the rich and powerful after the Industrial Revolution. The economy grew stronger because of industrialization, as did manufacturing and business. For people to work together and expand their businesses, it became necessary for them to organize events and meetings. Events could be hosted at a higher cost because people earned more money. The extension of transportation gave choices to build the quantity of events and gatherings. Trains and other new modes of transportation made it possible for people to get to and from events.

The development of the Internet and mobile phones had a significant impact on event planning. With the utilization of these hardware, correspondence can occur whenever of the day and from anyplace on the planet. Using a single, small, portable device, an individual can create, locate, register for, and record an event.

Then vs. Now

Registration

Then: Preceding the 1990s and 2000s, event coordinators needed to utilize manually written enrolment cycles and all reports were actually sent. It could require days to arrive at the appropriate spot and it was simple for records to get derailed.

Now: Online registration forms and documents can be sent instantly via email or uploaded to a drop box.

Locating

Then: In the days before the Internet, attendees had to use a physical map to locate an event, which could have been challenging and stressful.

Now: One basically has to type a location into Google Guides to get turn by turn bearings and even get another course on the off chance that they get lost or make an off-base turn.

Attendees

Then: Would you like to know who is going to an event? You once needed to put a call up to your companions or ask them face to face.

Now: Attendees can virtually see who is interested in or attending an event via social media and event organization websites.

Advertising and Finding Events

Then: Flyers, posters, and word-of-mouth were common methods of event promotion prior to the advent of the internet.

Now: Individuals can look for events using sites like Neighbourhood Jump and Facebook. Clients can type in their area and find many events they might not have even know existed!

The ability for an individual or organization to have greater control over event management is the most significant transformation that technology has brought about. Programming and sites permit individuals to development ads for events with easy-to-understand designs that are smooth and expert. Ticket deals and enlistment are coordinated in one spot. In the quick moving universe of the web, time is restricted and important. Websites and apps for event management like Local Hop save time and make it easy to create events.

4.4 EVENT MANAGEMENT

A public gathering for the purposes of celebration, education, marketing, or reunion is known as an event. Events can be grouped according to their size, type, and setting. A social or lifecycle event, such as a birthday party, engagement, wedding, or funeral, are all examples of events, or a career and education event like a job fair, education fair, workshop, seminar, debate, contest, etc.

Event management is the most common way of investigating, arranging, promoting, delivering, and assessing an event. Promoting a product, service, or idea in this way is different. On the off chance that an event is overseen proficiently and really, it tends to be utilized as an extremely strong special device to send off or showcase an item or administration. The executives require specific guiding principle to be sent to each component, interaction, and choice to legitimize proficient methodology and accomplish powerful and effective outcomes.

Event management is the use of venture the executives to the creation and improvement of huge scope events such celebrations, meetings, functions, weddings, formal gatherings, shows, or shows. Before launching the event, it entails studying the brand, determining its target audience, coming up with the concept for the event, and coordinating the technical aspects.

Typically referred to as event planning, the process of planning and coordinating the event can include budgeting, scheduling, choosing a location, obtaining required permits, coordinating transportation and parking, arranging for speakers or entertainers, arranging decor, ensuring event security, catering, coordinating with third-party vendors, and making emergency plans. Because each event is unique in its nature, the process of planning and carrying it out varies by type.

The event manager is the individual who designs and executes the event, assuming a sense of ownership with the imaginative, specialized, and calculated components. The overall design of the event, the creation of a brand, a marketing and communication strategy, audio-visual production, the writing of scripts, logistics, budgeting, negotiation, and customer service are all included in this.

A venue for an event can be on-site or off-site. In most cases, the event manager will oversee all aspects of the event while it is held at a rented event or entertainment venue. The venue may be given some of the tasks listed in the introduction, usually at a cost.

Corporate event supervisors book event scenes to have corporate gatherings, meetings, organizing events, career expos, item dispatches, group building retreats or instructional courses in a more customized environ.

Even the board programming organizations give event arranging programming instruments to deal with numerous normal exercises, for example, delegate enrolment, lodging booking, travel booking, or allotment of presentation floor space.

A new pattern in event innovation is the utilization of portable applications for events. There are numerous uses for event mobile apps. They can be utilized to hold moderately static data like the plan, speaker memoirs, and general FAQs. They can likewise energize crowd cooperation and commitment through intuitive apparatuses like live democratic/surveying, submitting inquiries to speakers during question-and-answer session, or building live intelligent "word mists". Versatile event applications can likewise be involved by event coordinators for correspondence. Alerts, notifications, and push messages enable organizers to communicate with participants. Through the app's surveys, they can also be used to get feedback from participants. With built-in networking features, some mobile event apps can assist participants in engaging with sponsors, organizers, and other participants.

4.5 EVENT TEAM

You really want a group to sort out an event. You cannot do everything without anyone else. Therefore, I do not need to go on about how essential a team is for your event. The majority of event mismanagement concerns team mismanagement.

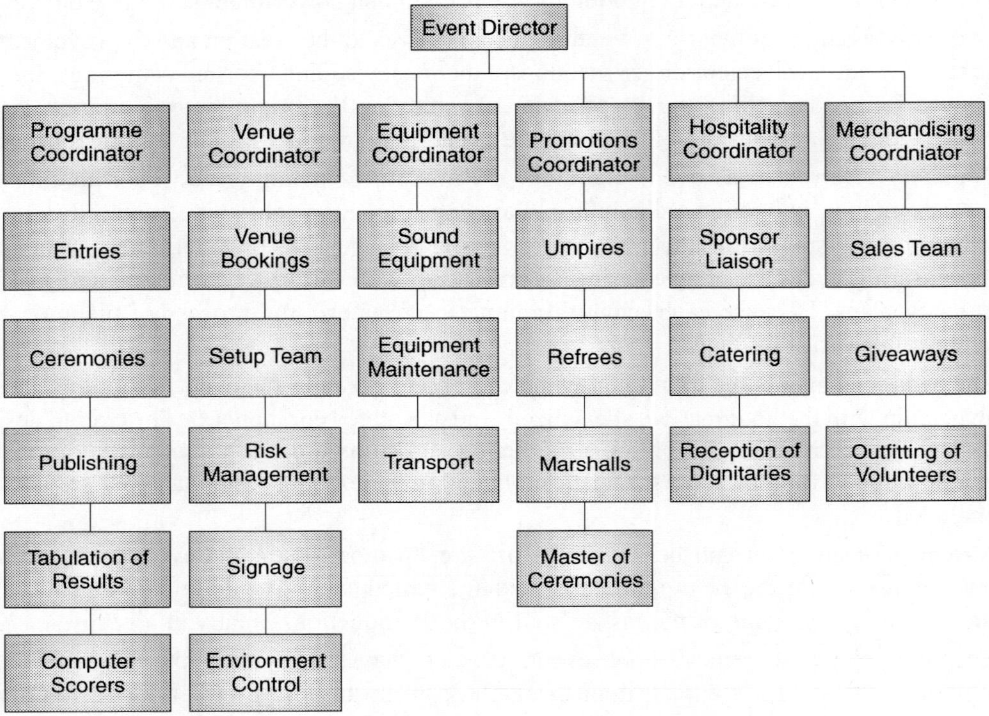

4.5.1 Do the Following Things for Effective Team Management

It is not sufficient to simply know the names, pictures, and job descriptions of your team members. You need to know a lot about their personality, way of life, likes and dislikes, family history, status, education, level of knowledge, customs, religion, and especially their needs and wants. By requirements and needs I mean their physiological necessities, well-being needs, social necessities, regard needs, mental necessities, and self-realization needs.

Everyone has various necessities and different needs to satisfy them. However, for some, getting noticed is more important than having a job. Others place a higher priority on job security. Decide the requirements of your colleagues and satisfy them to obtain ideal outcomes from them.

Physiological requirements

The need to have food, water, warmth, cover, and different things essential for endurance.

Well-being needs

It incorporates should be protected from physical and mental damage. It also includes financial and job security.

Social requirements

It is the need to feel a feeling of having a place and acknowledgment, need to be loved by friends, intimate partners, family, and social groups such as your team.

Regard needs

It is the need to get regard, acknowledgment, acclaim, and status.

The need to comprehend, learn, discover, and explore is referred to as cognitive needs.

Self-completion needs

It is should be awesome. It is the need to become everything, one is fit for becoming.

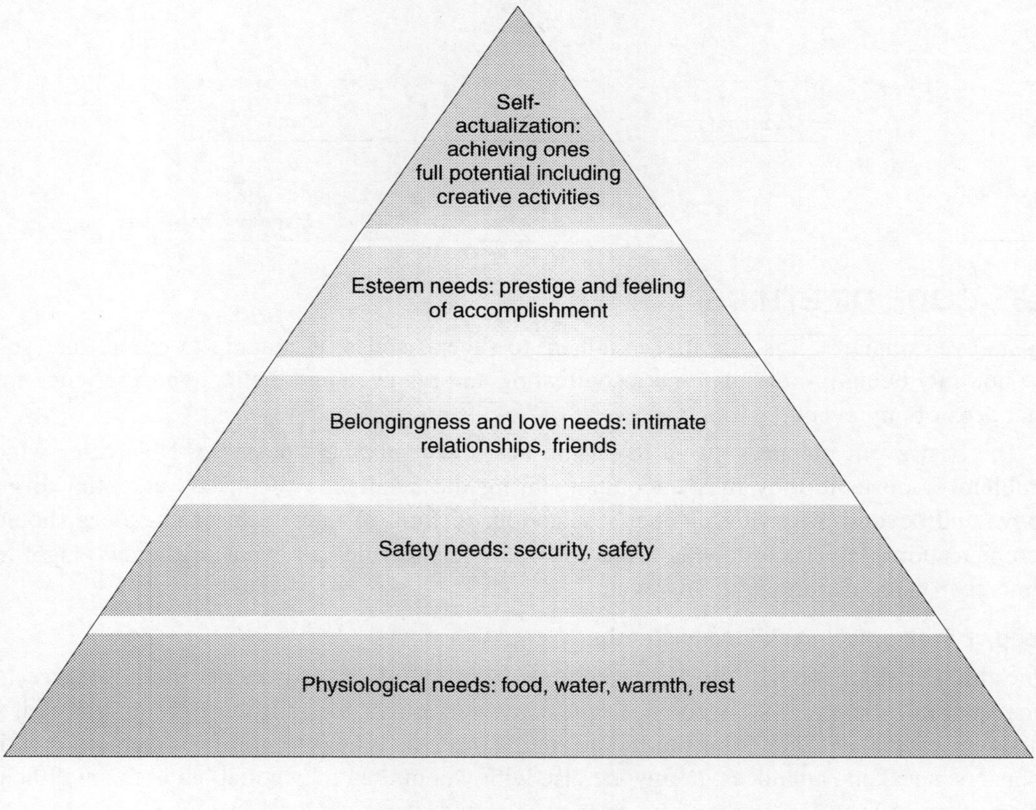

4.5.2 Hierarchy

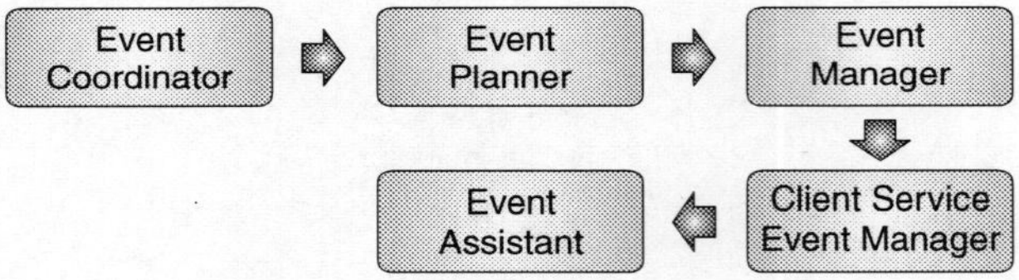

4.6 CODE OF ETHICS

As an event planner, it is essential to adhere to several codes of conduct to ensure that you are not only being professional but also creating an organized and distinctive experience for attendees of any event.

The best event planners strive to be the best event planners possible. No matter what problem or obstacle they may encounter during the event, they feel it is essential to go above and beyond. An event planner's behaviour in front of their team or attendees should be unquestionable. The following are a couple of sets of rules all event organizers ought to remember while dealing with any event.

Keep up with amazing skill consistently

One thing participant will always remember from any event experience is the degree of amazing skill the event staff gives. Event organizers ought to walk their groups through a rundown of dos and don'ts during the arranging system. When it comes to interacting with sponsors, speakers, attendees, or anyone else with whom they may collaborate, this will help ensure that everyone is on the same page.

Organizers ought to have a general elevated degree of information concerning any event. As the go-to person, it is critical to know the names and numbers of venue staff and third-party vendors in case you need them to step in at the last minute. The most important thing an event planner should always do is keep your cool and keep your cool. You never know what might arise, so make the code of professionalism your event mantra by repeatedly reiterating it.

Provide customer service 24/7

Event organizers ought to likewise keep the code of empathy. Very much like some other work, client support generally goes quite far in the personalities and hearts of beneficiaries. Be fair and recognize everybody you work with on an event. As you advance in your career as an event planner, the relationships you form at each event will continue to strengthen. As you rely on one another to repeatedly assist in the organization of amazing events, these relationships will eventually develop into more than just business acquaintances; rather, they will become your closest friends and family.

Recollect to not think about things too literally, and to not oppress any thoughts, concerns or ideas brought to you. Avoid being persuaded and remain true to the values you are working to promote for your event. When it comes to event planning, it seems like everyone has their own opinion, but as the leader of your team, you cannot let others take over. Even if you have to decline ideas from time to time, maintain a positive attitude, listen to your team, and treat them with respect. Remunerate your group when it appears to be legit, and show them you give it a second thought. Always act as a compassionate and responsible event planner.

Always avoid professional risks

There are a few regions that can turn into a gamble for event organizers. A portion of these areas incorporate tolerating gifts when not suitable, showing an unfortunate disposition while overpowered, giving terrible responses to partners, or offering private data when not satisfactory. In the end, it is critical for planners to always communicate, listen, and act professionally. The last thing you need is to become known as the organizer who never stays calm, or will add a speaker to the plan due to a payoff.

Ensure you audit event morals with your group, and assist them with understanding how to deal with dishonest way of behaving. As an event planner, finding the right people with whom to do business is essential. You ought to never endanger your expert or individual life regardless of what the circumstance might be. Maintain top behaviour and convention consistently during an event. A model here might be evening events where participants organization and blend following a lot of time meetings. Recall you are still at work, and should not get excessively private with participants, consistently keep an elevated degree of trustworthiness in these circumstances. Be the good example you maintain that your staff should turn upward to believe about how you need to be viewed as the organizer of an event consistently.

When dealing with all stakeholders, the ethical event manager or leader will show kindness, generosity, bravery, compassion, fairness, openness, patience, prudence, honesty, dependability, self-discipline, an appetite for the job, loyalty, stability, civility, and especially thoughtfulness.

4.7 CLASSIFICATION OF EVENTS

There are various rules for grouping of events. The fundamental one distinguishes between planned and unplanned events. Arranged events are the subject of investigation of event the board and they require arrangement, the board, leaders, and specific period. Impromptu events are mishaps, cataclysmic events, and other comparative, and they won't be thought about in this unit.

Events, which range in size from small community festivals to international trade fairs and the largest global sporting events like the Olympic Games and FIFA Football World Cup, provide a singular form of tourist attraction. One of the critical contrasts among events and conventional attractions is the timeframe over which they influence the host local area or district. Events are short-term, lasting only one or two days. However, larger events can last much longer (like the Kumbh Mela in India, which lasts for weeks), and fixed attractions typically attract visitors seasonally or over a longer period. Events are divided into four broad categories based on their scale and impact: Mega Events, Hallmark Events, Major Events, and Local Events. The key factors commonly perceived as deciding the apparent scale and effect of events are the degree of investment, crowd/onlookers, and media inclusion; what is more, how much an event produces critical worldwide interest for each.

1. Mega events

Major and mega-events are typically events that have true global reach and international appeal. These kinds of events have the potential to spur local development and provide a variety of economic, sociocultural, environmental, and other benefits, including those related to image, branding, and expanding the visitor economy, to name a few.

Uber events, as the biggest and most prominent of all events, perpetually, require the most critical and refined framework improvement, are regularly the costliest to host, and given the serious offering process for such events, commonly take the most significant length of time from commencement to conveyance. Additionally, they typically have the longest legacy period. However, cities and nations also have very few opportunities to host these extremely large events. Issues of foundation, offices, transport, and culturally diverse issues are a portion of the limits in the association of these events. Despite this, many nations continue to view the expenditure of resources required to bid for and possibly host these megaevents as one that can yield comparable returns.

The specific objectives and desired outcomes from a national perspective for the largest events may vary among potential host candidates depending, among other things, on their level of economic development, existing infrastructure, identified security needs, plans for urban regeneration, current and desired international image, maturity as a tourism destination, and sustainability credentials. Hence, obviously events give different likely heritages, contingent upon the necessities of the separate host city or country.

Getz (2005) characterizes them: According to Hall, a different author, "Mega-events, by way of their size or significance, are those that yield extraordinarily high levels of tourism, media coverage, prestige, or economic impact for the host community, venue, or organization."

Mega events get their name from the size of their attendance, target market, level of public financial involvement, political effects, extent of television coverage, construction of facilities, and impact on the host community's economic and social fabric (Allen et al., 2011).

2. Hallmark event

These are the events that set the programme apart from the rest. The spirit and soul of a host community are so closely associated with Hallmark events that they become synonymous with the location's name and gain widespread recognition. Hallmark events are very important to people who participate in them as well as to people who come to see them. They also get a lot of attention from the public, help build the image of the place, and keep and bring back the tradition. Exemplary instances of trademark events are Amusement Park in Goa, Dussehra of Kullu and Khajuraho Dance celebration. These events are connected to the very essence of these places and the people who live there. They also bring in a lot of money from tourists, give the locals a lot of pride, and get recognized around the world.

3. Major events

A major event is one that has a lot of people interested and is covered by the media. Significant events draw in enormous quantities of guests, and assist the coordinators with accomplishing great monetary outcomes. By and by of the board of events, these events are in many cases sports-situated, with a global standing, and characterized construction of rivalry for instance: Equation One Thousand Prix or exchange fair presentations held at Pragati Lady New Delhi.

4. Local events

A local event is one that is primarily staged for its social, amusing, and entertaining value and is intended primarily for local audiences. These events frequently result in a variety of positive outcomes, such as instilling community pride, enhancing a sense of belonging, and fostering a sense of place. They can also assist in promoting tolerance and diversity, introducing people to novel concepts and experiences, and encouraging participation in sports and the arts. Different nearby events are commended in India, for example, Lohrai, Baisakhi and presentations to show new items.The degree to which events are associated with a specific location is yet another criterion used in literature to classify them. As a result, there are events that are always held in the same community, events that are always held in a different community, events that are held simultaneously in multiple communities, or events that cover the entire region. As Getz (2008) makes sense of, super events, which generally happen in various local area, are ordinarily worldwide in their direction and require a serious bid to win them as a one-time event for a specific spot. Then again, trademark events cannot exist freely of their host local area, as well as territorial and neighbourhood events which are established in one spot.

4.7.1 Types of Events

Getz provides a typology of the most common types of planned events based primarily on their form, which clearly distinguishes them in terms of their purpose and programme. Some are for public festival (this classification incorporates purported community festivals which regularly contain an enormous assortment in their programming and expect to cultivate municipal pride and union), while others are made arrangements for reasons for rivalry, fun, diversion, business or mingling. They frequently require special-purpose facilities, and the managers of those facilities, such as sports arenas and convention centres, target particular kinds of events.

1. **Cultural celebrations**
   - Festivals
   - Carnivals
   - Commemorations
   - Religious events
2. **Political and state**
   - Summits
   - Royal events
   - Political events
   - VIP visits
3. **Arts and entertainment**
   - Concerts
   - Award ceremonies
4. **Business and trade**
   - Meetings, conventions
   - Consumer and trade shows
   - Fairs, markets
5. **Educational and scientific**
   - Conferences
   - Seminars
   - Clinics
6. **Sport competition**
   - Amateur/professional
   - Spectator/participant
7. **Recreational**
   - Sport or games for fun
8. **Private events**
   - Weddings
   - Parties
   - Socials
   - Business events and tourism

At last, all events can be classified as productive and non-benefit events. Special programmes that are primarily designed to improve the organizers', participants', or some organizations'public image are characteristic of nonprofit events. One more sort of non-benefit events is good cause events, contrived to gather reserves, not for the coordinators or members, but rather for a noble cause purpose. By and by, most of events are beneficial. Their social objectives are connected to the implementation of a variety of programmes—sports, cultural, artistic, business, educational, political, or scientific—while their economic goal is profit.

4.7.2 Categories of Events

Events that drive global the travel industry in huge numbers can be assembled into four principal classifications.

- **Specialty events:** Frequently with closely connects to the host objective, whether the association is artistic, culinary, experience sports, live concerts and so forth (for example, Agra live performance). This classification may likewise incorporate events at the more modest finish of the range, like Hemis Celebration of Ladakh. These kinds of events are easy to put on and do not cost a lot to organize, and they are more likely to have attendees from other countries who spend a lot of money.
- **Participatory games:** For instance, the world bosses' games, world police and fire games, ironman events, and junior games. These are 'destination' events which draw in a huge number of contenders from outside the host country, the majority of whom carry various individuals with them (life partners, companions, family) and frequently broaden their event related stay into a vacation.
- **Signature cultural events:** Events which gain a worldwide standing as 'must see' and incorporate, for instance, South by South West (SXSW) in Austin, Texas, Sonar celebration in Barcelona, White Evenings in Melbourne, or the Edinburgh Periphery Celebration and Hogmanay, in Scotland.
- **International sports events:** For instance, single or multi-sport events like the World Cup Rugby, the Visit de France, and big showdowns for different games (sports, swimming, tumbling and so on.). These kinds of events have the potential to not only attract many participants and spectators but also to receive extensive worldwide television coverage. They also have the potential to significantly raise the profile of the country as a destination and its brand. The Summer Olympic Games and the Football World Cup would be the biggest examples of this kind of event. However, smaller international sporting events have the potential to have a similar impact on a smaller scale and frequently involve less financial risk.

4.8 BENEFITS OF EVENTS

The likely advantages of facilitating significant events according to the point of view of the guest economy include:

1. **Structural expansion of the visitor economy:** Guests coming to a city or district for an event will add to a lighter economy, with guest consumption affecting livelihoods all through related supply chains. The host nation will gain in terms of employment, income, and improved living conditions because of the multiplier effect.

2. **Alignment of tourism with other strategies:** The requirements of hosting a major event can be used to promote an integrated whole-of-government approach and maximize synergies between relevant development and growth infrastructures. These infrastructures, which are built for events, are one of the most visible and lasting legacies for the city or region that hosts them and can have real effects on tourism growth.
3. **Marketing and promotion:** Pre-event branding, which is associated with the successful hosting of a major event, can provide long-term recognition of destination branding in key tourism markets, encourage attendees or participants to return, and provide a better understanding of the event's focus, such as sports, arts, and culture, food, and wine, etc.
4. **Environmental impacts:** The international focus that is frequently associated with major events can help prioritize work on an often neglected or underdeveloped built environment, increasing destinations' attractiveness and competitiveness.

A positive legacy can encourage community and stakeholder support for an event, represent a tangible return on investment, or justify public expenditure. In addition, ensuring that events are managed in an environment-friendly manner is becoming a high priority in terms of branding. However, strategic planning well in advance of the event, adopting a long-term perspective, and evaluation throughout the event lifecycle—from inception to post-event—are necessary for a successful outcome. Any foundation improvement should be worked with long haul use as the need, and in a perfect world with financing and assets reserved for the post-games time frame.

4.9 EVENT MANAGEMENT STRATEGY

Most people agree that events are a good opportunity generator for the economy and tourism, and they also bring a lot of social and community benefits to the place they are held.

The significant drivers of this technique are the social, and ecological advantages of local area events. A reasonable vision is expected to give guidance to movement later, thus the improvement of events. The executives procedure for Irwin. In fostering this procedure our goals are to:

- Acquire a sound comprehension of existing events and scenes.
- Accomplish lucidity in regards to the job and obligations of event the board organization to help and host events.
- Create a reasonable, result centered events programme which expands the capability of our contribution in events.
- Include in the events programme elements of the destination's culture, lifestyle, and environment;
- Seek after crusade which support events and which add to in general objective showcasing.

4.10 OBJECTIVES OF EVENT MANAGEMENT

Each event should have an obviously expressed generally point. Otherwise, the event ought not to take place. Events require a lot of focused effort and dedication. This responsibility can emerge from a veritable conviction among all members that the points are advantageous and that they will be helpful in the long haul.

Each event must have its own set of goals in addition to a broader goal. These goals must be clear and written in a way that lets you assess the event's success after it is over.

Goals ought to constantly be Savvy.

- REALISTIC set goals that the organizing team can realistically achieve.
- TIMED establish a timeframe for achieving the goals.
- SPECIFIC to the particular event and particular aspects of it.
- MEASURABLE express the goals in numbers and quantities.
- AGREED ensure that all team members are aware of the goals.

4.11 ROLE OF CREATIVITY

The capacity to create, bring into existence, invent into a new form, produce through imaginative skill, and produce something new are all hallmarks of creativity. We are socialized into accepting only a small number of permissible or normal things, so creativity in event management helps businesses by opening up new opportunities for problem solving and growth that would not be possible with more conventional methods. Creativity is not the ability to create something from nothing; rather, it is the ability to generate new ideas by combining, changing, or reapplying existing ideas. Creativity is also an attitude, the capacity to accept change and newness, the willingness to play with ideas and possibilities, flexible new points of view on issues from an imaginative methodology can prompt new and maybe up til now inconceivable arrangements.

Creativity among event management company managers has numerous benefits. A portion of these is recorded beneath:

- Obtaining advancement.
- Supervising teams in the workplace.
- Discovering unusual perspectives within the company.

The following is a list of each of the benefits of creative managerial skills and how they can be used in business:

1. **Accomplishing objectives and development:** At the point when event directors approach objectives according to an imaginative perspective, they gain the capacity to handily arrive at objectives more. An inventive chief sees extraordinary ways to arrive at these objectives. The creative manager can plan a route to new levels of success that other managers in the company cannot see, whether it is how to increase profit or expand product offerings.
2. **Promoting a positive attitude in the workplace:** As organizations develop and processes change over the long haul, lower-level staff can frequently feel disregarded.

By implementing unconventional strategies and concepts to include individuals and teams in the success of the business, creative managers present several opportunities to rectify this mindset.

Instead of taking ideas from the top, a creative manager might suggest that employees brainstorm ideas from their perspective. Representatives do not necessarily have a similar data as the board, so seeing issues or improving thoughts from inside could prompt new or significant thoughts and data to assist with shaping answers for issues.

3. **Tracking down improbable viewpoints:** An event management company must expand, change, and design its own path to success to succeed. Managers who are creative are open to novel ideas and points of view. Improbable points of view consider very interesting roads to be uncovered, which can be utilized to devise especially intriguing changes to help the organization flourish and develop.

4.12 EVENTS COMMITTEE

In event planning, the event team and committee are pivotal components for successful execution. The event committee holds the responsibility of making crucial decisions that shape the event's direction. Leading this team is often an event planner, who coordinates the diverse members' efforts. These teams benefit immensely from having individuals with varied backgrounds and experience, as this diversity brings a range of perspectives to the table. Among the team members, a marketing specialist plays a vital role by promoting the event to the target audience, ensuring optimal attendance. Collaboration is a cornerstone, where team members share ideas and tasks, fostering a sense of unity and cooperation. Effective communication within the team is equally vital, promoting understanding and aligning everyone toward the common event goals. Such collaboration and communication synergies ensure that the event planning process is both efficient and successful.

The events committee was established with the intention of advising council on short-term and long-term planning related to community, recreational, and cultural events in accordance with budgetary guidelines approved annually.

The events council endeavours to invigorate and empower events that address the issues of the local area and proposition the best an open door to give financial advantages and potential to showcase noticeable spots.

The events committee's responsibilities include the following:

- Exhort committee on proposals for gathering consumption before the yearly financial plan cycle.
- In accordance with agreed-upon budgets and employee delegations, fund, or co-fund any capital and maintenance improvements.
- Create and draw in new events.
- Look for alliances to create new events.
- Evaluate major council events at the conclusion of them and provide advice as needed.

	Financial Reporting	
Risk Management	Audit and Compliance Committee	Internal Controls
Compliance	External Audit	Internal Audit

4.12.1 Committee Structure

The big event committee structure

(a) Executive Director/ President

- Hold space for chief advisory group gatherings
- Plan and run chief advisory group gatherings
- Direct all methodology day of the event
- Plan and run—mock large event day
- Direct chief advisory groups
- Contact among client and partner
- Advisory group improvement - plan social exercises for the chief board
- Work with accomplices on member join and tasks to worksites

(b) Treasure Revenue

- Establish and control a budget
- Approve spending
- Keep track of all expenses

(c) Vice President Events

- Setup on the day of the event
- Reserve all facilities for the event
- Arrange all aspects
- Back stage management
- Work with the Executive Director for a 'mock' event
- Registration and other formalities on behalf of the organization
- Form a committee to visit each site
- Team management coordination
- Work on Team Manager Training
- Worth with the Parking Coordinator
- Create a parking plan
- Create and manage a team of parking volunteers
- Work with the Ceremony Coordinator
- Solidify entertainment

(d) Marketing Director

- Create and maintain a website
- Ensure that advertising guidelines are followed
- Collaborate with communication and marketing personnel
- Develop and implement an action plan for recruitment
- Create and implement marketing materials for recruitment
- Encourage registration for the Big Event at Get on Board Day and other events
- Produce videos to promote the Big Event
- Select the official spokesperson for the Big Event in consultation with the Marketing Advisor.

(e) Communication Sub-Committee

- Foster all limited time advertising things to make and balance flags nearby
- Plan shirt for advisory group and volunteers (work shirt and decent shirt)
- Update logo
- Correspondence another sub-advisory group
- Deal with all virtual entertainment accounts (Instagram, Twitter,
- Book appearances for morning news programmes
- Contact radio broadcasts
- Photographic artist/videographer day of the event
- Coordinate the gathering picture during opening event ofhost media upon the arrival of the Enormous Event

(f) Standards Sub-Committee

- Communicate with participating organizations
- Collaborate with the Marketing Director
- Participate in the Organization Expo at orientation
- Develop and implement an Action Plan for Recruitment
- Manage monetary donations
- Write thank-you notes to key players in the day and to any donors
- Gather any donations
- Communicate with Finance Director
- Govern sponsorship letters and make sure we deliver on what is on the letter to sponsors
- In-kind Sponsorship Coordinator
- Seek donations/sponsorships from various restaurants and stores for ceremony food, volunteer snacks, and water, and possibly for fundraising events

4.12.2 Coordination Among Committees

Co-appointment among sub-boards of trustees is the unification and reconciliation of the endeavours of gathering individuals and to give solidarity of activity in the accomplishment of shared objectives. It is a hidden force that binds all other management functions. Without the coordination of the activities that fall under the management function, no function can be carried out effectively. Coordination is useful in accomplishing the goals of the association. The process of coordination among sub-committees is not fixed. It prefers group activities rather than individual activities for coordination. The supervisors need to put forth exceptional attempts for coordination. Coordination is not something that just happens. Coordination prompts solidarity of activity. It is fundamental at each degree of the executives to accomplish the hierarchical objective.

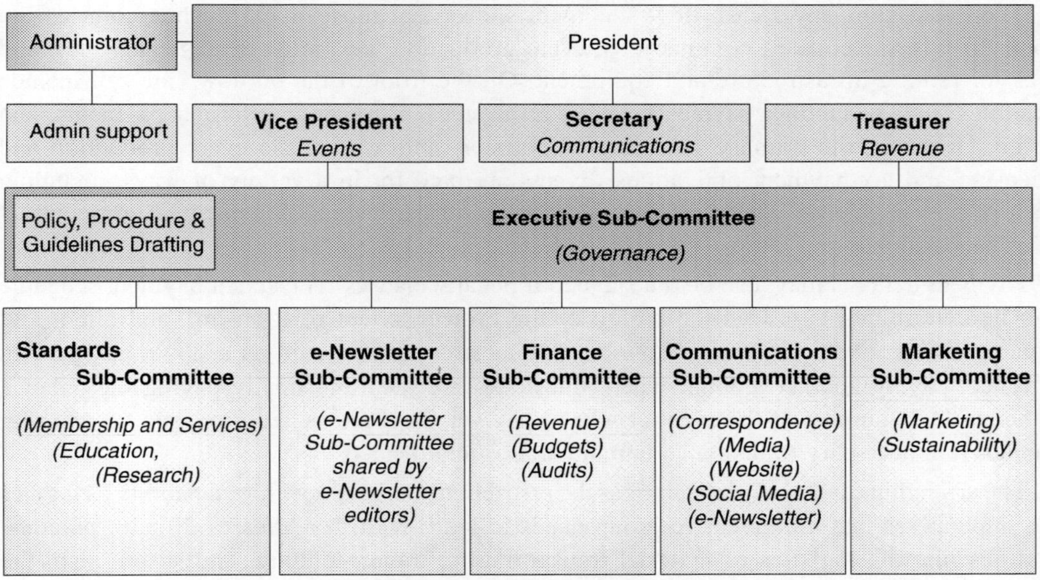

4.13 FUNCTIONS OF EVENT MANAGEMENT

4.13.1 Planning

The goal of planning is to maximize the use of all resources. Given the need for a variety of event activities and the complexity of the decision-making process, a cross-functional team is necessary in this case. The preparation of the event budget is an important part of any event that comes after understanding the client profile, the brief for the event, the target audience, and the expected number. The planning function is involved in micro-level event coordination activities like coordinating, facilitating, and discussing the technical specification with the creative team, lighting, stages, and sets. One of the most difficult tasks in the planning function is shortlisting artists and supporting artists in accordance with creative artists' wishes.

Additionally, it entails investigating different options for locating the event, the location, the conditions of the event, and gathering information to assist in deciding whether the event will take place indoors or outdoors. During the final task, comprehending licence, clearance, and other requirements. The event coordinator is tasked with the responsibility of arranging for the same whenever it is required.

Part of the planning process also includes deciding on soft issues like whether the show will be ticketed, non-ticketed, or fully or partially sponsored. Organizers then, at that point, do a gamble rating for the event. A planning function also includes determining the appropriate food and beverages to be served on the event as well as defining arrangements for the quality of hospitality and the dress code of the hosts/hostesses based on the audience profile. This is especially true given that the kinds of beverages served will have different security and other arrangements.

The event company's cash flow statement shows that most of its revenue comes from sponsorships, ticket sales, commissions, event production fees, artist management fees, and fees for renting infrastructure and equipment. On the front of the outflow, one can include headings such as supplier payments, venue hiring fees, artist, and performer payments, and so on. However, the primary sources of the major outflows are the event production and licensing and tax payment obligations. Events are paid for in a variety of ways, including cash or part payments, which are agreed upon by all parties and documented in a contract after negotiations.

Payment defaults may also be the subject of penalty clauses. The actual payment schedule can be determined based on the nature of the project, client relationship, and client and organizer objectives. This might involve paying a certain amount as a down payment in advance, paying another amount when milestones are met, and finally paying the balance either at the beginning of the event or when it is over. To meet the requirements for working capital, it is necessary to take a certain amount as an advance.

The arranging capability characterizes the restrictions of the innovative capability as it gives the imperatives that the inventive group needs to work with. It addresses difficult practical realities like the logistics of material transportation, travel, lodging, and so on. also, the systems administration, viz., media plan, promotion plans, standards printing, tickets welcome planning and printing. It tries to define and control the inflow and outflow of money prior to, during, and after the event to provide a complete picture of the flow of the event. Therefore, it is necessary for the planning function to play a significant role in event preparation. Planning also takes on a greater role as a function because of the limited time available for decision-making. The following is a list of some of the event planning services that must be handled by the organizers: Travel plans, general media needs, catering, china, and silverware, stylistic layout, mmbellishments and props, amusement, exhibitor needs, webpage, sound and lights, speakers, stage style, site, executives and so forth.

4.13 2 Organizing

These events ordinarily have a group-based workplace and a venture sort of association design and that obligation are relegated to the important staff individuals in the group for the event.

The members of the team share responsibility for coordinating the necessary arrangements. Understanding getting sorted out with regards to even the executives basically includes the depiction of the exercises expected for an event, distinguishing individual and group undertakings and appropriation of obligations to organizers. A clear division of authority and delegation of authority are also part of the procedure. Such an activity helps in making a deliberate design for clarityof jobs and positions. With almost every event, these structures change based on the resources available. Project based structure are more well known. The majority of an event's organizing is done by event coordinators. Beginning from reaching the craftsmen or entertainers and if there should arise an occurrence of nonappearance or dropouts, making backup plans is one of the main elements of the event facilitator. The event coordinator works with the artists to set the date, terms, and conditions after the game plan has been developed by creative functions and planning. Following this, the necessary infrastructure is organized and constructed. After arranging for some of the softer aspects of organizing, planning, and coordinating with professionals for the physical availability of the sound, lights, stage, sets, and seating follows. These include handling the press conferences, press releases, and other forms of publicityfor favourable ticketing coverage and invitation management. The genuine obtainment of consents and licences from different government divisions at last turns into the facilitator's liability once the arranging stage chooses the necessities,arranging for hospitality management, including things like the stay, food and drinks, hostesses, and so on. Part of the organizing function is getting in touch with sponsors to make sure that the event organizers' promises to their customers are kept. In a nutshell, organizing is the process of carrying out the event within the parameters established by planning.

4.13.3 Staffing

Event management staffing requirements are defined by functional responsibilities in a project type organization structure. The significance of group structure, insight, foundation, and skill of colleagues assumes a vital part in event the executives. It is the size and the asset accessibility in the events venture that to a degree characterizes the specific job of the staff. People with a variety of skills are needed to oversee a wide range of activities in event management. When recruiting for events, one tends to believe that candidates with a past background in the hospitality industry, sales, or advertising would be ideally suited to handle the stress and uncertain situations during the entire process. Events, as was mentioned earlier, are physical in nature. In contrast, in a small firm, there is a fusion of roles based solely on the availability of time and staff. A large group of talented and incompetent workers and work staff should be directed really. Practically, one can isolate the accompanying utilitarian level liabilities that should be tended to inside the group for a particular event as examined above in the segment on coordinating.

The person in charge of a particular event is known as the overall coordinator. When it comes to making decisions regarding the event, he holds the ultimate authority. The creative group is led by the creative manager. The project manager plays a crucial role in the planning process and is responsible for making the event a conceptual success. The creation directors are likewise involved from the arranging stage however their primary obligation is making the event an actual achievement.

4.13.4 Leading and Coordination

Interpersonal skills make up both the overall sum and substance of events. The primary objective of coordination is to achieve synergy among individual efforts to achieve the team's objective. The general facilitators should be chiefs with fabulous relationship building abilities. They are ceaselessly expected to spur the staff and other junior facilitators to buckle down given the actual idea of the gig, the time imperatives included and the oddball idea of the event.

The general organizer likewise ought to have the option to direct the promoting and project administrators and this might try and imply that the experience and aptitude of previous events should be given to relative newcomers given the deficiency of expert event supervisors. The overall coordinator must therefore possess excellent communication skills, patience without allowing too many mistakes to occur, and the ability to use both the carrot and the stick in a balanced manner. The ability to identify and manage issues is one of the managership qualities that an event manager must possess in addition to the aforementioned qualities.

4.13.5 Controlling

Assessment and revision of deviations in the event intends to guarantee congruity with unique plans is the significance of controlling. Assessment is an action that looks to comprehend and gauge the degree to which an event has prevailed with regards to accomplishing its motivation. The reason for an event will contrast as for the class and variety of event. Evaluation can be placed in its proper context using one of the two methods. The idea of assessment expressed above was a basic assessment recovering what turned out badly. A more useful concentration for assessment is to make proposals about how an event may be improved to successfully accomplish its points more.

To direct an assessment and estimation practice it is fundamental that the predefined goals of the events have been appropriately perceived. Since any evaluation of an event would be rather pointless if it was organized without a clearly defined purpose, the brief ought to include all the data that needs to be communicated. The fundamental assessment process in events includes three stages,namely,, establishing measurable goals and evaluating with sensitivity; evaluating the performance prior to, during, and following the event, and finally addressing plan deviations. We have discussed it in greater detail in a separate section on event evaluation because it is an important function on its own.

Events are a dynamic and quickly developing area that has clear cooperative energies with the travel industry. They have the potential to boost regional development, provide media exposure, stimulate the improvement of infrastructure, and encourage the formation of new partnerships for financing facilities for sport, tourism, culture, and leisure if they are managed and hosted effectively.

As a result, major events present a one-of-a-kind opportunity to rethink or reposition a location and to support the growth of cutting-edge infrastructure. As a result, the successful hosting of such events is now seen as a tool for economic growth, job creation, branding, well-being, and urban revitalization in many nations.

As part of a larger strategy to increase visitor numbers and spend, many cities, regions, and countries are now allocating significant resources to planning, attracting, and supporting major events. The ability to accurately assess the economic, social, environmental, and other added value of tourism events are just a few of the obstacles that face the cities, regions, and nations that host these kinds of events. Other obstacles include lack of funding and effective governance.

PROGRESS CHECK

1. Summarize the key experience of any mega event that you have attended.
2. Discuss the important features of private events with examples.
3. Highlight the impact of event on local community.
4. What is the role of Event Management Committee?
5. How can an organization's structure influence its functioning and effectiveness?
6. What is manpower planning, and why is it important for leisure and human services agencies?
7. How can a effective organizational structure contribute to the successful delivery of leisure and human services?
8. Write a short note on code of ethics of event management.

MULTIPLE-CHOICE QUESTIONS

1. What is the primary responsibility of an event committee?
   (a) Managing event logistics (b) Handling event finances
   (c) Overseeing event promotion (d) Making key decisions
2. Which individual is often responsible for leading an event team?
   (a) Attendee (b) Guest speaker (c) Event planner (d) Caterer
3. What is the benefit of having diverse members on an event team?
   (a) Reducing communication challenges (b) Streamlining decision-making
   (c) Ensuring unanimous agreement (d) Bringing varied perspectives
4. What role does a marketing specialist play on an event team?
   (a) Coordinating event logistics (b) Handling guest registrations
   (c) Managing event finances (d) Promoting the event
5. What does the term 'collaboration' mean in the context of event teams?
   (a) Avoiding all disagreements (b) Working independently
   (c) Sharing ideas and tasks (d) Micromanaging team members
6. How can effective communication benefit an event team?
   (a) It reduces the need for decision-making
   (b) It eliminates the need for diverse team members
   (c) It fosters understanding and cooperation
   (d) It speeds up event planning

7. An event manager must recruit personnel during which stage of an event management plan?
   (a) Negotiating the contract for the event (b) Coordinating the event
   (c) Staging the event (d) Scheduling the event
8. Event managers must post signs to direct spectators while
   (a) Negotiating the contract for the event (b) Coordinating the event
   (c) Staging the event (d) Scheduling the event
9. Who is the creative side of the event design industry?
   (a) Event planner (b) Event manager (c) Event coordinator (d) Event administrator
10. What does an event manager do?
    (a) An event manager helps choose themes of the event.
    (b) An event manager helps create menus.
    (c) An event manager helps with choosing entertainment.
    (d) An event manager helps with parking logistics.
11. Duties of leisure management staffs is considered a
    (a) Job specification (b) Job description (c) Job responsibility (d) None of these
12. It is advisable that the Event Director
    (a) Is solely responsible for making important decisions about the event
    (b) Consults with stakeholders before making important decisions about the event
    (c) Leaves import decisions about the event to stakeholders
    (d) Forms a committee to make decisions about the event
13. Which of the following is not a function of the event organising committee?
    (a) Provide advice to the event director
    (b) Take a share of the tasks involved in organising of the event
    (c) Develop the event management plan
    (d) Share in the process for making important decisions about the event
14. An event director should monitor the progress of the planning and organization of event tasks.
    (a) True (b) False

Answers to Multiple-Choice Questions

1. (d) 2. (c) 3. (d) 4. (d) 5. (c) 6. (c) 7. (b) 8. (c)
9. (c) 10. (a) 11. (b) 12. (b) 13. (a) 14. (a)

Chapter 5

Event Management Planning

Objectives

After going through this chapter the reader will be able to:

- Highlight different proportions of event planning.
- Understand the roles of different people adheres in this planning management.
- Be able to plan and develop a timeline for event management.
- Be able to review the planning and delivery of an event.

5.1 INTRODUCTION

Events allow organizations to showcase their activities or services in the community. Events are an important part of community life and it is a rewarding experience to contribute to a successful event. However, anyone who had been involved in running an event understands how daunting the task can be. This unit has been designed to provide insight to prepare a comprehensive 'event management plan'.

5.2 EVENT PLANNING

Event management can be regarded as the creation and development phase of either small or large-scale corporate managing powers to host parties, events, concerts, and conventions with a defined objective of optimum serving capacity to their guests. An event manager's job is to oversee and arrange every aspect of an event, including researching, planning, organizing, implementing, controlling, and evaluating.

Event planning is a process of creating, communicating, and implementing a more operational roadmap to guide the actions, policies, and decision-making. It should align with the strategic plan and assist in its implementation. The plan of an event management company is simply the document that lays out the resulting directions, actions, and implementation schedule. It is especially focused on delivering the operational horizon from one to three years.

These plans are typically created to guide the internal operations of an enterprise, summarize its operational and financial objectives for the near future, and to indicate how these objectives will be achieved and monitored.

Event management planning is a meticulous process that starts with defining clear event objectives to guide the entire endeavour. The event planner, a key team member, handles the coordination of logistics, ensuring that all components come together seamlessly. Employing the SWOT analysis—evaluating **S**trengths, **W**eaknesses, **O**pportunities, and **T**hreats—provides an effective strategic framework. Determining the event's date and time relies heavily on the availability of the venue. This schedule, documented in a run sheet, outlines each activity for the event. A budget is pivotal as it allocates financial resources to different aspects of the event, ensuring financial responsibility. During the pre-event phase, marketing efforts target the intended audience to maximize attendance. Despite careful planning, challenges may arise during the event. In such cases, successful event planners adapt and find solutions on-site to ensure a smooth experience for attendees.

This aspect presents a roadmap that helps to modify new opportunities in this field.

5.2.1 Benefits of Event Planning

- To define and practically apply good event planning and financial management practices in annual planning and day-to-day work.
- To provide logic and justification for prioritizing different tasks and decisions over others.
- To systematically define tasks, logic, roles, responsibilities, strategic alignments (internally and externally), timetables, and budgets.
- To present an opportunity for key players like stakeholders, boards, staff, and partners to get consulted when defining the key objectives.
- To provide frameworks for developing strategies related to manpower management, marketing, competitor analysis, and stakeholders.

5.2.2 Advantages of Event Planning

It help us to think ahead and prepare for the future, clarify goals, develop a vision, identify issues that will need to be addressed, choose between options whether a project is possible, make the best use of resources, motivate staff and the community, assign resources and responsibilities to achieve the best results.

Help to eliminate

- overambitious projects
- unsustainable projects
- undefined problems
- unstructured project work plans

5.3 FORCES AFFECTING EVENT PLANNING

It is important for event organizations to interact and transact with their environment as the business environment has a direct relationship with the organization. The interaction with the environment directly highlights the possible success or failure of an established organization.

The enterprise has little influence on the environment and therefore, it is important for the company to identify with the environment of its operation and devise its policies in relation to the forces in that environment. The forces affecting the external environment of business areas follows.

The political environment of any region or state influences the events to larger extent. This environment is influenced by the political organization, philosophy, government ideology, nature and extent of bureaucracy, and political stability. Even organizing an event may get various benefits from hosting the local policies from government policies.

In today's competitive world, most people have an urbanized approach to celebration. There are many community events and festivals in the urbanized world, celebrating their character of life. In India many festivals such as Durga Puja, Ganesh Chaturthi, Diwali and Dussehra are celebrated with enthusiasm and local participation. This aspect means event management companies that deliver optimum and professional approaches thoroughly.

Technology has put greater effort to dissolve issues related to defining social events more professionally. The Internet provides new possibilities for communication, information resources, and is an efficient marketing tool. Making connections between technology and event management puts together a great perspective in defining the professional management power in the event planning context.

Changing cultural diversity and generations in communities have resulted in shifting values that provide opportunity in both aspects. Diversity, unity, and equality are emphasized. Environmental and globalization awareness and quality are emerging as important values for event management companies. In India various events such as Jaipur Literature Festival, various trade fairs and travel arts promote the spirit of cultural synthesis.

Stakeholders groups, organizations, and individuals who have invested or have an interest in the success of events. The event stakeholders, organizers, customers and the community sponsors and other sponsors, partners supporting an event either financially or developing the considerate support in event planning and management. Guests and customers are stakeholders help because an event is organized for providing them a particular product, which is commonly leisure, education, or other service. The local community provides many resources for events, such as businesses, hospitality services and public places, staff, and volunteers.

The other forces that disturb event management are those that are considering event planning its perspective knowledge to hold programmes like local tourism bodies, facilities along with defining the perspective management with defining infrastructure within.

An event management company's stability and profitability are interdependent of its reliability to quickly identify and respond to changes in the external environment. Change is inevitable and having the flexibility to deal with unexpected market situations can mean the difference between survival and extinction for an organization.

The External Environment

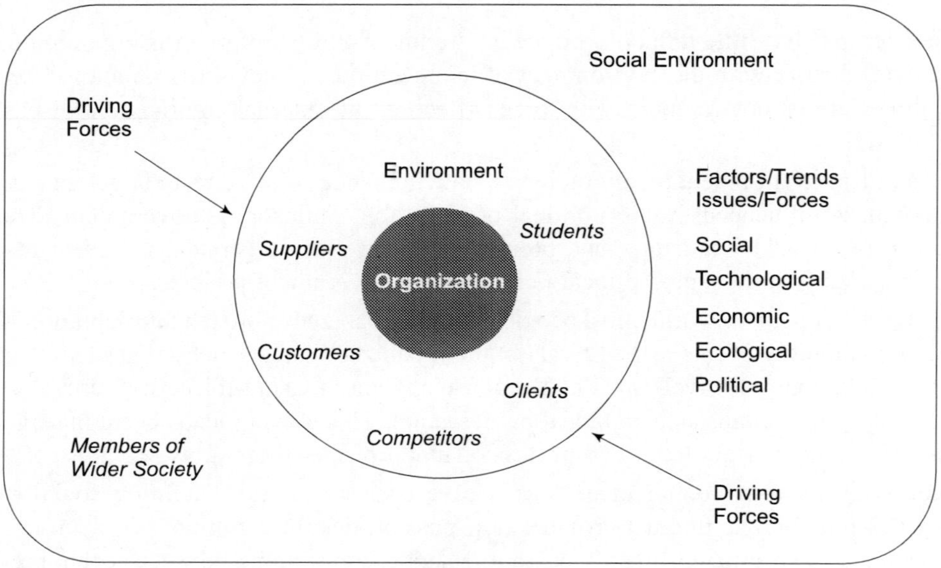

Fig. 5.1 External environment (Reference: K. van der Heijden)

5.3.1 Conducting an Environmental Scan

While external factors like government policy changes are one time unexpected, that does not mean one cannot prepare for them. The important way to define a business perspective to define an essential framework is an important aspect that is necessary. On the other hand, conducting the environmental scan is an important segment in event management.

An environmental scan is the process of methodically gathering, analyzing, and interpreting data about external opportunities and threats. It is a mechanism to collect relevant information about the outside world, the competitors, and the market position of the event management company.

One of the popular ways to define this performance measure is to develop environmental scan with PESTLE analysis.

- **(P) Political:** The extent to which a government may influence the economy and thereby impact organizations within a certain industry. This includes political stability, government policy and tax policy and trade.
- **(E) Economic:** How economic conditions shift supply and demand directly affects a company. This includes economic growth or decline, and changes in interest and inflation rates.
- **(S) Social:** Changes in the socio-cultural market environment illustrate customer needs and wants. This includes emerging trends, population analytics, and demographics.

(T) Technological: How innovation and development evolve a market or industry. This includes automation, technology awareness and adoption rates, and new services or products.

(E) Environmental: The environmental standards compile with event management composure to operate the market policies along with establishing meaningful applications thoroughly. Attitudes towards developing media with industrial and entertainment management are vital.

(L) Legal: The current legal allowances or requirements within countries or territories in which an organization operates. This includes requirements, labour laws, and consumer protection laws.

After one PESTEL analysis (sometimes known as PESTLE analysis), i.e., a thorough scanning of the environment external factors, identifies uncontrollable, organization should prepare for. It would be appropriate to develop a plan beforehand to understand material impact in this business.

5.4 STEPS IN EVENT MANAGEMENT PLAN

The steps involved in an Event Management Plan are studied following subheadings: Starting off and Feasibility.

5.4.1 Starting Off

The important thing that is necessary to consider when developing a new creation of an event is the individuals who will be involved. They need to develop innovative ideas to develop event planning. Thirdly, each concept needs to be put through a feasibility screening. Contingencies are a common element in various types of contacts where certain criteria need to be fulfilled.

The event can be organized by existing groups or the committee of clubs or an event planning company. In events an organizing team needs to be formed, and the type of event needs to be considered. Will the event be cultural, leisure, personal, or organizational, and will the organization be volunteer or professional, or both? The optimal size of a team is said to be around people to maintain good organization. The team member selection process needs to consider skills and experience, as members should complement each other's strengths and weaknesses. Typical tasks in a team are developing marketing, financing, health and safety, resource finding, recording and legalities, and. Hardship can be treated as the useful progress of a team's management power that needs to be modified significantly to develop optimum measure. Once the team has been formed, it must begin debating and coming up with ideas for the event.

Ideas for events can either come from somewhere else than the event organizer, such as community networks, individuals, and special interests groups, or the organizer needs to invent ideas. An occasion for brainstorming may be needed, and it is advised that brainstorming also includes consultation with stakeholders separately, or together with the team. The discussion should result in some creative ideas for the event according to the customer expectations.

The ideas should next be feasibility tested. The key aspects of the feasibility are how well organized, attend, watch, participate in, and pay for the event is considered. Understanding of operational, financial, and marketing factors is also required at this stage. All these segments related to the marketing a target, strategic developments, operative business measures and developing budgets that are essential to be considered in the primary phrase of event management context.

5.4.2 Feasibility

What are you trying to do and for whom?

What benefits to the participants can we build into our concept? What are the various plans to achieve this?

What are the pros and cons of each concept?

What is the best concept and how we will it get there?

5.5 OPERATIONAL PLANNING

An event can be successful with the result of careful, structured, and logical planning, which decreases uncertainty, centres attention to goals, and makes operation effective. Planning is probably the most crucial stage of event planning because it directly affects the event's success. Planning can help with coordination, concentration, and foresight. It can also be used to evaluate and manage the event's progress and outcome. A specific draft to develop a brainstorming important course is vital for each team member. Outcome of the feasibility needs to be formulated thoroughly in this aspect that is incorporated in event management along with the focus area. This would develop event focus area people that are incorporated within this context to understand various organizations' prospects.

A roadmap to develop the planning process needs to be created to understand the importance of team members. Outcome of the feasibility is an important aspect to develop optimum event planning system and process. The various activities proposed to organize meaningful events are being organized by individuals of event planners in this accord.

At this point in the planning process, ask these questions:

- Who are the key representatives from within the stakeholders to champion our event?
- What is our action team committed to?
- What particular strengths and experiences do committee members bring?

The planning phase requires the team to anticipate potential issues and develop solutions for emergency circumstances. To foresee such possibilities an analysis should be carried out to analyze the internal and external environments, including available dates and times, competing events, demand and capacity of the market, and potential venues and staff. The information acquired during this assessment should be used to determine the best course of action.

5.5.1 Finances and Budget

Every team member must be informed of the necessary financial outlays for event planning and management. For a public event, the financial matters become more complex involving studies on financial feasibility based on various financial techniques.

No matter the degree of intricacy, the financial arrangements must align with the event's goals.

The expenditure should be estimated through an identification and assessment process. To understand where the point of break-even is possible, the variable and fixed expenses must be identified. In terms of events, fixed costs involve the hiring of venue, staffing, marketing, and insurance, for instance, while variable costs are:catering, entertainment and accommodation at the completion of the total costs it is important that all fixed, variable, and other possible costs are calculated and included, to give a genuine picture of the cost side of the budget. Budget items to consider:

Staff time

- Marketing expenses (designers, printing, postage, etc.).
- Transportation venue.
- Guest accommodations (if applicable) food and beverage.
- Entertainment and recreation.
- Audio-visualequipment and production cost security (police), etc.
- Special needs (interpreters, etc.).
- Taxes and gratuities, service charges, etc.
- Contingency fund for unanticipated, last-minute expenses.

Admission fees and revenue-generating activities including games, pamphlets, food and sales stalls, products, transportation services, and parking lots are just a few examples of the many ways' money can be made and selling rights for broadcasting for instance. Moreover, events organized by governmental agencies may depend on a budgeted part of tax money, and funding for events can be sought at governmental agencies or official bodies, or sponsors. Public agencies and private foundations can make a grant to support a cause. Local governments may give grants to events that advance community spirit and unity.

5.5.2 Funding and Promotion

Organization commits money or any other resources to organize an event successfully in exchange for some promotional benefit to other organization who is helping by providing this kind of support. Company history should feature in the about page in their website. This is beneficial for both the organization. This funding is required for smooth cash flow and better organization of event. First need to check the budget and accordingly need to approach various organizations for funding the event. Event objectives, event background and event budget should feature in request for proposal.

5.5.3 Organize Team

Any major special event requires a dedicated team effort to manage every detail.

Where possible, the stakeholder involved with the activity should be invited to participate in the planning committee. Depending on the nature and size of your event, you might think about choosing an event manager or chair in addition to specific chairpersons for certain subcommittees, like:

- Venue, logistics and catering management (selection, contracts, permits, insurance, etc.).
- Guest management (invitations, RSVPs, greeters, registration, seating arrangements, etc.).
- Speakers/presenters (selecting, confirming, logistics, management, etc.).
- Activities/entertainment.
- Publicity/promotion (web presence, events calendars, printed programmes, media relations, signage, social media, etc.).
- Sponsor/partner management.
- Transportation volunteer management.

5.5.4 Blueprint of Functional Area

The growth of the event depends on finding a site and a venue. There may be several attractive choices of venue, in which case the organizers need to check each venue and spot which of them matches the requirements of the event best, is best priced, and is professionally managed. Attention is to be paid to appearance and aesthetics, sound, smell, and cleanliness of facilities and types of equipment.

The selection of the venue where the event is to be held will also depend on the purpose, concept, and theme of the event. It is the responsibility of the event planner to ensure that the chosen site is suitable for the intended event and that all relevant information and approvals are obtained for the event.

- When deciding on a suitable venue the following needs to be considered
- The anticipated size of the event and expected visitors
- Entrances and exits and car parking provisions
- Indoor versus outdoor requirements related to activities
- Requirements of people with special needs
- Access to infrastructure—power, water, communications, washrooms, etc.
- Risk management and occupational health and safety

5.5.5 Site Plan

A site plan is an overall framework indicating the ground layout of the event. Usually, event site maps will show the venue's perimeters, street entrances, stall placements, etc.

The site plan can be used by all significant stakeholders as part of the planning process, with consultation on the layout.

A site plan should be simple to understand and strategically distributed throughout the site in case of a major event. Staff and volunteers can utilize the site plan to set up the event, and it can be a great resource in case of an emergency.

When drawing the site plan, it is essential to use a simple format and include surrounding streets and landmarks. The site plan must be clear and show all important event features.

All entrances and exits information centre paths used by vehicles.

Path for pedestrians only.

Locations of the food and other stall holder's stage and temporary structure locations seating configurations shade and/or shelter emergency access routes.

Entertainment sites rides, jumping castle toilet facilities.

Waste bins/refuse sites first aid posts drinking water sites.

Approved liquor consumption areas no-alcohol (dry) areas.

5.5.6 Security Check Posts

Another very important consideration of special events is crowd management. A first step in this endeavour is estimating the number of attendees to develop a sound monitoring and control plan. Understanding the expected audience's characteristics and the need to compare various crowd control measures for various event kinds are both crucial.

A comprehensive security plan is a must to properly control events, protect attendees, and provide a fun and secure environment. A good security plan will assure the right number of law enforcement and security personnel. It will address training, logistics and scheduling.

Maps of the event are and surrounding areas should be developed. These security plan should involve everyone associated with the event. The security plan should address the possible adverse behaviours of individuals or groups. Large events should consider a command post that coordinates all event activities. These posts should be open before the public enters the event area and should operate until after the event is completed.

5.5.7 Power Lighting

It is essential that the event organizer review and make necessary arrangements for the supply and installation of any electrical/power requirements for the event, such as the use of generators, extension cords and cables.

It is important to ensure that adequate safety guidelines are followed that electrical leads do not create trip hazards. Lead joints and connections are not to be accessible to the public or exposed to damp conditions, temporary electrical leads must be flexible cables and double adaptors and piggy-back plugs are not to be used.

5.5.8 Water

Water is required for multiple uses such as catering, entertainment for cleaning purposes before, during and after the event.

All taps located within the selected venue should be checked to ensure they are in good working order prior to the event. Where any deficiencies are identified they are to be reported to the concerned management at the earliest possibility to enable the problem to be repaired prior to the event.

5.5.9 Sanitary Facilities

The event organizer is in charge of making sure that participants have access to sufficient restrooms. The number of restrooms to be offered will depend on several variables, are given below.

5.5.10 Anticipated Crowd Numbers

The gender of patrons (women require more facilities than men) in the duration of the event.

Are the toilets accessible to people with limited mobility and parents with small children to ensure toilet supplies are restocked and for safety and cleanliness regularly wastewater management?

Availability of a plumber through the event for repair sand blockages, temporary structures and staging.

Tents, marquees, and portable stages all qualify as temporary structures and if being used at an event should be marked on the site plan.

5.5.11 Risk Management

Risk management is the logical and systematic process of eliminating or minimizing the adverse impact of activities which may give rise to dangerous or damaging situations. This requires the development of a framework within which risks can be identified, evaluated, treated, and monitored. Successful event management requires dedication risk management.

There are four basic types of risk that organizations that host events must consider.

Understanding the general types of risk facing an organization can provide a better understanding of the actions required to minimize exposure to risk. The four main categories of risk are:

- Physical risks involve injury, also cause the damage or destruction of property.
- Financial risks affect the financial situation of an organization or event and could include increased insurance premiums, cost overruns or costs associated with injuries.
- Moral or ethical risks involve the loss of quality of participant experience and confidence, adverse publicity and damage to an organization or event's image or reputation.
- Legal risks are losses and costs arising from legal actions for breach of a law, standard or guidelines or breaches or statutory duty of care. For instance, a restaurant or food vendor that does not adhere to the rules set forth by the local government regarding food preparation.

These hazards should be handled with an appropriate action plan for prevention and management. An emergency should be designed. The aim of an emergency plan is to minimise the threat to life and damage to property. As a result, the risk analysis ought to be included in the event plan. Depending on the complexity of the situation, precautions can range from first-aid personnel to open emergency access routes to entire catastrophe preparations.

Good atmosphere can make an event highly successful in the same way as a negative atmosphere can cause an event to fail. Good ambience is created through good and sufficient stimuli of visitors' senses and therefore the physical environment of the event is important, which together with the physiological, emotional, and cognitive reactions among the guests, become the ambience.

5.6 MARKETING

When brands throw parties, trade shows or brand launch events, one of the best ways to grab media attention is to have celebrities presence. To select celebrities the following factors should be considered:

It is advisable to make a list of celebrities you would like to have at the charity event. Once you have compiled a list of potential celebrities to get in touch with, you should be willing to trim it down.

You should make a list of potential celebrities whose personal interests and favourite causes are similar or matches the interests of events.

Make a plan entailing three methods of how to get into contact with the celebrity. It may be a good idea to reach the celebrity's publicist when doing a charity event.

Bringing celebrities to events because:

Celebrities get mediator tendons to cover the event.

Celebrities provide photo opportunities that will later make the event appear even more exciting–especially the sizzle reel.

Celebrities can impact the brand bases through social media and raise awareness of the event.

Celebrities are PR friendly, providing content for public relations story development.

Celebrities excite other event attendees, whether they are distributors, C-level executives, or the public.

When the plan is in place, and the event management team has agreed upon a general budget as well as the type of celebrity to approach, it is time to create an offer letter outlining the deal points. The letter specifies what the star must do (social media, the red carpet, meet-and-greets, product photographs, interviews, etc.), along with the time they are expected to come and depart.

5.6.1 Promotional Tools

Each special event will be marketed differently depending on its purpose, objectives, and markets. Marketing needs to be aimed at the target market, meaning the potential attendees. The team needs to determine whether the target market is a specific group or the public, and whether groups of special interests can be attracted. The physical area and the population from where an event may attract visitors, is called catchment area.

The importance of an event usually determines the catchment area of the target market, which grows in relation to the size of the event and links the complexity of the marketing directly to the complexity of the event.

Knowing the target market helps organizers reach and sway it to spread the word about the event and persuade potential attendees to come. Various strategies for event promotion are used to attract the potential customers. Awareness should be created through campaigns, advertising and public relations with the stakeholders.

Website: Every yearly event should have a website that provides crucial information. This is a great place to promote and advertise.

Newspapers: Local and regional papers will usually publish feature articles on events, especially if they are well written and have photographs attached. To avoid having to retype articles and images, it is crucial to email them as attachments.

Radio stations: Many local radio stations have early morning talk shows which welcome event celebrities as guests. What a great way to promote at no cost. Stations will often trade sponsorships for advertising spots. It is important to establish a good relationship with station officials putting vendor applications online, photographs for media, and updates.

Television stations: Most TV stations have shows and post-community calendar advertisements on their websites.

Posters: Posters are a must for most events and festivals. Many festivals design an annual logo to reflect their theme and use it on their posters and T-shirts. In high traffic areas, posters of varied colours and sizes should be displayed.

5.7 PREPARING THE EVENT OPERATIONS

The right people, supplies, and equipment should be available as the event day draws near. Everybody who is part of the event should be appropriately briefed right before the event so they can be efficient in their job. The leader of the team needs to be good at communicating and delegating as the situation can be in a constant state of flux. The team members should be equipped with mobile phones, so they can contact each other at all times. A controlled system for delivery acceptance should be established.

5.7.1 Managing Chief Guest

Many chief guests and celebrities enjoy spending time with their fans and have no issue with interacting with fans. Many famous people host events where they encourage their followers to attend so they can meet them, sign autographs for them, and pose for photos with them. Following are a few occasions where famous people meet fans.

Special events where the celebrities will stop on the red carpet to sign autographs and take pictures with fans are important.

Award ceremonies are also a place where celebrities will stop on the red carpet to interact with their fans.

To meet fans in person, celebrities often invite them to their book signing and record release parties.

Celebrities will even invite their favourite fans to VIP parties to interact with them to a certain level.

However, many celebrities are very cautious when it comes to allowing fans to get up close and personal because some fans become obsessed with the celebrity. Following are some safety measures used by celebrities when connecting with their fans.

When a celebrity is out and about, security officers will safeguard them from aggressive and irrational admirers.

The celebrity will have a publicist who is the go-to person if a fan wants to contact them personally.

The celebrity will take care to limit the amount of personal information posted on their social media profiles so that admirers cannot access it.

The celebrities will have staff who will check and monitor their social media activities to ensure there is no hacking of their social media accounts.

5.7.2 Event Entertainment

It takes extraordinary entertainment for an event to be remembered. Usually, the entertainment matches the theme. Festivals are known for providing continuous entertainment, which covers the entire kaleidoscope. Event entertainment may include:

Amusement rides, pony rides, vocalists, etc.

Dancers parades, crafts fair, food fair, street dances, magicians, etc.

5.7.3 Close-down, Survey and Legacy

An event's close-down comprises both physical and administrative components. The physical close-down will have be taking apart and removing of the equipment, whereas the administrative side of the close-down will involve filing, completion of accounts and paying bills, and collecting feedback.

The administrative side of the close-down willing Volvo picking up comments noting down verbal feedback, but also the settling of accounts and bills, acquittal contracts, along with an evaluation of how contractors and suppliers have done their job. The outcome will show the success in financial terms especially.

5.7.4 Event Survey Techniques

Conducting surveys or providing feedback forms during and after the event to gauge attendee satisfaction. Evaluating your success against the aims and objectives you identified at the beginning of the event planning process. Preparing a SWOT analysis to examine the strengths, weaknesses, opportunities, and threats associated with your event is essential.

5.7.5 Strength and Weakness

Strengths of the event may include:

- Strong attendance numbers.
- Wide range of food and beverages available, satisfaction with entertainers.
- Ten new members recruited because of event.
- Some examples of event weaknesses are: Too few volunteers, limited media coverage, expenditure exceeds income.
- Events are often celebrations of creativity and cultural uniqueness, local customs, lifestyle, and talents, and can thus have significant cultural impacts. Preservation and revitalization of unique cultures and traditions can be promoted by events. Some events leave social legacy or intangible impacts. The image and awareness of an area for tourist destination, social integration may improve, and a community's pride, happiness, and confidence may all increase.

5.8 EVENT PLANNING TIMELINE

5.8.1 High-Level Planning: Six Months Ahead of Event

- Establish event's objectives.
- Recruit event committee, solicit trust representative, select an event manager, or chair, and establish sub-committee chairs.
- Identify venue and negotiate details.
- Develop master plan and settle for the event's cost estimates(e.g., room rental, food & beverages, equipment, speaker fees, travel, etc.) and create a budget.
- Create communications plans (ensure staff and/or volunteers are identified to manage specific tasks, e.g., media relations, VIP coordination, printed material design and printing coordination, online/social media, etc.)
- Identify and confirm speakers/presenters/entertainers. Determine sponsorship levels/amounts.
- Identify and contact potential sponsors/partners.

5.8.2 Four Months Ahead of Event

- Determine VIPs and create RSVP tracking document (e.g., spreadsheet) speaker/presenter liaison:
- Finalize presentation/speech topics.
- Request bio-information, photo.
- Make travel and accommodation arrangements.
- Have legal review contracts; obtain signatures as appropriate, etc.,venue/logistics.
- Investigate need for any special permits, licences, insurance, etc. Determine and arrange all details regarding menu, A/V equipment, facilities, parking, signage, etc.
- Review security needs/plan for the event with venue manager communications plan.

- Request logos from corporate sponsors for online and printed materials on develop draft programme.
- Create draft event script (e.g., MC, speaker introductions, thanks, closing, etc.).
- Develop media list and prepare media alert/release, backgrounder, and media kit materials (e.g., speaker info, photos, etc.).
- Create event page on website.
- Create social media accounts/pages a needed consider developing promotional video for YouTube and Facebook page.
- If you are hosting a public event, consider registering your event on a variety of online event calendars, such, rotary club, etc.

5.8.3 Two Months Prior to Event

- Send reminders to contact list regarding registration/participation presenters/speakers.
- Confirm travel/accommodation details.
- Request copy of speeches and/or presentations.
- Sponsorship: Follow-up to confirm sponsorship and under writing publicity.
- Release press announcements about keynote speakers, celebrities, VIPs attending, honourees, etc.

5.8.4 One-Two Weeks Ahead

Schedule a meeting for all committee chairs to confirm all details against master plan – and ensure back-up plans are developed for a situation (e.g., plans for bad weather, back-up volunteers as VIP greeters, additional volunteers for registration or set-up, etc.)

Finalize the event script and inform all hosts, greeters, and volunteers of their responsibilities and schedules.

Final seating plan, VIP place cards, etc. Ensure that, as necessary, stage seating or front row reserved seating is provided for each trustee who will be present.

Provide final RSVP numbers to caterer.

Make print and online copies of any speeches, videos, presentations, etc.

5.8.5 One Day Ahead

Confirm media attending, ensure signage's place.

Ensure registration and media tables are prepared and stocked with necessary items (e.g., blank name badges, paper, pens, tape, stapler, etc.).

Ensure all promotional items, gifts, plaques, trophies, etc. are onsite.

5.8.6 Event Day

- Appoint someone to arrive early to attend to important event details.
- Ensure you have copies of all instructions, directions, phone numbers, keys, extra parking permits for VIP guests, seating charts and guest lists with you.

- Check-in with each Committee Chair to ensure the important the amiss on track.
- Bring water for speakers.
- Bring anemergency kit (kleenex, band-aids, safety pins, etc.).

5.8.7 Post Event

Conduct a post-event survey to learn what people enjoyed about your event, and where you have room to improve.

Conduct a post-event meeting and thorough evaluation of objectives vs. outcomes,

Gather all receipts, documentation, final attendance data, donations, etc., and update budget. Implement post-publicity plan –thank attendees for participating and promoting your ongoing programmes and how they can support youth rough out the early joining, volunteering, or making a sustaining donation.

Send thank-you letters to sponsors of volunteers speakers/presenters, donors of media in your thank-you notes, be sure to remind the recipients of the event's success.

5.8.8 Greening the Event

It is important to remember that events can harm our environment. By making the right decisions, we may significantly lessen its effect. The following advice can help you lessen the impact of your event.

- All events should aim to use the minimum amount of energy required. Minimize lighting needed by making use of natural light wherever possible. Water usage should be kept to a minimum.
- Tap water should be supplied to eliminate mileage and waste arising from bottled water.
- Recycling facilities are made available on site to match the types of wastes likely to be produced.
- Just what you will need and use soon should be ordered.
- Aim to re-use where possible. Food items like fruit that have been stored for later consumption and recyclable printed materials may fall under this category.
- If they are needed, provide reusable name badges, and collect the badges at the end of the event.
- Influence your suppliers, e.g., caterers should be asked to minimize waste caused by excess packaging and non-recyclable containers. Ensure over-catering is minimized.
- Aim to use recycled paper (min 80% recycled content) and print or copy double sided where needed.

Events vary widely in the variety, type, scale, and purpose. They range from large-scale international events such as the Olympic Games down to small-scale, local events such as a school exhibition day. They may also involve a range of activities or they could focus on just one activity or for one target group. Important processes like social development and personal expression are usually sparked by events.

PROGRESS CHECK

1. Highlight the various environmental factors that affect planning of events.
2. Write a note on event planning timeline.
3. Highlight the role of any two promotional tools in marketing of event.
4. Discuss with examples the role of celebrities in event management.
5. Describe the various phases involved in planning of an event.
6. Elaborate the various aspects involved in preparing a blueprint of functional area.

MULTIPLE-CHOICE QUESTIONS

1. What is the initial step in event management planning?
   (a) Evaluating event's success (b) Setting up ticket sales
   (c) Defining event objectives (d) Selecting event vendors
2. Which team member is responsible for coordinating event logistics?
   (a) Marketing manager (b) Entertainment coordinator
   (c) Venue owner (d) Event planner
3. What does the term "SWOT" stand for in event planning?
   (a) Special workforce and objectives team
   (b) Strategic workflow for organizing tasks
   (c) Strengths, weaknesses, opportunities, threats
   (d) Successful ways of organizing techniques
4. Which element is crucial for establishing the event's date and time?
   (a) Attendee preferences (b) Availability of event staff
   (c) Weather forecast (d) Venue availability
5. What is a 'run sheet' in event management?
   (a) A list of promotional materials (b) An outline of event expenses
   (c) A schedule of event activities (d) A summary of vendor contracts
6. What role does a budget serve in event planning?
   (a) It ensures entertainment quality (b) It guarantees event success
   (c) It allocates financial resources (d) It creates event objectives
7. Which stage of event planning involves promoting the event to the target audience?
   (a) Pre-event (b) Event execution (c) Post-event (d) Event evaluation
8. How can event planners manage unforeseen challenges during an event?
   (a) Ignoring them to maintain the flow (b) Adapting and finding solutions on-site
   (c) Cancelling the event immediately (d) Shifting blame to vendors
9. Contingencies are a common element in various types of contacts. What do these specifically entail?
   (a) Monetary remuneration
   (b) A non-disclosure or confidentiality clause

(c) A list of services
(d) Dependence on the fulfilment of certain criteria

10. Which of the following sections should be included in an RFP (request for proposal)?
    (a) Event objective (b) Event background (c) Event budget (d) All of these
11. On which of the following pages should a company describe its history?
    (a) The about page (b) The content page (c) The home page (d) A separate page
12. Maria and Gian are planning a 60-person dinner party for their wedding anniversary. They would like to have an open bar. To calculate total beverage costs for the night, Maria and Gian need to determine __________, followed by __________ .
    (a) the average cost per beverage; how many ounces per beverage
    (b) the average beverage number of beverages consumed per person; the average cost per beverage
    (c) how many ounces per beverage; how much total liquor is available
    (d) the cost of the most expensive beverage; the cost of the least expensive beverage
13. Mr. Valdez is reviewing the capital expenditures section of his master budget. Which of the following transactions would appear in this section?
    (a) His hiring of 50 labourers to build an extension to his hotel.
    (b) His annual costs for material production.
    (c) His purchase of land surrounding his hotel for expansion plans.
    (d) His hiring of 200 employees to work in the expanded portion of his hotel.
14. Which of the following should be developed first
    (a) The events marketing strategy (b) Sponsorship proposals for the event
    (c) Event plan (d) A work breakdown structure
15. Which aspect must be considered when developing an event marketing plan
    (a) The personality that brand is trying to convey
    (b) Target audience
    (c) Lasting impression to leave an audience
    (d) All of the above

Answers to Multiple-Choice Questions

1. (c)	2. (d)	3. (c)	4. (d)	5. (c)	6. (c)	7. (a)	8. (b)
9. (d)	10. (d)	11. (a)	12. (b)	13. (c)	14. (c)	15. (d)	

Chapter 6

Aspects of Event Management

Objectives

After going through this chapter the reader will be able to:

- Grasp the significance of budget preparation.
- Understand the role of marketing in event management.
- Concentrate on the idea and benefits of planning.
- Comprehend the different administrative abilities expected in event management.
- Assess the job of criticism in event management.

6.1 INTRODUCTION

Event management is the cycle by which events are characterized, arranged, observed, controlled, and conveyed with the end goal that the concurred benefits are understood. Events are novel transient undertakings embraced to accomplish an ideal result. For successful event management the board members of the event team need to plan and execute events properly. To comprehend the worth of event management, it is important to comprehend the basic idea of an event, the central qualities of event, the board processes, how achievement is assessed, the jobs, obligations, and exercises of an event manager and the mastery required; also, the setting wherein events are to be performed.

Events achieve change, advancement, innovativeness, and event management is perceived as the most productive approach to overseeing such change. To guarantee an effective event arranging it is vital to comprehend and value the job of stage director, significance of marketing of different properties with proper initiative, and meaning of planning and significance of input.

6.2 BUDGETING IN EVENT MANAGEMENT

Event budgeting is a crucial aspect of planning and executing a successful event. Its primary purpose is to allocate financial resources effectively to ensure that an event stays within its financial limits and meets its objectives. Fixed and variable costs play a significant role in event budgeting. For instance, while entertainment fees might fluctuate (variable), venue rental is a fixed cost that needs to be accounted for. One essential concept in event budgeting is ROI, which stands for return on investment. It measures the financial gain or loss generated from an event relative to its costs. The break-even point in an event budget refers to the moment when total costs match total revenue, indicating that an event has neither gained nor lost financially. To accommodate unforeseen expenses, a contingency fund is included in the budget. This fund helps cover unexpected costs that may arise during event planning or execution. When developing an event budget, various approaches can be employed. Activity-based budgeting involves estimating expenses based on the key components of the event, ensuring a comprehensive financial outlook. By understanding these concepts and employing effective budgeting strategies, event organizers can create memorable experiences while staying financially responsible.

An event spending plan is the all-out amount of cash dispensed for the specific reason for the event for a particular timeframe. The objective of financial plan management is to control event costs inside the supported spending plan and convey the normal event objectives.

According to the point of view of an effective event is one that meets four achievement models: that the event's degree is followed through on time, it is conveyed inside financial plan and, once conveyed, it measures up to the quality assumptions of the contributor and the recipients. For event chiefs to find true success they should focus on gathering those standards.

Most event administrators burn through majority of their endeavours on finishing the event on time. They invest majority of their energy on overseeing and controlling the timetable and will generally disregard observing and controlling the financial plan.

6.2.1 Budget Management

Budget management comprises a progression of undertakings and steps intended to assist dealing with the expenses of the event, the means are:

- Characterizing the budget
- Executing the move
- Controlling the budget
- Refreshing the budget

Inputs for Budget Preparation

Inputs: Inputs for the event budget management incorporate the accompanying reports or well spread of data:

- Event agreement or introductory budget
- Asset prerequisites
- Asset quotes
- Movement length gauges

Historical information

- Economic situations
- Donor and association strategies

Outputs: The event group involves the above-mentioned data to foster three significant archives for the event:

- Cost measurement by activity
- The event budget
- Budget fluctuation report

Event budgeting is performed on the underlying phases of event arranging and as a rule is lined up with the improvement of the event plan. The means related with budgeting are exceptionally reliant to both the assessed lengths of errands and the assets allocated to the event. Budget management is the interaction by which expenses or costs caused on the event are officially recognized, supported, and paid. Buy request structures are finished for each arrangement of related event costs, for example, counselling administrations, gear, and material expenses. Contingent upon the approval level the buy request structures are endorsed by the event supervisor and recorded by the money unit for following, contributor revealing and examining purposes. Budgeting fills in as a control component where real expenses can measure up to and estimated against the budget. The budget is in many cases a genuinely set boundary in the execution of the event. At the point when a timetable starts to slip, cost is relatively impacted. At the point when event costs start to raise, the event supervisor ought to return to the event plan to decide if the degree, budget, or timetable requirements changing.

6.2.2 Criteria in Budget Development

To foster the budget, the material expense factors related with event errands are recognized. The improvement of expenses for each errand ought to be basic and direct and comprise of labour, material, and other direct expenses. The expense of playing out an errand is straightforwardly connected with the staff relegated to the undertaking, the length of the errand, and the expense of any non-work things expected by the undertaking. Asset necessities include figuring out what assets (individuals, hardware, administrations, and material) and the amounts of those assets are expected to finish the event. The events, scope articulation, authentic data, asset data, and approaches are inputs used to decide the assets for the event. The fundamental result is a rundown of asset necessities that give the premise to budget assessing and budget controls, and give significant data to the event asset management process.

There different kinds of heads in which event cost can be gathered are as per the following:

1. **HR:** They incorporate counselling administrations; comprising of ideal individuals with the aptitude and abilities expected to finish the exercises on the event plan. Individuals might come from the association, or employed however long the event would last. Relationship building abilities likewise incorporate specialists who bring a general specialized mastery that is not found in the association or in the neighbourhood work market. The event will foster a rundown of the human asset prerequisites enumerating the skill level, areas of involvement, instruction, and language necessities. This data will be utilized in the asset management cycle to secure or get the ideal individuals.

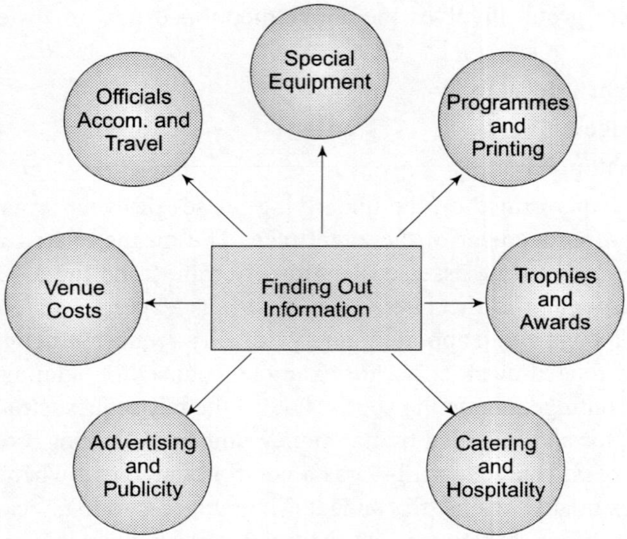

2. **Hardware and material assets:** Equipment include all the specialized tools required for the event, from water siphons to electrical generators that will be utilized by the event or conveyed to the recipients, it additionally incorporates the requirement for vehicles and office hardware like PCs and printers. The materials incorporate a more extensive class of necessities, for example, utility administrations, for example, power, phone lines, admittance to the web, office material, office space and utilized by the event. The material may likewise incorporate materials that will be utilized to construct transitory offices or food and shows that will be conveyed to the recipients.
3. **Other expenses:** This incorporates expenses of setting, showcasing, unique courses of action for events. This expense will be reliant upon the accompanying:
    - the length of the event;
    - the member gatherings;
    - the scene or office; and
    - the size of the event as far as number of member.

6.2.3 Budget Control

Checking and controlling the event budget guarantees that suitable event changes are taken care offor the budget pattern, that data about approved changes are imparted and remedial moves are made by those in control. The activity of budget control is likewise a course of dealing with the budget.

Controlling the budget is a basic obligation of the event supervisor, and it is similarly critical that the association characterizes the jobs and obligations of all gatherings engaged with budget control. Generally, the money division's liability is to record, track and screen the budget from an expense bookkeeping viewpoint and creates reports for the association management and the contributor as a feature of the consistence prerequisites, for example, guaranteeing the right records are appropriately utilized and recorded.

The money unit isnot answerable assuming the event budget is the obligation of the event director who utilizes the reports and screens the budget and decide whether the assets are utilized by plan and recognize any deviations, changes or adjustments to the budget.

Budget execution

Budget execution is the movement to check whether the event costs are being executed by the budget plan and distinguishes deviations and foster remedial activities. The technique uses to screen that the budget relies upon the bookkeeping framework utilized by the association to follow costs. Assuming that the bookkeeping framework records what assets are accessible. The bookkeeping framework may just show genuine costs and doesnot consider the contacts, buy orders and other financial responsibilities that are not represented on the overall record.

Bookkeeping reports regularly report on solicitations that have been paid to date. The event director requirements to follow genuine uses and all money related responsibilities made to merchants or advisors as agreements or buy orders that may be kept in the bookkeeping framework once the solicitations are paid. In any case, simply by taking a look at the bookkeeping reports might give the feeling that the event has more cash that what is really accessible.

Remedial activities

Some event might incorporate a predefined limit by which an event might be under- or over-budget during the event execution stage. It is generally set as a little level of the aggregate, on the off chance that the event is over as far as possible, the event director makes restorative moves to welcome the budget in the groove again. These activities might incorporate compromises that should be examined with management and the contributor, compromise include decreasing the degree or bringing down the quality of event.

Remedial activities might incorporate utilization of elective choices to deliver the comparative result utilizing various data sources, the event director will execute the restorative activities and screen their exhibition to check whether they are successful in lessening the event costs and assist with welcoming the event in the groove again. Remedial activities should be talked with the event group and the staff responsible for the exercises so that changes are executed.

6.3 SUCCESS OF THE EVENT

There are various parts engaged with event assessment. The event results are those quantifiable changes that can be seen because of the event's effective finishing. These quantifiable outcomes and advantages will be recognizable inside the designated populace once the event is finished, deciding the degree to which the distinguished goals were accomplished. The outcomes and advantages measure the advancement toward accomplishing the general arrangement.

Results are the present moment and medium-term impacts of the event on the partners. Instances of results incorporate new information, expanded abilities, expanded understanding, and expanded support in different event related exercises.

6.3.1 Understanding Key Performance Areas (KPAs)

Key execution markers include the main exhibition objectives across all parts of group association in an event. Compelling KPAs ought to be:

- Settled upon by all gatherings before the event starts
- Significant to the target group
- Quantifiable estimations that can be shared and investigated across hierarchical divisions whenever
- Coordinated toward the advantages the event tries to convey
- A reason for basic dynamic all through the event
- Lined up with targets and vision plan
- Reasonable, financially savvy and custom fitted to the association's way of life, requirements, and time span
- Brought together with authoritative endeavours
- Intelligent of an association's prosperity factors
- Well defined for the association and the specific event

By and large, KPAs are strong management instruments to achieve association wide achievement. Holding track of exact measurements back from changing groups can recognize where more course is required or where motivators, plans and different assets, like preparation, ought to be assigned in future.

6.3.2 Scope of KPAs

While the extension and terms of an association's KPAs might vary from one event to another, there are different kinds of information that can be useful to any association. Top event management benchmarking measures remember return for venture (return on initial capital investment), efficiency, cost execution, process duration, consumer loyalty, plan execution, representative fulfilment, and arrangement with vital business objectives. Instances of KPAs inside event management include:

- Event plan
- Gauge to event finishing
- Current advancement excess
- Work costs spent each month
- Current asset portion

Knowing how, where, and why event budget digressed is significant in finding waste and shortcoming and for arranging better for the unanticipated difficulties intrinsic to most events.

Deviation of planned hours of work: What's more, understanding which groups needed to exceed all expectations can assist with building a significant motivating force and prize programme and further develop time designation arranging.

Percentage of milestones missed: Events shift over their life cycle. Recognizing achievements and accomplishing objectives are essential to keeping up with event energy. At the point when an excessive number of achievements are not accomplished or are moved, representatives might feel disappointed. Distinguishing when achievements are missed can assist with restarting an event and moderate comparative difficulties later .

Cost variance: Keeping accurate records related to cost variance can provide a detailed profile of which teams and processes are most efficient. It can also help companies decide whether an event was worth the investment and assist managers in deciding whether to initiate similar events.

Motivation: Event managers can use_KPAs not only as a performance management tool, but also as a motivational tool. When all teams are united with common goals, their individual contributions can shine. Team competition, incentives and rewards can be a powerful motivating tool to keep event momentum pushing forward. Using quantifiable and consistent KPAs can help event managers assess event goals in an objective, fair and powerful way.

6.3.3 Event Feedback

Collecting event feedback holds immense importance as it enables organizers to enhance future events. Surveys are a commonly used method to gather insights, where attendees are asked about their experiences and impressions. One common metric used in event feedback is the net promoter score (NPS), which measures attendee satisfaction and their likelihood to recommend the event. While closed-ended questions provide quantitative data, open-ended questions offer attendees the opportunity to provide detailed explanation, fostering deeper insights. This quantitative data is invaluable, as it allows organizers to objectively analyze areas of improvement. By implementing relevant suggestions from feedback, event organizers can continually refine their events. Ignoring feedback risks stagnation, while embracing constructive feedback ensures that each event becomes a better experience for attendees.

Event execution and achievement are not generally simple to quantify. Saddling the force of areas of strength for an exhibition pointer strategy can assist event supervisors with driving their groups to better expectations, more prominent objectives, and effective events. A properly planned assessment plan follows key component for the effective execution and management of an event. An assessment plan depicts the cycle and gives the apparatuses to quantify progress in executing the event, it additionally surveys how actually the event resolved issues and accomplished its goals. The central part of assessment plan is the criticism from different partners after the effective fruition of the event.

Achievement factors decide the positive results of carrying out events. They must be recognized by event implementers from the origin stage. Be that as it may, event conditions

Operational	On-time performance	Event management software
	On-budget performance	Business budgeting software
	Number of attendees	Event booking platforms
Brand awareness	Social shares	Social media monitoring tools
	PR mentions	PR monitoring tools
	Word of mouth	Online survey software
Customer satisfaction	Net Promoter Score	Specialized software
	Reviews & testimonials	Online review sites
Business impact	Attendees	CRM software
	Partners	
	Sponsors	
Revenue	Ticket sales	Event ticketing sites
	Other guest revenue Sponsorships	Business budgeting software

are dynamic; consequently, an extremely durable observing of these variables is required. At whatever point the event chief ought to impact specific elements to build chances of achieving achievement measures.

Impact indicators: The targets and 'sobjective give the structure to event assessment. Accomplishment of every goal is estimated by its going with results and advantages (results). Accomplishment of the event objective is estimated by influence pointers. The assessment of these pointers will quantify the degree to which the ideal change has happened. The pointers should be quantifiable and reported, and ought to incorporate objective numbers and global positioning frameworks. The assessment will consider the marker, the instrument for following the pointer and the objective number or circumstances toward the finish of the event time frame. Reference to the pre-award status of the marker and last objective for the pointer will enormously aid event assessment.

6.3.3.1 *Methods*

The event is probably going to have a few goals to assess, and a few unique techniques for assessment may be required.

What strategies will be utilized to quantify the outcomes and advantages? What records will be kept up with? The assessment plan should incorporate the strategy used to decide if the goal was achieved, and whether the ideal change really happened.

One such strategy is revealing technique as a vital piece of the assessment plan and the recurrence and people in question should be determined:

- What number of absolute estimations will be taken?
- How regularly will the information be gathered and by what implies?
- How will be managed the information?
- How might the information be dissected and what structure will the report take?

Reporting: Reporting as well as assessing the last event results, one ought to routinely screen and assess the event's advancement in doing work plan exercises, finishing event targets and remaining inside the endorsed event budget.

This cycle assessment decides if the event was led in a way steady with the arrangement and whether the event exercises added to the progress of the event. As such, was the arrangement followed, and was the arrangement successful in accomplishing the targets? This piece of the assessment plan is utilized to really deal with the everyday and week-to-week exercises and is the premise of standard advancement reports ready for the event's funder.

Numerous funders require covering progress had towards accomplishing the effect pointer target numbers, and yearly providing details regarding the outcomes and advantages framed in the event work plan.

The essential partner will have various perspectives of the outcome of an event. The client will be centred around the results of the event, the expectations. The attention will be on the objectives and targets of the event, particularly on the degree and quality parts of the expectations. In specific occurrences, time and costs issues are of optional significance however could be similarly all around as significant as the previous angles. The degree and nature of the event has been recognized as the most persuasive variable among the components of the iron triangle. The exhibition in cost and time timetable will be estimated, like extension, against the last qualities and the general extent of the changes. Certain differences can be legitimate; however, the outlandish change will impact the judgment regardless of whether the event was a triumph. Free of the above mentioned, the view of progress can be affected by issues, for example, responsiveness of the group to client demands for changes, dependability at gatherings, correspondence or the scarcity in that department, character conflicts and others issues. These issues can be gathered into camaraderie and client fulfilment, and are more enthusiastically to gauge and evaluate.

This unit gives a guide in figuring out the job of stage supervisor, to achieve the goals by depicting how the branding is to be executed, observed, and controlled, distinguishing the job of administration to successfully speak with partners, job of budgeting and criticism in overseeing events.

An event is transitory, interesting, and the result of a multi-layered and logically explained process that creates an answer for a particular goal. For the undertaking to find true success, the event should be achieved on time, in budget, and to the proper degree expected to fulfil the goal. For progress to be accomplished, the event director should be talented and work in a climate which empowers an event group to work. Greatness in event management ought to be seen as the positive pattern in the exhibition of fruitful events in a continuously elaborative way to create the deliverable outcomes.

PROGRESS CHECK

1. Write a short note on event feedback.
2. Highlight the role of branding in successful management of events.

3. What do you understand by budget? What factors should be kept in mind while preparing a budget of event management company?
4. Define feedback. Discuss the role and importance of different types of feedback in management of an event.
5. Highlight the responsibilities of an event manager in case of live theatre performance.
6. What strategies will you adopt to implement a successful brand management strategy for your firm?
7. What is the importance of budget control for an event management firm?
8. Elaborate on the various leadership qualities required in event management.

MULTIPLE-CHOICE QUESTIONS

1. What is the primary purpose of event budgeting?
   (a) Enhancing attendee engagement (b) Determining event objectives
   (c) Allocating financial resources (d) Selecting event dates
2. Which of the following is an example of a fixed cost in event budgeting?
   (a) Marketing expenses (b) Entertainment fees
   (c) Venue rental (d) Variable staffing costs
3. In event budgeting, what does ROI stand for?
   (a) Return on investment (b) Running on-time information
   (c) Realistic operational income (d) Revenue output indicator
4. When creating an event budget, what does the term 'break-even point'refer to?
   (a) The point where ticket sales begin
   (b) The maximum budget limit
   (c) The point where total costs equal total revenue
   (d) The minimum number of attendees required
5. What is the purpose of including a contingency fund in an event budget?
   (a) To cover unexpected expenses (b) To provide discounts for attendees
   (c) To increase marketing efforts (d) To reduce ticket prices
6. Which budgeting approach involves estimating expenses based on the event's key components?
   (a) Historical budgeting (b) Incremental budgeting
   (c) Zero-based budgeting (d) Activity-based budgeting
7. What is the purpose of collecting event feedback?
   (a) Selecting event dates (b) Evaluating event budget
   (c) Improving future events (d) Managing event logistics
8. Which method is commonly used to gather event feedback?
   (a) Creating a guest list (b) Sending out invitations
   (c) Conducting surveys (d) Hiring event staff
9. What does NPS stand for in the context of event feedback?
   (a) New performance standards (b) National participation survey
   (c) Net promoter score (d) Notable presentations

10. Which question type is often included in event feedback surveys to measure attendees' satisfaction?
    (a) True or false (b) Yes or no (c) Multiple-choice (d) Open-ended
11. What is the benefit of using quantitative data in event feedback analysis?
    (a) Encouraging personal opinions (b) Providing detailed explanation
    (c) Allowing for subjective responses (d) Offering measurable insights
12. How can event organizers utilize feedback to enhance future events?
    (a) Ignoring feedback to maintain creativity (b) Implementing relevant suggestions
    (c) Discouraging attendee opinions (d) Focusing solely on positive comments
13. Which of the following is not used for event evaluation
    (a) Staff meeting and report (b) Food and stall holder income
    (c) Incident report by security staff (d) Attendance register

Answers to Multiple-Choice Questions

1. (c)	2. (c)	3. (a)	4. (c)	5. (a)	6. (d)	7. (c)	8. (c)
9. (c)	10. (d)	11. (d)	12. (b)	13. (d)			

Chapter 7

Basic Qualities of Event Personnel

Objectives

After going through this chapter the reader will be able to:

- Understand event environment and regulations.
- Recognise the importance of management abilities in planning an event.
- Stress the value of human connection.
- Investigate the significance of personal etiquette in event planning.

7.1 INTRODUCTION

Activities in event management go beyond merely instructing workers on what to perform. It is essential for event managers to have a firm grasp of the fundamentals of business theory, the state of the company's finances, and the ins and outs of their industry's technological landscape and regulatory framework. While event managers may not be the most high-profile employees, the success of the company depends on their efforts to ensure that everyone works together well. There are certain skill sets that you should have as an event manager, and bring to the event team, to effectively manage the event's conflicting restrictions and the event. The application areas you need to master include: industry norms and standards, the event environment, and general management and people skills. It is important to remember that the industry experience is not in a specific subject but rather the competence needed to organise the tvent. While familiarity with the field is helpful, rest assured that the event team is there to back you up every step of the way. If, for instance, you oversee planning and executing a sporting event, you need not be an expert in the sports, since your team will include actual athletes who can lend their knowledge to the task at hand. We will learn the ins and outs of becoming a good event manager in this lesson.

7.2 KNOWLEDGE OF STANDARDS AND REGULATIONS

When we talk about standards, we are referring to recommended practises and procedures that may help with event organization but are not strictly required. When we talk about regulations, on the other hand, we are talking to the set of rules that must be followed to pull off a successful event, such as the restrictions imposed by the government via legislation. If you are a professional, you know that you must abide by any rules and regulations of your field, company, or event has in place. Regulations and standards are present in every field. If you know which ones are relevant to your event, you can better prepare for them and assess potential dangers.

Certain competitions call for expertise in a narrow range of fields. The events that make up these regions have certain characteristics. It is possible to categorise them according to the field in which they operate (hotels, transportation, etc.), the division in which they work (accounting, marketing, legal, etc.), the field in which they work (software engineering, transportation), or the field in which they are managed (procurement, research, and development, etc.). Typically, the focus of these uses is on rules, regulations, and the particular requirements of the occasion, the client, or the business. Examples of such regulations include the fact that most government agencies have separate procurement procedures for their events, laws which do not apply to the sports event. requirements for food and hygiene in hotels are of relevance to the hospitality business, but to a festival event designer, such requirements are of little to no importance. To put your expertise to good use, you must remain updated on industry developments. Keeping up with the latest developments is essential in, else you risk falling behind.

If you want to succeed in event management, it helps to have some prior expertise in the field. Even if you plan on bringing in specialists, it is still a good idea to familiarise yourself with the nitty-gritty of your event's potential uses.

7.3 UNDERSTANDING THE EVENT ENVIRONMENT

Your event setting is complex, and there are numerous facets to learn about it. On one level, you should learn about the local culture and society to better plan your event. Concerning the inhabitants, demographics, and education of this area. In the diplomatic and political sphere, familiarity with cultural differences across nations is essential. The next step is to consider the event's physical surroundings. This includes things like time zones, the number of countries involved, and the ways in which your event will be carried out differently depending on whether it is being held in just one location or by a global team spread across five continents.

Let us look at some concrete instances of cultural differences. In the United States, it is common practise for strangers to use one other's first names. Europeans are more formal than Americans, preferring to use their surnames in professional situations even when they are familiar with one another. Their communication style is much more formal than that of the United States. Despite their penchant for independence, the Japanese place a high premium on traditions like respect for elders, group solidarity, and loyalty. The Japanese, on the other hand, are known for their indirectness of speech and their emphasis on communal identity over personal one. Most of the world, including the Japanese, places a premium on working hard and achieving one's goals. The Indian culture values a clear separation of power and respect for established hierarchies.

How something is perceived may be heavily influenced by cultural norms that vary greatly from country to country. The cultural variations of their customers led to unforeseen problems for several big American and European telecommunication corporations in the 1990s, for example, when they were expanding into new countries in Asia. Telecommunications infrastructure developed by western firms followed the same blueprint in Asia as it did in Europe and the America. However, social norms around how to speak were not the same. In certain regions of Asia, the use of call waiting is seen as rude even if it is commonplace in the West. If the team had properly documented the event setting's prerequisites and enlisted the help of the client, they may have avoided this cultural gaffe.

Since, somewhat predictably, individuals conduct things differently across nations, even the smallest of differences may become a source of conflict. Date formats are one of the simplest but most egregiously common instances of this. I need to know what day and year February 8th, 2018 is. Although the date may vary from country to country, in North America it is celebrated on February 8th and in Europe (and most of the rest of the globe) it is celebrated on August 2nd. It is crucial that all parties understand the timeline and deadline definition structure being employed.

Beyond the question of dates, the variety of practises and cultures has a far-reaching effect on events and technology. If your organization offers its wares on a global scale, you can oversee an event to launch a brandnew website for the business. Simply translating the webpage into multiple languages does not solve the underlying problems with grammar, syntax, and presentation. Making ensuring the translation is accurate is a given, but the presentation layer will have its own culturally specific needs. Given that Arabic and Hebrew are written right to left, the right half of a web page may catch the eye of a Middle Eastern visitor before the left does. Similarly, other civilizations attribute various meanings to various colours. The colour white, which represents innocence and fresh starts in the United States (think wedding dresses) but death and mourning in Japan (think funeral shrouds), is not a popular choice for backgrounds on either continent.

Table below summarizes different meanings of common colours:

Colour	United States	China	Japan	Egypt	France
Red	Danger, stop	Happiness	Anger, danger	Death	Aristocracy
Blue	Sadness, melancholy	Heavens, clouds	Villainy	Virtue, faith, truth	Freedom, peace
Green	Novice, apprentice	Ming dynasty, heavens	Future, youth, energy	Fertility, strength	Criminality
Yellow	Cowardice	Birth, wealth	Grace, nobility	Happiness, prosperity	Temporary
White	Purity	Death, purity	Death	Joy	Neutrality

Managers of such events may be asked to facilitate intercultural exchanges. Before managing an international event, they should gain an understanding of the cultural factors at play and,try to familiarise themselves with local customs, courtesies, and business protocols. The success, timeliness, breadth, and depth of an event may all be impacted by cultural factors, which the event organiser must consider.

7.4 MANAGEMENT KNOWLEDGE

Your understanding of events and your general management abilities will be put to the test when you take on the role of an event manager. We are thinking here about things like your event planning skills, your event execution chops, and your event control chops, all the way through to your ability to lead the event team and see it through to a successful completion, all while meeting the event's goals and staying within its restrictions. Event managers skills include: ability to close sales, willingness to work long hours and negotiating skills.

Planning and executing an event areis just half the job. General management abilities that help the event manager see the event through to a successful conclusion are an inalienable part of the job of an event manager. Risk and reward, money, and accounting, people, and stress all play a role in the successful administration of an Eevent, which is not unlike to the management of a company. Competence in event management is a universal need. Therefore, it is crucial for those in the event management industry to excel in tasks such as planning, organising, controlling, and conflict management.

7.5 INTERPERSONAL SKILLS

Success, as we all know, depends on strong interpersonal connections. Building and maintaining trusted connections with staff and customers is essential for any manager to succeed. Achieving unprecedented success is the reward for every event manager who puts in the time, effort, and even emotion required to establish relationships both inside and outside. The phrase indicates that you should develop a personal connection with a crucial member of your company's staff. In this case, ease of access is crucial. The manager might make an impression as a mentor simply by greeting everyone and showing appreciation for their efforts.

7.5.1 Trustworthiness

Among the many desirable qualities in a leader, integrity has gone the extra mile to become just as important as confidence and ability. As the event landscape flattens, the most important differentiator between winners and losers has shifted from raw strength to the power of relationships.

To what degree you come across as an honest and trustworthy boss in the present digital era will decide your career trajectory. Honesty and integrity are qualities that promote collaboration, open lines of communication, and mutual respect at all organizational levels. Integrity and candour are at the heart of trustworthiness. It is the most important factor in a company's success.

7.6 DELEGATION

A professional event manager will have the skills necessary to assign work effectively. To do this, you must have an in-depth familiarity with the people involved, including their strengths, weaknesses, areas of expertise, and interests. The key to the fairest outcome is using this information and assigning duties to the correct people. Employees are more likely to have faith in their supervisor if they are given work that plays to their strengths. As a result, those in charge of organising events need to strike a balance between micromanaging their staff and stepping in when things go poorly.

7.7 COMMUNICATION

Communication skills are essential for event personnel to effectively communicate with attendees and colleagues.Communication takes up an average of 90% of an event manager's time. As a result, they need to be effective communicators who push for the free flow of information without ambiguity. The responsibility of an event manager includes keeping their staff always informed. Everyone working on the event must have a clear understanding of their roles, responsibilities, deadlines, and the event's overall budget, timeline, and quality expectations. The whole event will come to a stop if the crew does not know their roles and responsibilities and how to carry them out. It will be impossible to keep tabs on the event's development if you have no idea of the personnel strength involved. Finally, the event will not get off the ground if you are unsure of what the customer wants from you. Who needs what information and when may be summed up as "event communication." Interpersonal communication involves symmetrical communication in event management.

A well-thought-out communication strategy is essential for each event, although not all events will use the same channels of contact or distribution strategies. Is there a common website, will people need to meet in person, or can things be handled with only the mail and e-mail? The communication management plan details how the stakeholders' needs will be met in terms of communication, including the types of information to be communicated, who will communicate it, who will receive it, how it will be communicated, how often, and by what means, as well as how the plan will be updated as the event develops, who will handle escalations, and what terms will be defined.

7.7.1 Striving for Feedback

The difference between a successful and unsuccessful event is frequently the quality of the feedback given to the team members. Therefore, it is imperative that all event managers prioritise this factor.One of the most essential qualities in a manager is the capacity to take criticism seriously.

There is always a way to become better, no matter how skilled you already are. You will improve as a manager if you learn to take criticism constructively and change as a result. A savvy leader will see this as the key to improving the group's performance.

When you ask for and implement suggestions from your group's members, you strengthen your standing with everyone. Everyone's admiration, commitment, and loyalty are through the roof because of this quality. It is crucial to develop this quality as a manager, since it will serve you well in many situations.

7.7.2 Negotiation

Managers of events must engage in bargaining for the benefit of the event. All events need negotiations between the event management, the sponsor, and the event team and the event's stakeholders, suppliers, and consumers to create an arrangement that satisfies everyone.

If you are in the process of negotiating a contract with a new location, service, or vendor, keep the following guidelines in mind. A meeting planner may make better use of the tools and techniques available to them by adhering to these basic principles.

- Always keep your cool and act professionally.
- Remain calm and collected.
- Stay out of petty power struggles and ego clashes.
- Spend some time in advance collecting the necessary information.
- Talk to the decision-makers on site or with the appropriate stakeholders.
- Keep in mind all the following Dos and Don'ts.

DO

- Set forth your meeting's goals and intentions.
- Be well-versed in the specifics of the event and the needs of your customers.
- Make hard copies of the agenda accessible to attendees.
- Establish essential links across all departments and locations.
- Be sure to check in regularly.
- Use advice from your friends.
- Act morally.
- Take note and listen carefully.
- Be aware of your financial limits.

DON'TS

- Put price above quality.
- Put in an excessive request.
- Demand to be treated as the ultimate arbiter.
- Neglect a vendor's bottom line and business requirements.
- Intensify and exaggerate need.

7.8 LEADERSHIP

Leadership is the capacity to inspire and mobilise others to achieve shared goals. Leaders mobilise followers around a shared vision and motivate them to action. A competent event manager will be able to get everyone involved in the event excited about the event's potential and its significance. As the team's leader, the event manager may motivate the staff to come up with creative ways to get the job done despite any problems that may arise.

Effective managers/heads

- They are reliable since they provide as promised. They are trustworthy and reliable, always delivering on their word.
- They take care to behave in accordance with the desires of those they lead. They know exactly what people expect of them and what they are capable of.
- They have faith in people's innate dignity.
- They are honest about their shortcomings. They understand that trying to cover up an error undermines trust and credibility.
- They provide a friendly and open atmosphere.
- They aid others in achieving their goals and in gaining a sense of self-worth.
- They are not too insistent, either. They push their team to the limit, but they also know when to pull back.

Successful event management relies on coordinating the efforts of many individuals. The rules, procedures, and culture of any company are exclusive to itself. Every organization has its share of political alliances, competing motives, competing interests, and power battles. A successful event manager is one who is aware of and sensitive to all the underlying dynamics at play in each organization.

7.9 MOTIVATION

An inspired workforce is a more productive workforce. The event manager's ability to inspire the team to strive towards their goal with enthusiasm and a strong sense of purpose is an ongoing effort. Various team-building activities may help get the group fired up and working together towards a common goal. Rewards and commendation play a significant role in inspiring people towork hard. Management and the event managers are most suited to carry them out, since they are official means of recognising and encouraging excellent conduct. When utilising incentives, it is important to consider people's unique tastes and cultural backgrounds. Not everyone like the spotlight, but it may bring forth the best in those who do. This means that people's unique qualities should be celebrated. It is important to employ both monetary and non-monetary incentives to motivate people. Motivation depends on expectations that increased effort to achieve an improved level of performance will be successful.

7.10 PROBLEM SOLVING

The ability to solve an issue lies in one's capacity to zero in on its essence, search for a workable solution, and then make the call to put that answer into action. issue definition is the starting point for any effort to fix the issue. Problem-solving skills helps event personnel anticipate potential challenges and plan accordingly. Understanding the issue's origin and impact is crucial to defining the problem, which is where root-cause analysis comes in. The symptoms of a problem will persist throughout the event's lifetime if the management does not address the underlying source of the issue. Attempting to alleviate a discomfort may sometimes cause worse damage. Analysing the underlying causes of a problem, rather than just the symptoms, may help you find effective solutions to that problem. After a problem's cause has been acknowledged, a choice may be taken about how to best deal with it.

Members of the stakeholder community, the event team, the event management, and other interested parties may provide suggestions on how to proceed. Any workable answer must consider not just the issue at hand, but also its origins and consequences. Timeliness is also important since missing the chance to solve an issue requires making a new choice. To provide one concrete example, while planning a first-time special exhibition in a certain location, organisers have to ensure that their exhibitors are prepared to face the region's unique cultural norms and linguistic barriers.

7.11 TEAM MANAGEMENT

Managers of events need to be inspirational leaders, but they also need to be leaders in terms of getting things done. As a result, the ability to lead a team effectively is now considered crucial for managers.

Team management is all about getting things done the correct way, whereas team leadership is all about getting people fired up. Putting one's vision into action is what this is all about. Therefore, managers need to be experts in delegating tasks, establishing objectives, assessing performance, and mediating conflicts. Organizational skills help event personnel stay organized and manage various tasks efficiently.Event personnel often need to adapt to unforeseen situations is known as adaptability. Teamwork skills helps event personnel work well in teams and collaborate effectively. Time management skills ensures that event personnel complete tasks within set timelines.

Managers of events are also responsible for ensuring that the group itself functions efficiently. Managers must organise the many personalities, routines, and eccentricities that make up a team to ensure that tasks are accomplished on time and within the budget. They determine the guidelines and procedures that make progress possible.

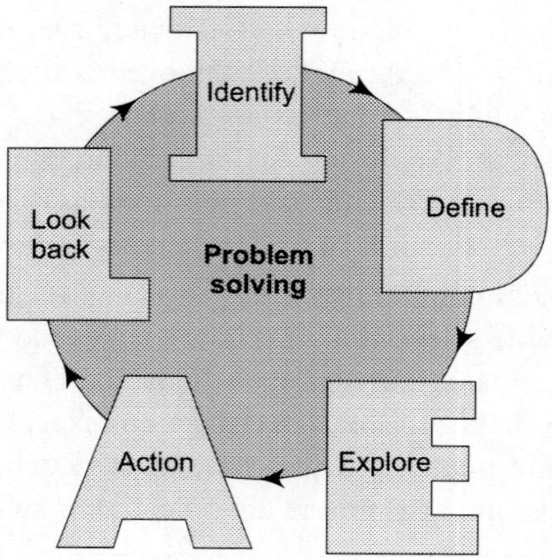

7.11.1 Set Personal Example

To effectively lead by example:

- Putting your aspirations on paper and having faith in them.
- Success is in your future.
- Finding the most important outcomes.
- Changing how you seem and act to show that you have made it to the next level in your career.
- Strategies for coping with pressures from inside and outside.

Keeping and cultivating high-performers is essential, as is cultivating an inspiring environment in which exceptional work may thrive. Choose which jobs to assign by first noting down the following criteria for each one:

- Can anybody on your team handle this responsibility?
- Just what is it that prevents you from delegating the work?
- To delegate a work efficiently, you must consider how you would like to assign the task.

7.12 RISK MANAGEMENT

When things do not go as planned, it is tempting to blame the event planner. No matter what the specifics are, everyone always asks whether the project manager could have anticipated this and taken measures to mitigate it. Good risk management may help prevent unpleasant surprises, which event sponsors tend to dislike. The lack of urgency associated with hazards causes many event organisers to not take them seriously. Managing and reducing any threats to your event will keep you in command of the situation. The knowledge of what may go wrong is the talent necessary for good risk management. Identifying risk is a crucial first step for every event organiser, since doing so early increases the likelihood that the risk will not materialise.

However, that is not the end of it. The process of identifying risks should be followed by a strategy for mitigating those risks. Assigning a likelihood, a cost, an owner, and mitigation techniques appropriate for the risk and the client's appetite for things going wrong are all part of this process. These secondary plans of action need to be included into the primary plan and monitored as well.

Significant gains may be achieved via prudent risk management. Customers will be more satisfied with your services since you will be able to better meet their needs and utilise their resources effectively, resulting in a greater return on investment. While they certainly benefit, you do as well since you will not have to waste as much time fixing issues or putting out fires caused by unpleasant situations. Mastering risk management as an event manager requires early identification of potential problems and the development of suitableresponses to eliminate any possibility of such problems from occurring. Event personnel need to handle stress and pressure,knownas stress management skills.

7.13 MULTITASKED

Several activities need to be coordinated at once at different points in the process of arranging an event. Your to-do list may include: negotiating a hotel contract; meeting with the client to talk about possible speakers; reserving a caterer; interviewing rental providers; investigating entertainment choices; and more. That is just for one gathering. When you throw in the planning of many events at once, the outcome is a complex balancing act. Successful event planners need to be able to juggle many responsibilities at once and keep the event running well without letting anything go by the wayside.

The key to success is learning how to set priorities and stick to them without becoming side-tracked or feeling overwhelmed by the sheer number of things that demand your attention. The ability to maintain composure, concentration, and adaptability are hallmarks of the effective multitasker.

7.14 DECORATION

When properly decorated, a reception hall may be transformed into a scene straight out of a guest's wildest dreams. The successful completion of any special event, from wedding receptions and conferences to ceremonies, is the product of meticulous, and imaginative beautification efforts. Decorations for an event are a subset of event planning that focuses on creating a certain mood for guests. Décor is mainly concerned with the aesthetics of the event, including the beauty of the tables, the chairs being nicely positioned and sometimes covered, the emphasis (stage), flowers and arrangement kinds, colour matching, and so on. An eventsmanager with a knack for decorating is someone who can make any event memorable. People remember the atmosphere of a party long after the food, drinks, and other entertainment have faded from memory. People and businesses alike would often fork out a sizable sum on event decorations because of the significant role it plays in conveying their sense of style and taste to guests.

An event's decorations are crucial for creating the desired atmosphere, highlighting the significance of the occasion, and evoking the desired emotions. The decoration, which may range from simple crepe paper streamers to elaborately crafted displays of colour and beauty isan important part of any celebration since they establish the tone for the rest of the day.

Large events may be difficult to decorate for because of the volume of people, merchants, and equipment that must be seen. The event's colour scheme, which should mirror the selected theme and be represented in advertising materials, commercials, and flower arrangements, will help bring the entire thing together into a spectacular feast. Therefore, it is essential for an event manager to be creative, to value novelty, and to provide employees the flexibility they need to bring out the best in the organization.

7.15 PERSONAL ETIQUETTES

According to Webster, etiquette consists of "the forms, manners, and ceremonies established by convention as acceptable or required in social relations, in a profession, or in official life". To behave with courtesy and decorum is an example of etiquette. It is not just one of these things, but rather it encompasses everything on this list. We will be concentrating on the following five aspects of business conduct:

- Attitudes at work.
- Social Interactions.
- Protocol for phone calls.
- Dining manners.
- Etiquette for written communication.

7.15.1 Work Etiquette

Workers at your event may demonstrate excellent manners by adhering to these guidelines, which cover every facet of the office setting.

- Maintain punctuality. Do not be late to the workplace or any meetings. Complete assignments on time and maintain regular reliability and punctuality in the office.
- Maintain a nice demeanour and be polite while interacting with others.
- Recognise what is expected of you in the workplace and how to act accordingly by developing your interpersonal competence. Pay close attention to regulations and policies.
- Recognise the importance of teamwork, embrace the company's founding principles, and think positively about your coworkers.
- Be as polished as possible in your presentation. It is crucial that you keep yourself neat and tidy. Be presentable as is customary in the workplace.
- Put on a winning mentality. Those who are willing to take risks and show originality are invaluable.
- Be adaptable. Your reputation as a cooperative worker will rise if you can adapt to new situations and ideas.

7.15.2 Personal Appearances

Personal and professional appearance should be updated to reflect the achievements you have achieved thus far. Planning is required to:

- Develop an impressive mode of accomplishment, and keep in mind that you can never go back and change a first impression.
- You can tell a lot about a person by how they keep their workstations, which is both visually appealing and crucial to their productivity.

7.15.3 Meeting People

Your ability to interact with others is mostly defined by the words and actions you use in social situations. Good manners are shown by firm handshakes, direct eye contact, and formal introduction.

When meeting new individuals, eye contact is also very important. Making direct eye contact conveys self-assurance, social competence, and openness to others. Making direct eye contact conveys confidence and professionalism.

Proper introduction: Preliminary interactions aid in forming bonds. Whose name is spoken first is determined by rank. When introducing someone, it is customary to start with the most prominent person in the room and work your way down the list. The following is the recommended sequence for introductions: Relationships spanning generations, from junior to senior executives, and from coworkers to clients. Do not complicate the introduction. You may explain your link with the folks you are presenting by providing some background about them.

Telephone etiquette: Telephone etiquette is equally as essential as in-person manners when communicating with others. The way you behave on the phone says just as much about you as the way you act in person. Always aim for a same-day callback in business talks, and remember to stick to the subject. Keep them on wait for no longer than 30 seconds at a time. If you want someone to call you back, always leave your number. Many CEOs also keep a call record so they may look back on past conversations and learn something new. In-person or over the phone, attentive listening is always important.

Dining etiquette: A great deal of business is done around the dinner table in today's corporate world. It is crucial to know how to act while entertaining or being entertained in any social setting, whether it at the workplace or a restaurant. learning how to order your food, what utensils to use, and how to use them correctly, as well as learning basic table manners, may help alleviate some of the stress that might arise when eating out. The stress of eating out may be reduced by coming prepared.

- Allow the host to set the pace whenever feasible.
- Seek advice and opinions from others.
- Do not choose the most costly or cheapest item on the menu as your meal.
- Do not consume messy or difficult to chew meals.
- Do not have a drink even if your friends do.

Correspondence etiquette: It is crucial to follow up meetings with written contact, whether you have just met someone or have known them for a long time.

1. Send a thank-you letter or letter of follow-up within the next 48 hours. Always use proper business letter format, whether you are sending a memo or a formal letter.
   - Regardless of whether they are married, women should always be addressed as "Ms".
   - Be sure to end your letter with your signature.
   - Check for typos and spelling mistakes whenever you proofread.

   The following are common components of letters:
   - **Opener:** An informal and informative introduction to yourself and your letter's purpose is essential.
   - **Justification:** What you want and why you want it are both reaffirmed and justified in the second paragraph.
   - **Closing:** In your closing, ask the recipient to take the requested action or make the requested request on your behalf.
2. Despite its relative youth, email etiquette does have a few hard and fast rules.
   - You may use email, but please avoid all-caps messages and proofread carefully.
   - Always use a subject line when sending an email.
   - Put some thought into the subject line.
   - Spell and use language correctly.

   Use a signature wherever possible; if you do, make sure it clearly states who you are and provide at least two methods to get in touch with you (phone and fax). The importance of using correct business etiquette in generating a favourable impression is growing. These outward signs are crucial to your career advancement.

7.15.4 Time Management Skills

The main issue in time management as event manager is in the process of monitoring, analysing, and amending your plan until it works after you have established your lists of things to accomplish and prioritised them. To be effective with your chosen approach to time management, you will need to develop abilities like as:

- One of the most essential things to remember if you are having trouble with time management is that good planning is a talent that can only be developed through experience and exercise. You cannot expect to sit down and come up with a foolproof plan of action. A first try may not be successful. Some level of irritation is to be anticipated; nevertheless, you should not allow this to discourage you from trying. Simply making lists is not enough to successfully manage your time. Plan and manage your time carefully, but do not be discouraged if it seems like you are getting less done than before. Details in your time plan may make or break your approach, so it is best to sort out the kinks at the start of the semester when stress and work load are low. There is no way to know what will work without first trying it and failing. The rewards will be there for you when you need them later in the semester if you can make it through the first few weeks.

- Self-evaluation is a fundamental aspect of developing a reliable method for managing one's time effectively. It is difficult to improve at time management since there is no one except yourself to provide you with feedback on how well you are managing your time. So, it is important to take a quick look at how your time management strategy is faring every day. Examine the status of completed tasks and the reasons for their completion or lack thereof. Is it possible that you just overestimated or underestimated your study session's potential! Do you let others disturb you when you are working, or are you able to keep working and yet socialise with others! To keep developing your abilities, you must critically evaluate the factors that contribute to the success or failure of your time management strategy. Always take the time to evaluate your results, both good and bad.
- You should keep in mind that your schedule is not set in stone, as this will allow you to be more flexible with your time. As such, it is important to have the awareness to recognise when you are really making progress towards your goals as opposed to just banging your head against a wall, and to adjust your approach accordingly. Do not interrupt a brilliant thought during writing your essay because you have only allotted an hour for it. Figure out how to differentiate between a smart, deliberate choice to delay a task in favour of doing anything else and mindless procrastination. To get some distance from a problem or regain your concentration, it may be helpful to take a little break and attend to another event.
- Don't be too hard on yourself if you make mistakes, but keep an eye out for negative trends and figure out where they are coming from. Your chances of success will increase if you prepare for the unexpected and leave some wiggle room in your schedule. Strategic thinking is essential for effective time management. There are a few stages to this process. In this case, the first step is to plot out how you will spend your time. Second, you check in to see if anything has changed. Am I succeeding in my goals? Just how much fun am I having? How challenging is it? The third step is to determine why the strategy succeeded or failed. If it was successful, you may consider expanding its usage. If the strategy fails, adjust and try again.
- Awareness of the significance of time management, of how you are managing your time, and of what works or does not work for you is the common thread that runs through all these processes. Time management knowledge acquisition is a never-ending process. Your ability to observe and learn from the time management practises of others will increase as you increase your own awareness. It will be simpler to adjust to changing circumstances if you have a wide variety of time management tools at your disposal, such as those posed by examinations, a thesis, or juggling a full-time job and a family. Be observant, tune in to conversations on time management, and never stop trying new things. In today's competitive job market, the ability to manage one's time efficiently is invaluable. You may be confident in your ability to manage time in

practically any scenario after graduation if you can learn to do it in the chaotic and unstructured atmosphere of college.

- Time management should not be seen as an aim. To put it simply, it is a tool. The only way to get really great results from yourself and the people around you are to tie it into the process of defining and achieving objectives.
- Timing is everything in event management, therefore being able to keep to a strict schedule is essential. Managers of events must master their own schedules as well as those of their teams. To boost output, efficiency, and effectiveness, as well as cut down on time spent, they need a firm grasp on how much time they spend on certain tasks.
- Assembling a timetable is a crucial part of every event manager's job. Timelines and task breakdowns can help you reach your targets. Planners of special events are responsible for establishing timelines and adhering to them.

Prioritisation is a crucial part of scheduling and managing projects, which is why time management also involves this skill. Managers of events require time management skills to focus on what is most essential and cut out the distractions. To successfully plan and schedule a project, time management is essential. So, the ability to manage time effectively is crucial for every event organiser.

PROGRESS CHECK

1. Leadership and communication both play crucial roles in managing a team effectively, so let us talk about that.
2. The importance of etiquette in successful people management is highlighted.
3. Determine the key elements of the external business environment that have an impact on your event management.
4. Describe the significance of cultural sensitivity in event planning.
5. To what extent do interpersonal connections matter while planning an event?
6. Write a note on team management.

MULTIPLE-CHOICE QUESTIONS

1. What quality is essential for event personnel to effectively communicate with attendees and colleagues?
   (a) Punctuality (b) Technical expertise
   (c) Creativity (d) Communication skills
2. Which quality helps event personnel stay organized and manage various tasks efficiently?
   (a) Flexibility (b) Attention to detail
   (c) Interpersonal skills (d) Organizational skills
3. Event personnel often need to adapt to unforeseen situations. Wqhat quality is crucial in such scenarios?
   (a) Patience (b) Leadership skills (c) Resourcefulness (d) Adaptability

4. What quality helps event personnel work well in teams and collaborate effectively?
   (a) Independence (b) Technical knowledge
   (c) Analytical thinking (d) Teamwork skills
5. Which quality ensures that event personnel complete tasks within set timelines?
   (a) Enthusiasm (b) Multitasking ability
   (c) Initiative (d) Time management skills
6. What quality enables event personnel to resolve conflicts and maintain a positive environment?
   (a) Technical proficiency (b) Diplomacy
   (c) Innovation (d) Conflict resolution skills
7. Event personnel need to handle stress and pressure. What quality helps them remain composed?
   (a) Spontaneity (b) Resilience
   (c) Intuition (d) Stress management skills
8. What quality helps event personnel anticipate potential challenges and plan accordingly?
   (a) Artistic creativity (b) Humour
   (c) Analytical skills (d) Problem-solving skills
9. Which quality allows event personnel to understand the needs and preferences of diverse audiences?
   (a) Self-confidence (b) Technical expertise
   (c) Empathy (d) Cultural awareness
10. Event personnel often represent the event and its organizers. What quality is crucial for maintaining a professional image?
   (a) Flexibility (b) Social media proficiency
   (c) Spontaneity (d) Professionalism
11. What quality is essential for event personnel to effectively manage budgets and financial aspects?
   (a) Enthusiasm (b) Creativity
   (c) Financial literacy (d) Financial management skills
12. Event personnel often need to lead and guide teams. What quality helps them inspire and motivate others?
   (a) Patience (b) Technical knowledge
   (c) Vision (d) Leadership skills
13. An individual's motivation depends on
   (a) Whether path-goal relationships are clarified
   (b) Expectations that increased effort to achieve an improved level of performance will be successful
   (c) Their effective performance
   (d) The necessary direction, guidance, training, and support is provided
14. Which one is not a required event managers skill?
   (a) Ability to close sales (b) Knowledge of food and wine pairing
   (c) Willingness to work long hours (d) Negotiating skills

15. What should be avoided for effective communication during event process
    - (a) Personal remarks
    - (b) Respect to audience
    - (c) Tone of speech should be high
    - (d) None of the above
16. Interpersonal communication involves
    - (a) Asymmetrical communication
    - (b) Symmetrical communication
    - (c) Professional communication
    - (d) None of the above

Answers to Multiple-Choice Questions

1. (d)	2. (d)	3. (d)	4. (d)	5. (d)	6. (d)	7. (d)	8. (d)
9. (d)	10. (d)	11. (d)	12. (d)	13. (b)	14. (b)	15. (a)	16. (b)

Chapter 8

Events and Activities

Objectives

After going through this chapter the reader will be able to:

- Learn about the numerous kinds of happenings.
- Investigate the value of displays, obviously.
- Investigate why festivals are so well-attended.
- Bring attention to the many aspects of celebrations.

8.1 INTRODUCTION

Multiple tiers of activities, from the neighbourhood to the country to the world, are being planned today. Cultural preservation, tourism promotion, and community improvement are all bolstered by these gatherings. Although the return on investment for some fundraising events is lower than that of others, these events are still frequently incorporated into a larger fundraising strategy due to the visibility they bring to the organization and the opportunities they present for engaging a wide range of people in its work.

8.2 EVENTS AND ACTIVITIES

Creating or enhancing any form of event is possible. When a new management team is tasked with expanding an event that has already begun, we speak of it as its development. In this scenario, the event will already have a set structure and procedure in place, thus the new team's job will be to revise and improve it to restore the event's former prominence or make it more applicable to the current climate. If the event is novel, the planning group must determine a need or goal they want to achieve before doing anything else. In the case of events that become annual traditions, the event organiser will need to come up with a fresh idea every time to keep the event fresh and exciting for attendees. Accordingly, the following categories are used to generally classify events:

- Private occasions
- Business events

- Charity activities
- Living events

8.2.1 Private Events

People who choose to celebrate personal milestones privately are referred to as "private event" hosts. To create these one-of-a-kind occasions, we use specialised event planners to take our clients' wishes into account as we strategize every detail. What follows are some instances of this type:

- Wedding
- Celebrations of marriage
- Celebrations of birth
- Occasions of note

Since private events may be catered to a wide range of clientele, the sector is varied. Celebrations, especially weddings, sometimes need the use of a private event space so that the hosts may enjoy their event in peace and quiet.

People that only want a select group of people to attend their event hold private parties. A guest list will be used to restrict access to certain events from the general public. The events management industry is dominated by the private sector, with several firms engaging in commercial activity. Clients may either do the legwork themselves, which can be time consuming, or they can submit an inquiry to an agency, which will reduce their workload and may even help them save money by negotiating better prices with potential event venues.

8.2.2 Leisure Events

Leisure is defined as any activity pursued by a person for reasons other than those required by his or her employment, family, or community responsibilities. This might be for the purpose of rest and recreation, intellectual growth, social interaction, or the unrestrained expression of artistic talent.

Motivational processes are also required for engaging in recreational activities. One of these motivations, known as pushing motivation, is the urge to leave one's present position, while the other, known as pulling motivation, is the wish to visit new areas. The many events provide people a place to meet others who share their interests and have similar experiences. Individuals' interests in leisure activities and events may be explained by their pursuit of a variety of goals, including improved health, psychological respite, a more vibrant social life, and expanded skill sets. Participating in these kinds of activities helps people in many ways, including their overall well-being, health, and growth.

8.2.3 Corporate Events

Conference tourism is a subset of group tourism that deals specifically with the organization of meetings and other types of group gatherings.Networking event focuses on exchanging ideas and knowledge among professionals.

8.2.3.1 Meetings

The role of the event planner is to ensure that the corporate meeting is conducted in accordance with the rules, even though doing so may appear like a simple task. Meetings have several purposes, and two of them are inspiring employees and building strong teams. The most crucial aspect of organising a productive meeting in any field is thinking through the choices that will be made as a consequence of the gathering.

8.2.3.2 Incentive Events

The purpose of the event is to encourage participants to reaffirm their devotion to the company and its products. Employees may require engagement programmes, and consumers may be losing interest, both of which suggest that an incentive event may be beneficial to reinvigorating the brand. Brief yet unforgettable is the goal for these occasions. As a planner, your first step should be to figure out why the event is being held. Employees may be energised by motivational speakers, while consumers might enjoy the atmosphere created by a comedic performance or live band. This event has a lot of room for spontaneity, so hopefully it will be fun and interesting for everyone involved.

8.2.3.3 Business Dinners

A business dinner is a time-honoured tradition that may be used to honour significant company achievements and show appreciation to deserving personnel. However, you should still give some thought to how the event should feel and what its overall theme will be. A middle ground is necessary here. As with any gathering of this kind, food will play a vital role. The dinner's vibe should be reflected in the kind of service provided, therefore this is something the event planner must keep in mind.

8.2.3.4 Launch Parties

A launch party is a great method to get the word out about a client's upcoming product or service release and get people excited about it. Parties are a common way for businesses to network and connect with new clients, and they often include presentations and speeches by prominent figures in the industry. In addition to providing entertainment, they could also hand out freebies or hold a raffle. The timing and specific needs of guests during such a celebration are essential considerations for the venue.

8.2.3.5 Award Ceremonies

Management of award ceremonies to honour employees or acquire and delight customers are becoming more and more common. Considering that we live in a culture that is eager to recognise and reward excellence, award ceremonies are an essential sort of gathering. Television viewers often tune in to watch award shows like the academy awards, the Grammys, and the Olympic Games. It is common practise for businesses and other organizations to regularly hold awards ceremonies to recognise and celebrate their own. In-house meeting planners, marketing departments, or external firms manage these events.

In the event of an internal awards ceremony, the corporate board room or a nearby restaurant would be ideal venues. Large-scale community events provide special issues for planners. Particularly if these are community-oriented awards, the organisers will need to decide on menus and confirm that the venue has everything, including a guest speaker, for the gala dinner event. You may spread the word about your organization's goal and encourage potential future awardees by having them hear from some of your guest speakers. As before, the event organiser has a wide variety of options, including well-known figures, local celebrities, and even members of the event's own staff. Attendees need to be kept amused both before and after the ceremony begins. The nature of the occasion guides the selection of appropriate entertainment. An awards ceremony invitation should capture the excitement and excitement of the event to which it is attached. Colourful logos from the event's sponsors are essential for every community gathering.

8.2.3.6 *Conferences*

Conferences and seminars are a kind of educational event that may be used to swiftly increase the workers' knowledge base or to demonstrate the company's competence in a certain field. There should be plenty of time for questions and comments from the audience and for the speaker to field them. To successfully organise such an event, it is crucial to keep the goal in mind at all times. Therefore, whether the clients want to expand staff knowledge for increased efficiency or educate customers about a new product, an event organiser will require a suitable site.A technology expo is an example of business conference.

8.2.3.7 *Exhibitions*

There is a wide variety of labels for gatherings whose primary goal is to facilitate commerce between buyers and vendors. One such example is the usage of interchangeable terms such as "Trade Fair", "Trade Exhibition", and "Trade Show" to refer to the same event. Fairs may be either general, which is gaining popularity, or sector-specific.

8.3 CHARITY EVENTS

Individuals may generate money for a cause close to their hearts by participating in charity activities like:

- Balls for the society
- Competitive sports
- Auctions for a good cause

Sponsorship of participants is optional in just a small fraction of charity activities, and these events might be anything from marathons to triathlons:

- Promotional events
- Funded bike races
- Skydiving with a sponsor
- Fundraising strolls

A charity fundraiser walk may be considered a fundraising event although its charity fundraiser.

Since any person may attend a charity event or donate to one.The charity events sector is very inclusive. By choosing a worthy local charity or charitable event, one may garner tremendous goodwill by donating to a charity within the community, and this is an important aspect of these activities. It is good for company in the long term because of the relationships and connections that are forged. There is mutual benefit when a company sponsors a non-profit organization. The company underwrites the expenses of a charitable event, which in turn, provides the company with free or low-cost marketing opportunities to the public. The effectiveness of an organization's efforts to get corporate sponsorship is directly related to the value it provides to prospective sponsors.

8.4 LIVE EVENT

Staging, scenery, mechanicals, sound, lighting, video, special effects, transport, packaging, communications, costume, and makeup are just some of the production equipment and services utilised by the performing arts to make their live audiences feel like they could not be anywhere else but at that very moment. A wide variety of production support tools and services are discussed in this article, along with their interrelationships. Art exhibition typically involves showcasing artwork, sculptures, and crafts. In talent show individuals competing against each other to showcase their skills.

8.4.1 Music Events

Cultural and societal norms are reflected in music festivals. Entertainment events are also popular nowadays like fashion shows. Many fundamental human needs, such as the need to contribute, to create, and to feel like oneself, are met via them. Since music festivals are a natural element of modern culture, they cannot be understood apart from the wider structures in which modern civilization operates. From this vantage point, we can see how music festivals nest inside societies, which in turn, nest within the planetary ecological systems that make life possible.

Attending a music festival is a novel method to fulfil many requirements at once:

- To participate in a social event
- Being involved in a creative endeavour
- To have a sense of belonging to a group

The four key stakeholders and their interactions have been determined:

- The institution
- The viewers
- Creators of art
- The providers

8.5 SPORTS EVENTS

Sporting activities are a staple of leisure time. The basic objective of sporting competitions is, via different computations, to establish a performance sequence for the competitors. In the event of a competition, the regulations of the relevant sport and/or the description of the contest will dictate the format of the challenge. But in competitions one can challenge oneself without risk, can learn personal and professional competencies, can gain positive personal features like the desire to struggle, exhibition play, subordination of personal interests, stamina, helping others, etc., all of which are indispensable in one's life. Various types of sporting events are marathon, athletics, boxing, etc. Dance class involves engaging in physical exercises and stretches.

8.5.1 Benefits of Sports Events

- The tourist sector benefits from sports investments.

It contributes to economic expansion because of full restaurants, cafes, and stores.

- Increases your community's visibility and goodwill.

It makes a brand-new product, a brand-new place to visit.

- Makes the most of the resources available in your area.
- Improves corporate partnerships and community ties.

Opportunity and fun for young people are created.

- Target high-value visitors, particularly those who are likely to return.
- Make people feel good about visiting there.
- Raise public interest in sports and sporting activities.

8.5.2 Hosting a Sports Event

As a first step, the event organiser must collect the necessary paperwork or requirements from the rights holder. Create a methodical strategy to quickly collect and organise the relevant data. The bid is the organisers' first formal offer to the event rights holder on behalf of your community. Many of the items asked for are essential to the success of the event, thus it is important that the map appropriately depicts the community's resources. In the case that a community lacks a necessary resource, details on how those needs might be fulfilled for the event itself must be provided.

8.5.3 Sports Event Planning

Fundraising, membership recruiting, boosting public awareness, and celebrating are just a few of the reasons why sporting events are conducted. No matter the scale of the event (national, regional, county, or local), careful and extensive preparation in advance is essential for its success on the big day.

8.5.4 Meeting the Challenge

It is no easy task to organise and carry out large-scale athletic events in accordance with the many strict requirements that must be met, such as those listed below:

- There is zero wiggle room in the schedule, since all the due dates are set in stone.
- Sports stadiums, the athletes' village, and other development projects like new hotels must be finished in time for the games.
- Everything that goes into organising, staging, and hosting the events will be broadcast across the world, so any slip-ups on the side of the host city or country will be instantly and universally scrutinised.

Because of these considerations, good governance, openness, and procedural controls are crucial when organising and hosting large sports events. Complex interdependence, which may arise because of exponential expansion, provide additional difficulties.

- Multiple interconnected projects, each with its own set of complexities (e.g., evolving designs, needs, prices, and priority).
- The number of parties with a vested interest in the outcome of choices, the handling of risks, and the production of deliverables.

Keeping tabs on earnings and development in venues, particularly the interdependence of venues with infrastructure and/or venue development and event management.

8.5.5 Ground Rules for Sports Events

- The event's goals and objectives should be clear to the whole planning team and coordinating committee.
- Ground conditions, traffic and pedestrian paths, terrain, placement of available facilities (such as water, power, audience capacity, etc.), and other factors should all be considered in a site appropriateness evaluation of the venue.

Someone has to be put in charge of the event, both before it happens and on the day of the event itself. At the earliest feasible point in the planning process, duties, roles, and authority should be assigned. When planning a large-scale event, it may be beneficial to form subcommittees of experts in certain fields. The Event Safety Management Team's responsibilities include communicating with the police, fire department, city officials, current venue management, stewarding and security companies, staging and electrical firms, and health and safety coordinators. Throughout the event's preparation and execution, there should be open channels of communication between all parties involved.

- For the sake of transparency and documentation, all arrangements and financial dealings leading up to the event should be reduced to paper.
- To avoid missing any crucial steps, it is important to establish goals and timelines for the time leading up to the event.
- The event organiser guarantees that all volunteers are aware of their responsibilities on the big day, and that there will be enough "free hands" to handle any unforeseen situations.

- Make sure that any assistants you employ have received the proper training and tools to do their jobs effectively.
- Make preparations for unforeseen circumstances, such as severe weather, emergencies, health and safety concerns, insurance claims, etc.
- The 'who', 'what', 'when', 'why', and how' questions are fundamental to every successful event strategy.

8.5.6 Greening the Event

Keep in mind that unexpected occurrences might cause damage to our natural surroundings. If we make smart decisions, we can lessen our effect significantly. Here are some suggestions for lessening the blow.

- Energy efficiency should be a priority for all activities.
- Reduce artificial lighting by letting in as much natural light as possible.
- Use as little water as possible.
- Tap water should be provided to save the cost and environmental impact of transporting bottled water.
- On-site recycling facilities are provided in accordance with the anticipated waste streams.
- Only purchase what you know you will use soon.
- Recycle and reuse items if at all feasible. This includes things like fruit that can be stored for later consumption as well as reusable printed documents.
- Name tags should be provided if necessary and collected when the event has concluded.
- Suppliers, such as food service providers, may be influenced to reduce their usage of non-recyclable packaging and packaging materials. Reduce the likelihood of serving too much food.
- Print or duplicate on both sides of the paper and try to use recyclable paper (at least 80% recycled content)

8.6 FESTIVALS

Festivals fulfil three categories of needs: physiological, social, and introspective. In addition, Crompton established a framework for his research that considers the following seven factors:

(a) **Novelty:** Visitors are motivated by the desire of seeking new experiences.

(b) **Socialization:** Visitors are energised by interacting with the community.

(c) **Prestige/status:** The need to put oneself forward socially by way of making appearances at notable gatherings.

(d) **Rest and relaxation:** Motivation to go away from the stresses of everyday life and recharge the mind.

(e) **Education value/intellectual enrichment:** Cause for growth attending a festival and picking up some fresh information.

(f) **Enhancing kinship and relations/family togetherness:** Strengthening familial ties and the motivation to spend time with relatives.

The entertainment, food, drink, music, art, and games during a festival are only some of the highlights. The finest festivals foster a feeling of togetherness among their attendees.

8.6.1 Festival Planning

Organizing a festival planning team

A lot of people are required for the event to go off without a hitch. The planner of the event has to anticipate everyone who needs to be engaged and make sure they are on board and aware of all the particulars. They will likely need to coordinate the efforts of several people, including the venue management, a public relations professional, a talent agency, performers, and other event personnel and volunteers.

Festival site: It is important to think about a lot of different factors before settling on a location for the event. One of the most crucial aspects is the kind of the event the firm intends to organise. You can get an idea of how many people are likely to show up at each potential venue by looking at their locations and populations. Finally, think about how convenient the venue is to travel to for both vendors and guests.

Book the festival entertainment: The promoter of such an event typically scouts, negotiates, and books the performers. When selecting what course of action to follow, this individual will give careful thought to several factors. Sales of the band's albums and the number of tickets they were able to move at recently held shows at local venues are both solid indicators. The promoter has an intimate understanding of the local taste in music. When booking live shows, the promoter will typically coordinate with the band's managers to iron out the details, such payment and lodging.

Festival entertainment: Unique entertainment is essential for making any gathering remarkable. The entertainment is often related to the event's theme. Festivals are well known for their seemingly endless streams of entertainment that span the full spectrum. Some examples of event entertainment are:

- Theme park attractions,
- Riding ponies
- Vocalists
- Dancers
- Parades
- Display of handmade goods
- Expo on food
- Karate exhibitions
- Fireworks
- Live music

- Club scenes
- Magicians
- Famous attendees
- Contests
- Art exhibitions

8.7 INDIA AS EMERGING DESTINATION

The Indian government's Ministry of Tourism (MoT) is committed to making India a top location for event planning. New Delhi, the country's capital, has long been the top choice for meetings, conventions, and exhibitions. Business conferences and meetings held in this city are a delight for attendees because to its many attractions, which range from historic landmarks to first-rate shopping. For morethan forty years, international gatherings have been convened at The Ashok in New Delhi. The pillar-free Convention Hall at The Ashok is a favoured site for the most influential businesspeople and government leaders. It spans an expansive 16,435 square feet. An outdoor theatre, cocktail bar, and banquet hall can be found on the hotel's third level at The Ashok. Other than the Taj Palace, Maurya Sheraton, Le Meridien, etc., the other hotels in the capital with great conference facilities include the Vigyan Bhawan, the Habitat World Centre, and the many more.

With a visit to Agra, home of the world-famous Taj Mahal, a business trip may easily be transformed into a memorable cultural experience. You may host your convention, conference, or meeting in comfort at the Jaypee Palace Hotel and Convention Centre. The conference venue has cutting-edge amenities including a satellite uplink, simultaneous translation services, and audiovisual recording equipment to accommodate its maximum capacity of 1500 attendees. This venue''s expansive banquet hall can accommodate up to 350 people, with a separate pre-function room that can accommodate an additional 200, and an adjacent garden that can accommodate an additional 300. Several domestic and international conventions have been held at the hotel with great success.

India's Ministry of Tourism supports the India Convention Promotion Bureau (ICPB), which was established to market the country as a site for international conventions and expos. India's overseas offices, in addition to IMEX Frankfurt and IMEX Las Vegas, EIBTM Barcelona and AIME Melbourne, participate in International MICE Tourism trade fairs on behalf of the country's national airlines, hotels, travel agents, tour operators, tourist transport operators, conference organisers, etc. With the help of the Global Incredible India media campaign and road shows and seminars put on by India Tourism offices across the world, India is also being marketed as a top destination for MICE events. Convention centres are included in the programme for large revenue generating projects, for which the Ministry of Tourism offers central financial assistance.

8.8 INDIA TRADE PROMOTION ORGANIZATION (ITPO) PROFILE

ITPO is the government of India's primary trade promotion organization, with a mission to highlight India's many accomplishments in the realm of international trade and investment.

When it comes to fostering the expansion of India's commercial ties, ITPO is a vital cog. ITPO grants permission for and controls many expositions in India to ensure that no efforts are duplicated and that correct scheduling is maintained. It oversees the maintenance and upkeep of India's state-of-the-art exhibition centre, which is renovated regularly to ensure peak performance. In addition to its open display area of 10,000 square metres, Pragati Maidan's covered exhibition space of 61,290 square metres is spread over 16 rooms on its 123 acres of magnificent land in the centre of India's capital, New Delhi. As a result of its modern exhibition rooms, Pragati Maidan is attracting an ever-increasing number of international trade show organisers and attendees.

Both domestic and international traders may take use of ITPO's substantial infrastructure, marketing, and information resources. ITPO's regional offices in Bangalore, Chennai, Kolkata, and Mumbai work together to promote commerce throughout the country. Each office has a unique profile of operations that contributes to the overall success of the nationwide initiative.

Additionally, ITPO is helping state governments establish Regional Trade Promotion Centres (RTPCs) in several state capitals and key cities around the country. ITPO has taken the lead in organising the construction of convention centres and trade exhibition complexes in the cities of Kolkata (West Bengal), Bhopal (Madhya Pradesh), and Srinagar (Jammu and Kashmir), in close collaboration with the respective state governments and industrial development corporations/boards of these jurisdictions.

8.8.1 Activities and Services

- Pragati Maidan, located in the centre of Delhi, is a massive trade show facility that we manage.
- Pragati Maidan, India's premier exhibition centre, hosts several trade shows and other types of events each year.
- Facilitating the usage of Pragati Maidan by other Indian and international exhibition organisers for the purpose of organising trade exhibits and exhibitions.
- Prompt and thorough assistance to international purchasers in locating vendors, creating itineraries, scheduling visits, and even accompanying them as needed.
- Building long-lasting relationships between businesses in India and those in other countries.
- Helping Indian businesses create and modify products that satisfy the needs of international customers.
- Buyer-seller meets and other unique India exhibitions are organised to facilitate interactions between buyers and sellers.
- Coordinating international department store and mail-order house promotions featuring products made in India.
- Attending trade shows and other events in other countries.
- Setting up exhibits for potential international customers.
- Seminars, conferences, and workshops on commercial topics.

- Supporting initiatives to increase exports by smaller and medium-sized businesses.
- Promoting exports and importing locally by doing market research.
- Promoting India's international trade via involving and supporting India's state governments.

8.8.2 Access to Business Data Through the Internet at the Business Information Centre

The expansion of tourism in any nation is directly tied to the rise in business travel. go and tourism companies across the globe are seeing India as a promising market and have begun offering deals and incentives to Indians planning to go abroad. Businesses and big groups may take advantage of discounted prices and tailor-made itineraries from travel firms. Reduced visa prices, free visas, e-visas, and visas upon arrival are just a few of the visa changes that have been proposed by various nations to attract more tourists. Large ballrooms are being built by hotel chains for the express purpose of hosting conferences, and these establishments are also providing their corporate clientele with specialised services, discounted accommodation rates, and carefully crafted menus. The efforts of the ITPO, the Ministry of Tourism, and other state governments are contributing to the growth of the country's events industry.

PROGRESS CHECK

1. Break out what MICE management entails, and how it works.
2. To further promote event management, it is important to highlight the role that government organizations play.
3. Define the value of recreational activities in boosting tourism.
4. What are the most important details to think about while planning a business lunch or dinner?
5. Define the value of an exhibit in the context of product promotion.
6. Provide specifics on your athletic accomplishments in several different competitions.
7. Write a short note on exhibition.

MULTIPLE-CHOICE QUESTIONS

1. Which type of event focuses on exchanging ideas and knowledge among professionals?
   (a) Networking event (b) Sports event
   (c) Concert (d) Art exhibition
2. A marathon is an example of which type of event?
   (a) Cultural event (b) Sporting event (c) Social event (d) Academic event
3. What type of activity involves solving puzzles and riddles to escape a locked room?
   (a) Cooking class (b) Team-building activity
   (c) Escape room challenge (d) Painting workshop

4. A fashion show is an example of which type of event?
   (a) Business conference (b) Educational seminar
   (c) Entertainment event (d) Health and wellness event
5. Which type of event typically involves showcasing artwork, sculptures, and crafts?
   (a) Food festival (b) Trade fair (c) Art exhibition (d) Music concert
6. What kind of activity involves participants working together to achieve a common goal?
   (a) Solo performance (b) Team-building activity
   (c) Individual competition (d) Personal development workshop
7. A charity fundraiser walk is an example of which type of event?
   (a) Cultural event (b) Recreational event
   (c) Corporate event (d) Fundraising event
8. What type of event gathers people to celebrate a specific cultural or religious occasion?
   (a) Business conference (b) Wedding reception
   (c) Holiday party (d) Fitness class
9. Which activity involves individuals competing against each other to showcase their skills?
   (a) Collaborative workshop (b) Networking event
   (c) Talent show (d) Meditation session
10. A technology expo is an example of which type of event?
    (a) Educational seminar (b) Art exhibition
    (c) Concert (d) Business conference
11. Which type of event allows companies to showcase and demonstrate their products?
    (a) Health and wellness event (b) Trade fair
    (c) Music festival (d) Book club meeting
12. What kind of activity involves engaging in physical exercises and stretches?
    (a) Art workshop (b) Dance class
    (c) Poetry reading (d) Cooking demonstration
13. Which of the following are not types of event?
    (a) Corporate (b) Community (c) Product (d) Arts
14. Which type of event is used to honour and motivate key staff?
    (a) Award ceremonies (b) Board meetings
    (c) Product launches (d) Annual shareholder meeting

Answers to Multiple-Choice Questions

1. (a)	2. (b)	3. (c)	4. (c)	5. (c)	6. (b)	7. (d)	8. (c)
9. (c)	10. (d)	11. (b)	12. (b)	13. (d)	14. (a)		

Chapter 9

Event Management: Concept & Design

Objectives

After going through this chapter the reader will be able to:
- Understand the guidelines and could able to organize event.
- Plan and prepare the event.
- Analyse the concept and design the event.
- Evaluate the event and plan the logistics.

9.1 INTRODUCTION

Event considering any kind of activity and managing these activities are considered as event management. Whether it is a wedding, a festival, a corporate event, a private party, a sports event, a birthday party, a conference, or a meeting, event management may be described as the art of offering any live experience. When planning an event, it is important to choose someone with the artistic and technical chops to pull off the desired atmosphere.

9.2 GENERAL GUIDELINES FOR ORGANISING SUCCESSFUL EVENTS

1. Event objectives

For what reason are we holding this gathering? What is it that we want folks to feel or experience? Without defined goals, it is hard to organise a successful event. Successful event management often hinges on having well-defined goals.

2. Budget planning

After determining the goals, financial planning is the most important element of event management. You may lessen your exposure with careful budgeting. If you have an unlimited budget, it is simple to put on a wonderful event, but if you have a restricted one, you will need to use some savvy event management skills.

3. Know your target audience

It does not matter what kind of event it is, but if it is meant to promote a new product, you should know who you are selling to. It is crucial that you find out so that you can tailor the event to their needs. Because getting people to think about a product must be your event's main goal.

4. Timelines

Setting deadlines and committing to action. Catering, digital, and electronic setup, and venue preparation are just a few examples of the many tasks that must be carefully planned and coordinated in advance of any major event. Event management's emphasis on punctuality is crucial.

5. Venue selection

Finding the correct location may seem like an easy task, but it is crucial for the success of your event. For this purpose, you will need to do investigation, negotiate contracts and costs, and cultivate business partnerships.

6. Manage suppliers

Organising and managing one's suppliers is a crucial aspect of any event's success. And there are always many vendors involved in every event. There are a variety of vendors, from caterers to lights, that must be contacted, shortlisted, price negotiated with, and contracts finalised with. From then, the event's success hinges on the competent administration of all vendors, who must be held to strict deadlines and budgetary constraints.

7. Marketing and communication

Delivering a crowd need promoting the promise of what the event will give; it is never a matter of 'if you build it, they will come'. Today, this is done via a wide variety of digital, social, and traditional marketing methods.

8. Thinking sustainably

Planning events with an eye on minimising negative effects on people and the planet.

9. Managing risk

Event planning is difficult because there are so many moving parts and so many ways for things to go wrong. It is crucial for event planners to have a thorough understanding of the potential dangers that might arise during their event, as well as methods to lessen those dangers and a solid backup strategy in case of emergencies.

10. Backup plan

A contingency plan is an essential part of any event's preparations.

9.3 EVENT CONCEPT DESIGN AND ANALYSIS

Event concept refers to the overall theme and idea behind the event.The success of an event depends on having a well-defined and well-executed idea that serves the event's goals, the requirements of the intended audience, and the interests of other important parties. The target audience and their interests are a key consideration when designing an event concept. The 5 W's (what, why, who, where, and when) should be asked and answered as part of the event planning process.

Type and scope of proposed event?

This calls for careful analysis of the event's key activities and attractions, which will vary depending on the event's genre (whether musical, athletic, artistic, or cultural). It is standard practice to include several supplementary and secondary activities, in addition to the primary features and attractions, to broaden the appeal and participation of the event to a wider audience.

Listed below are some main and subsidiary attractions:

- The grand reopening
- Live/DJ/background music
- Central and peripheral food and drink
- Interacting with others and making connections
- Presentations and/or speakers
- Famous people, actors, and singers
- Firework
- Contests, games, and races
- Product and exhibitor displays
- Act or stage production
- Involves dancing or dancers
- Shops and market booths

The event's location and venue, with its own distinct characteristics, history, and tradition, should be considered when deciding on the event's feature mix and programming aspects, as they may be included into the event to enhance its results. The movement of attendees at the eventis known as event flow. Lighting, décor, and musiccontributes to the ambience and atmosphere of an event.The arrangement of physical elements within the space refers as layout when considering the design of an event space.

Aspects like programming need thought to strike the right balance of activities to suit the requirements of all the participants. Depending on the nature of the event, a committee made up of several organizations interested in the event might be one approach of finding and planning appropriate activities.

When planning a recurring event, it is important to make sure it is as exciting and engaging as the first time around by including some new features while yet preserving the staples of the original event. The purpose of event mood board is to visually communicate the event concept and design. Colours can evoke emotions and set the event's tone. To make the event more engaging and memorable interactive element may incorporate in event design.

What is the event supposed to achieve?

It is essential to keep the event's goals in mind while decisions are made about the event's scope and the elements inside it. Take the event's purpose as an example: does it aim to unite the locals, draw in tourists, or do a little bit of both? Given the constraints of time, money, and other resources, optimising every event requires a delicate balancing act between competing priorities.

For whom is the event for?

To do so successfully, organisers need to give careful thought to the demographics of the event's intended audience as well as the expected turnout. To maximise attendance at your event, you must get as much information as possible on your intended audience. Which begs the question: who are they? Where do you think they could be residing? They need to know how to get to your event. When do these folks typically go out? What kind of entertainment will they be expecting at your event, and how well-equipped do you plan to make it for them? How many of your clients are new to you against how many of you have had before? When and how can people purchase tickets? I was wondering how frequently they attended functions. How sizable is this industry as a whole? How large a turnout would you want to see at this event? If so, how many people do you anticipate serving? Questions like these are essential for understanding your target demographic.

Location and venue

Location and venue are the two most important aspects to think about when choosing a place to hold an event. The setting refers to the actual place where the action takes place, whether it is a city, a hamlet, or any other physical spot. The venue is the location where the event will take place; this might be a pre-existing facility or a blank slate.

Depending on the specifics of the event at hand, deciding where it should take place might be an easy or difficult task. However, the selection criteria below must be adhered to, and it is imperative that the event's goals and purpose be considered while making venue and location options:

- Marketing: In marketing, it is essential to cater to your demographic. Branding helps create a consistent visual identity for the event.
- Functional: Practical in terms of scale, storage capacity, and ergonomics.
- Operational: Accessibility, stage size, electricity, water, amenities, parking, and tickets are all operational factors.
- Risk management Including preventative measures, crisis planning, and emergency planning.
- Financial: Economically viable within certain limits.
- Aesthetic: Aesthetically pleasing and fitting for the occasion.
- When choosing a location for your event, it is not only the building itself that matters, but also the surrounding environment. Inns and other places to stay are many in the neighbourhood.

- The availability of nearby hotels for attendees and spectators.
- Preferred modes of transportation to and from the venue.
- Parking and drop-off services.
- Location with relation to transportation hubs and airports.
- Loading docks and exhibit entrances.
- Construction and roadwork projects are in the works.
- Other events that draw attention away from the one being held.
- Any additional activities that may impede access for vendors or guests.

There is a wide variety of indoor locations from which to choose, including but not limited to museums, schools, colleges, universities, galleries, conference centres, nightclubs, restaurants, leisure facilities, hotels, tourist sites, and historic structures.

The list of possible outdoor locations is long: parks, streets, theme parks and zoos, marketplaces, sports grounds, national parks, squares, vineyards, and open agricultural land.

Once you have decided on and reserved a location for your event, you can begin making site plans to illustrate where everything will go. Important factors consist of points of entry and departure, points of interest, points of activities, points of sale, points of service, and so on. There are additional factors to think about if the event is going to take place outside, such as the placement of barriers, stages, car entries, infrastructure, restrooms, and first-aid stations. The aesthetics of the event experience are important, but so are the event's practical and safety needs, so keep these in mind while designing the venue.

Time of year, day of week, start and finish?

Appropriate dates are determined by factors such as the intended audience, the nature of the event, the availability of appropriate venues, the nature of the market, and the preferences of the event's organisers. The duration of the event is of equal importance, whether it is a full-day or half-day event or is it only going to last for a few hours. It may or may not be possible to choose when to hold an event because of the nature of the event or because of some other combination of criteria.

When choosing when the event will take place, it is important to think about how other similar events could draw attention and resources. Knowing what other events are happening in the region or target market is crucial for anticipating how many people will show up and how they will behave while there, as well as how these factors will affect the accessibility of facilities, personnel, and even parking spots. Dates to avoid and dates when the event would be more successful might be determined by studying supply and demand dynamics within the local market.

Longer events need more activities because of the need to keep attendees entertained for that amount of time; however, those costs may be spread out over more days and ticket prices might go up, all dependent on the event's infrastructure needs. The requirements and expectations of those with a vested interest in the event's outcome should be considered when settling on a time frame for the event. To calculate how long an event must go on for, first determine which parts of the programme may run simultaneously and which must follow a strict order. It is important to think about things like the event's audience, transportation, local traffic, weather, and daylight hours when deciding when to start and end the event, in addition to the length.

9.4 EVENT EVALUATION

Steps Involved in Writing the Evaluation of an Event

The next time you and your team plan an event, you may make it more successful by learning from the experience. The key is to reflect on your actions and figure out where you went wrong.

The best time to evaluate an event is either just after it ends or the day following. Gather your team for a debriefing after the event.

Step 1: Determine the extent to which event and advertising objectives have been achieved

Even if your event was wildly successful in terms of attendance and buzz, on a commercial level it was a bust if you were not able to reach your event and advertising goals.

Step 2: Get feedback from your clients and target audience

A feedback form is a useful tool for gathering customer opinions. Include a customer feedback section on your exit pass form to increase the likelihood that customers will fill it out. Exhibits cannot be removed from the building without first obtaining an exit permit, which can only be done by filling out the corresponding form.

Include a space for comments on the voucher to get input from your intended audience or event attendees. A visitor must complete out the survey and return it to an employee before receiving the coupon. People are hesitant to provide written feedback, thus these strategies are necessary for collecting it.

The following are some inquiry topics for your comment sheet:

1. Did you have fun? Explain why you answered "no" if possible.
2. Why do you like it so much, exactly?
3. In what ways do you dislike the event?
4. If there were any difficulties, what were they?
5. If you could change one thing about this gathering, what would it be?
6. Select one that best describes how you feel about the services we provide and explain your reasoning.

Hospitality:	Excellent, good, average, poor
Catering:	Excellent, good, average, poor
Transportation:	Excellent, good, average, poor
Management staff behaviour:	Excellent, good, average, poor
Management staff services:	Excellent, good, average, poor

7. Would you be interested in attending our next gathering?

9.5 EVENT LOGISTICS

Event logistics is the discipline concerned with the planning, control, and management of the flow of resources and the physical and immaterial activities involved in the production of an event.

9.5.1 Event Logistics Management

The success of every event depends on meticulous organization that considers the details of each programme and place of stay in the planning stages, as well as throughout the event's execution and management. Any potential adjustments need to be included into the larger strategy as soon as possible. That is why being able to 'foresee the unforeseen' and come up with a perfect solution on the fly is so important. Always keep in mind the following factors:

- Organising the venue
- Distribution and storage
- Loading schedules and delivery management
- Managing traffic flow
- Asset management, freight, and bump-out planning, etc.

9.5.2 Tips and Importance of Event Logistics

The following are helpful strategies for organising events and managing one's time that have proven effective in the past:

1. Planning

The logistics of any event cannot be handled without careful preparation. Make sure your strategy is sensible before you commit to it, since this will increase your productivity.

2. Set specific goals and objectives

Providing an accurate description of your intended outcome might be challenging. Time management strategies might be of use here. Learn to tell your objectives from your goals. Aspirations are high and widespread. If you want to do anything, you should "split" it up into smaller, more manageable chunks.

Consider the scenario if you need to plan a gathering, for instance. Planning it 'on time within the approved budget' is your objective. Getting there requires doing a few key things.

- Managing and maintaining the website.
- Invitee selection and event planning.
- Where to have the party and how to plan the activities.

3. SMART technologies

Separate the overarching objective into manageable steps, and then write them out in detail. Make use of SMART methods here:

- Specific
- Measurable

- Attainable
- Relevant
- Time-based

For instance, 'increase online sales in Singapore by 25% by the end of 2018' is a SMART goal since it is specific, measurable, attainable, relevant, and time-bound.

4. Fix plan of action

Plan out the steps and outcomes of an event's logistics on paper or on an app.

5. Prioritise

Is there a plan if there is a long list of things to do? Is there anything you need to do right now, or can it wait? Look at the whole list and rank the situations. For this priority-setting assignment, you may want to use time-tracking software.

6. Execution

How do you ensure that what was intended is carried out without hitch when even the best-laid schemes sometimes fail but make use of solid backing for success.

7. Focus on the task

If you want to succeed at managing the logistics of an event, you need to zero in on one thing and ignore everything else. How would you recommend doing this? Consult the experts!

8. Delegate

People frequently worry that the person they have entrusted with a task will not be able to handle it or will do a lousy job of it. Taking that tack will prevent your subordinates from developing professionally. Cooperate openly with your employees and delegate tasks that are not crucial but time-sensitive. Have faith in them. You will have more time and the other workers will be inspired.

9. Clean up your email

Chaos in your mailbox slows down work: Disorganization in your inbox slows you down because you waste time reading messages twice, searching for the relevant items, and being sidetracked by spam. Use computerised event planning software to prevent this from happening. Set up filters and folders in your email service so that everything is neatly filed away.

10. Control time

Keep your work and leisure time under control.

There are a plethora of other offline and online businesses and event logistics checklists that might:

- Consulting and technical assistance
- Planning
- Coordination of dispatch
- Shipping and handling

- declaration
- Services related to transportation
- Particular transportation services
- Quick post
- Unloading
- Placing order
- Shipping to the trade show booth
- Tailored attention
- Warehousing of unused shipping containers
- Warehousing
- Regulation of shipping
- Safety in transit insurance
- Air travel, charter flight planning
- Saloon/disco/conference hall charters on trains
- Hotel reservations using international databases and regional affiliates
- Tour schedules
- Transfers and transportation
- Assistance in obtaining visas, etc.

Organizing an event is a challenging task but with proper planning well in advance could may make an event successful. Logistic planning and proper check may eliminate the last-minute hassle. Right evaluation could make the right judgement of an event and make it more meaningful and successful for next event organization.

PROGRESS CHECK

1. What are the guidelines one should follow to organize a successful event?
2. How 5 W's plays a vital role on event design?
3. Write an essay on event logistic management.
4. Write a short note on event evaluation.
5. What is SMART technology?

MULTIPLE-CHOICE QUESTIONS

1. What does the term 'event concept' refer to?
   (a) The physical location of the event
   (b) The main sponsors of the event
   (c) The overall theme and idea behind the event
   (d) The timing and schedule of the event

2. Which of the following is a key consideration when designing an event concept?
   (a) The number of attendees
   (b) The cost of admission
   (c) The target audience and their interests
   (d) The availability of parking spaces
3. What role does branding play in event design?
   (a) It does not impact event design
   (b) It helps create a consistent visual identity for the event
   (c) It determines the event's location
   (d) It affects the weather conditions for the event
4. Which element contributes to the ambience and atmosphere of an event?
   (a) Number of restrooms available
   (b) Lighting, décor, and music
   (c) The size of the event's logo
   (d) Availability of free Wi-Fi
5. What does the term 'event flow' refer to?
   (a) The movement of attendees at the event
   (b) The direction of wind during the event
   (c) The organization of chairs and tables
   (d) The audio quality of the event's speeches
6. When considering the design of an event space, what does 'layout' refer to?
   (a) The event's social media posts
   (b) The arrangement of physical elements within the space
   (c) The choice of event's date
   (d) The event's registration process
7. What is the purpose of an event mood board?
   (a) To display a schedule of events
   (b) To showcase sponsor logos
   (c) To visually communicate the event concept and design
   (d) To list emergency contact numbers
8. What is a 'call-to-action' (CTA) in the context of event design?
   (a) An announcement of the event's dress code
   (b) A statement encouraging attendees to engage in a specific action
   (c) A list of event sponsors
   (d) The event's location coordinates
9. How does the choice of colours impact event design?
   (a) It doesnot affect the event experience
   (b) Colours have no psychological impact on attendees
   (c) Colours can evoke emotions and set the event's tone
   (d) Colours determine the menu options for the event
10. What is the purpose of incorporating interactive elements in event design?
   (a) To increase the number of attendees
   (b) To decrease the event's duration

(c) To make the event more engaging and memorable
(d) To reduce the overall event cost

11. Which of the following is not a part of logistics
(a) Product scheduling
(b) Replenishment
(c) Procurement
(d) Meandering

Answers to Multiple-Choice Questions

1. (c) 2. (c) 3. (b) 4. (b) 5. (a) 6. (b) 7. (c) 8. (b)
9. (c) 10. (c) 11. (d)

Chapter **10**

Event Management: Key to Success

Objectives

After going through this chapter the reader will be able to:

- Know the concept of organizing a successful event.
- Plan the mission and objectives of event.
- Understand environmental, social, and economic parameters of event management.
- Prepare an event proposal and analyse SWOT.

10.1 INTRODUCTION

Event management: Key to success describes how effective planning organization and coordination contribute to achieving successful and memorable events that meet objectives and engaged participants effectively. In an increasingly competitive landscape mastering event management is essential. Skilful coordination of logistics, resources and creativity ensures seamless execution, leaving a lasting impact on attendees and stakeholders alike. Navigating the intricacies of event management demands meticulous attention to detail. From conceptualization to execution, it demands adaptability, communication, and innovation to craft experiences that resonate and deliver remarkable outcome.

10.2 ORGANIZE A SUCCESSFUL EVENT

1. Begin early

Get the planning process rolling as soon as possible. You should realistically start organising your event four to six months in advance if it is a huge event. Even for smaller events, a month's notice is required. Make sure all vendor contracts are finalised a few weeks before the event to keep things running smoothly in the last days leading up to it. Effective communication ensures clear coordination among all involved parties and stakeholders.

2. Remain flexible

Things will evolve as we work towards the perfect execution of the event. You need to be adaptable and able to satisfy the needs of your guests no matter what the circumstances of your event are, including the time, place, or nature of it. Considering the availability and preferences of the target audience need to select date and time.

3. Negotiate

Despite what many retailers may have you believe, there is always room for haggling. Try to negotiate a reasonable price, but keep in mind that there will always be unexpected expenses associated with the event. Before meeting with a seller, set a price range and then offer to pay 5-10% less than that range. Despite whatever resistance they may put up, your vendor really wants your business.

4. Assign responsibilities

Divide the event into manageable chunks (registration, food, transportation, etc.) and give each member of your team a specific responsibility within that larger whole. Since they oversee their own division, they will be more attuned to changes in the finer points.

5. Create a shared document

The cloud allows for simple and effective teamwork because to its central location. Make sure everyone is on the same page by compiling all the pertinent information about the event into one comprehensive handbook or document. This should include everything from vendor contracts to guest lists to the venue's layout. Each member of your team may check the shared document for clarification, and any discrepancies will be immediately apparent.

6. Have a backup plan

Event planning is notoriously difficult, and it is not uncommon for something to go wrong, such as a forgotten item or a late arrival by a key figure. Identify the most crucial elements of your event and develop a backup plan for each. whether many problems develop in the future, prioritise them to determine whether they can be fixed or whether they need to be eliminated totally from the event.

7. Do a run through

Conduct a full rehearsal of the event around two weeks beforehand. Set up a meeting with your staff and go over the whole process, from planning to execution, in advance. At such gatherings, issues may be discussed and addressed before they become major problems. Schedule one last dress rehearsal at the venue a few days before the big event.

8. Photograph everything

Because a picture is worth a thousand words, sharing happy photographs from your event online is a great way to show how successful it was. Investing in a professional photographer is a good idea if you have the means to do so, as they will know what kind of shots are needed and will likely contact you to acquire additional details. Inquire for a variety of photographs to ensure you have got everything covered, such as a wide-angle shot of the whole room, some shots of the event's logo, and a tonne of shots of the attendees having.

9. Get online

The best approach to boost your online visibility is to host an event. Make use of Twitter to spread the word about your event by creating and promoting a unique hashtag. Similarly, you may organise an event on Facebook and ask attendees to mention it in their posts. When the party is finished, post images online and urge viewers to tag themselves.

10. Follow-up immediately

It is easy for event planners to make the mistake of taking some time off once the event ends. Even if the event's planning phase is over, it is vital to show the event's success by actively following up with participants through email or social media.

10.3 THE EVENT AIMS AND OBJECTIVES/MISSION

To ensure the success of your event, it is essential to have defined goals and outcomes in mind. Though they may be created and fine-tuned as the project develops, it is crucial that the goals and objectives of your event be specified and agreed upon from the start.

Your event's goals reflect the major reasons for holding the event and the broader strategic course you want to take. Simply said, objectives are a set of purposes that have been granularized into measurable endpoints to improve the efficiency and effectiveness of event delivery and assessment.

Impacts and results from events may be positive for a wide range of parties, including event organisers, host communities, participants, spectators, sponsors, and the media. Events should be developed and planned with these various groups in mind to optimise good outcomes, which in turn encourages stakeholder participation.

If you want to define goals and objectives for an event, one way to do so is to think about the effects it may or should have and work backwards from there.

10.3.1 Environmental Aims Could Encompass

- Urban and rural revitalization is a focus.
- Upgraded public utilities and amenities.
- Reduce your carbon footprint by recycling more and using less energy.
- The creation of new gardens and parks.
- Raising people's consciousness of ecological problems.

10.3.2 Social and Cultural Aims Could Encompass

- Raise people's consciousness of a place, time, event, custom, cultural practise, artistic expression, historical period, geographical region, social group, etc.
- Increasing civic pride and group solidarity.
- Recognising the importance of community organizations and problems.
- Community involvement has increased.
- Posing novel and difficult concepts.
- a broader view of the world.
- Methods of teaching, learning, and community service.

10.3.3 Tourism and Economic Aims Could Encompass

- Advocating for Monmouthshire as a tourist destination and enhancing its reputation as one.
- A rise in the number of visitors.
- Extending visitors' stays.
- Bringing in visitors' off-season and elongating the peak season.
- A rise in commercial and business prospects.
- Economic stimulation and the production of new jobs.
- Promotion of the local community via the media.
- Supporting regional producers of food and drink.
- Featuring handcrafted items made in the area.

10.4 SETTING EVENT OBJECTIVES

Goal-setting is the next step after determining the event's overarching purpose. Financial goals, marketing goals, attendance goals, etc., should all be established in connection to the many facets of the event. The importance of setting goals cannot be overstated, as they serve as guides for what it is you should be working towards, as well as indications of progress that can be tracked and evaluated. Goals should be SMART to achieve this:

- Tailored to certain venues during the event.
- Capable of being measured numerically.
- Conceivable by both the event planners and the participants.
- Having some bearing on the event's stated goals.
- In accordance with the event's schedule.

Here are a few examples of SMART goals:

- Six months before the event, a questionnaire will be sent out to all the town's companies.
- Online ticket sales will bring in ₹5,000 in advance of the event.
- Promotion to raise non-local tourist numbers to 10% over the previous year's levels.
- Commitment to recycling 80 per cent of event trash.
- The goal is to boost park-and-ride service use by 20%.

10.5 SWOT ANALYSIS IN EVENT PLANNING

Products/Services Research

When planning a corporate event, it is your duty as the event manager to learn as much as possible about the goods and services that will be shown and sold by your business client.

- Learn more about the firm's advertising strategies.
- How does the firm plan to increase and strengthen the public's perception of its product (its "brand image")?

- How much money do the firm and its goods are making?
- Who exactly are the product's end users?
- What are the product's key features?
- What are the product's benefits and drawbacks in relation to those of its rivals?
- All this research will later help you in making an effecting promotional campaign for your corporate event.

SWOT analysis: After receiving completed surveys and specific input from event attendees, you should do your SWOT analysis. First, the SWOT Analysis looks at the event's strengths and weaknesses, which should be evaluated while taking into, account the original event goals and objectives. Strength may be the event satisfactory report after evolution and weakness could the smaller number of staff. A SWOT analysis also examines the event's opportunities and risks. Opportunities are prospects for improvement and threats are potential future impediments.

Opportunities for improvement could include:

- Increasing attendance at future events obtaining More Sponsorship Assistance
- Continuing future events in to the evening to attract a wider range of attendees is vital.

Future threats might include:

- Event disruptions due to inclement weather.
- Loss of key organizing personnel, leading to a lack of direction for future events, inability to cover event costs due to limited income is vital.

In SWOT analysis:

'S' stands for Strengths

'W' stands for Weaknesses

'O' stands for Opportunities

'T' stands for Threats

It is a method for assessing the positives and negatives of your project to help you prepare for the future. SWOT analysis may also be performed on your company.

Strengths: These are characteristics of your project or organization that will aid in realising its goals. Examples include a skilled event crew, great motivation, positive press, a sizable piece of the market, etc.

Weaknesses: These are aspects of your project or organization that are counterproductive to reaching your goals. Lack of motivation due to, among other things, social loafing, a lack of resources, a lack of event planning expertise, a lack of media and business connections, etc.

Opportunities: Here, we are talking about all the things outside of the project that will help us succeed. Consider factors like low levels of rivalry, a thriving economy, official endorsement, access to cutting-edge facilities, etc.

Threats: These are elements of the environment that work against the project's goals. There is a lot of competition, there is not much help from the government, the weather is horrible, the infrastructure is not great, the lab our rate is expensive, the raw materials are not available, etc. You should do a SWOT analysis before creating an event plan to come up with a strategy that makes the most of your project's strengths and chances while mitigating its weaknesses and threats.

10.5.1 Analysis Report

Write a report outlining your findings after investigating the market, your rivals, your product, or service, and doing a SWOT analysis. Your study should be documented for future assessment purposes. You may use the results of your investigation to convince businesses to donate to your cause.

10.6 EVENT PROPOSAL

The purpose of event proposal is topresent a detailed plan and concept for an event to potential clients or sponsors. First and foremost, request for proposal (RFP) and your customer should be reflected in your event proposal. Since event planning entails tailoring the event to the client's goals and budget, your proposal should portray a personalised and distinctive event. An event proposal template may serve as a starting point for your writing, but each proposal should be unique and highlight your ability to meet the needs of the customer.

A Note Before You Start

Event proposal includesevent concept, budget, schedule, venue details, and proposed services. A detailed outline of the tasks and responsibilities for each aspect of the event considered as scope of work in event proposal. To demonstrate a clear understanding of the client's objectives and how the event will meet them to know the needs of clients' in details for the success of an event.

The first step is to get down with a potential customer and talk about the event, its goals, the expected turnout, and any other details they would want to provide. Not only should the meeting's date, time, and venue be written down, but also any suggestions for the event's theme, catering, general aesthetics, colours, or ambience.

Formulating an Initial Plan for the Event Proposal

To provide transparency and show how funds will be allocated for different aspects of the event is the primary purpose of including a budget breakdown in an event proposal. Each proposal must be tailor-made to the specific needs of the customer. As a service industry, event planning relies on the quality of the service provided, the individuality of the planner, and the uniqueness of the event itself to attract and retain clients. Proposals should be well-written and researched to provide the customer a clear picture of what you have in mind.

1. **Introduce yourself and the project.** Start out with a quick summary of who you are and what you do in the event planning industry. Be as descriptive as possible, elaborating on topics like how long you have been in company and your prior experience. Like

the author›s biography on the dust jacket or back cover of a book, this part is often included towards the conclusion of certain plans.

2. **Write an attractive event description.** Include a brief overview of the event itself, including topics such as its purpose, expected length of time, expected number of attendees, and potential locations mentioned in your meetings. To add as much appeal as possible to this area, you should, if you are not a talented writer, discover or pay someone who is.
3. **List all services provided.** Keep reading because this is a crucial portion. The customer must be aware of the precise nature of the services you will provide for this function. The many features and offerings are neatly laid out in a bulleted list format. The client can easily understand what you will accomplish and who you will work with using this method, which is especially useful for smaller events like wedding showers and celebration meals. Larger events that consist of numerous parts, like a cocktail hour or a luncheon, may benefit from having separate sections in which the services given for each part are detailed.
4. **Show your previous work.** Photos from comparable events you have organised in the past are a great way to demonstrate your skills. Pictures are worth a thousand words when it comes to convincing a customer of your abilities and giving yourself peace of mind that your aesthetic sensibilities align with theirs. When it comes time to start building, having something to measure against may greatly improve efficiency.
5. **Incorporate monetary information throughout.** The client's attention may be riveted by the proposal's descriptions of the event and its setting, but it is likely to transfer to the budgetary specifics. Keep the language and tone of all business and facts consistent; otherwise, everything might come to a halt. Create a section titled "Proposed Costs" and use it to walk the customer through the various parts of the event, explaining the costs as you go and include pricing throughout the proposal. Your customer should be able to perceive your proposal as a sequence of phases, each of which includes a distinct set of services and associated pricing. Give the customer an opportunity to visualise the event and the associated costs by providing a full overview that specifies the price for each item and its function.

Last Words

The last section of your proposal is a note of gratitude for their time and interest. Give your website, email, and phone number so that potential customers may reach out to you with inquiries or, better yet, to employ you for the project.Post event evaluation ensures to assess the event's success, identify areas for improvement, and gather feedback for future events.

10.7 EVENT MANAGEMENT TOOLS

Use Sales force and Hub spot to track your event attendees and build lasting connections.

A customer relationship management system (CRM) is a must-have for any events company that values its clientele. Your customer data will be neatly organised in a top-tier customer relationship management system like Salesforce or HubSpot.

If you want your event to result in sales or donations, your customer relationship management system is crucial. After collecting customer data, you may monitor and adjust each client's experience over time by using a customer relationship management system.

But a good CRM also helps you manage connections with sponsors, partners, and other vendors. As a result, you may use this resource as the nerve centre for planning the event's human components.

Boost attendance with Eventbrite's streamlined ticketing and registration process.

Most of the ticket and registration sales now occur online, but not all platforms are created equal.

You should be able to manage the whole event from start to finish with the aid of your online ticketing platform, not only make purchases. It should also provide you with insightful data and statistics to help you make well-timed strategic choices. And by connecting with popular social media platforms like Facebook and Instagram, it should help you boost turnout.

Eventbrite's built-in visual analytics, charts, and reports provide you a wealth of information on the individuals who will be attending your event. The Eventbrite Organiser app also allows you to monitor attendance and ticket sales in real time using your mobile device.

It is essential that all the tools you use in your event preparation sync seamlessly with your event management technology.

Use email to interact with prospective guests using Emma and Mail Chimp.

According to a recent poll conducted by Eventbrite, 73 per cent of event professionals see email as a priority marketing method to enhance in 2019. There is no better way to contact prospective guests or keep in touch with them.

Meanwhile, over half of event pros anticipate that email will be a less effective sales tool in 2019. To monitor your progress and boost your sales, an email marketing platform is essential.

Two of the most reliable email marketing platforms are Emma and Mail Chimp. By using them:

- Build professional-looking email marketing campaigns that stay true to your brand's aesthetic.
- If you want to get the most out of your email marketing, segment your contact lists by category (possible attendees, registered attendees, repeat attendees, etc.) and send each subset of recipients tailored messages.
- Set up recurring and automatic email sending

Having your email service sync with your event ticketing service is a huge time saver, and both Mailchimp and Emma do just that with Eventbrite. That way, you can avoid having to manually add attendees to your email lists (and the associated risks of human error and forgetfulness) whenever someone purchases a ticket to your event.

Asana: Plan your event down to the last detail.

Asana is our go-to tool for keeping track of all the moving components in event planning, thus it is essential that we include it here. Asana is a project management app that facilitates efficient project planning, team priority tracking, and increased output quality.

Create a project in Asana for each event you oversee and fill it up with each action in the work-back schedule. Then, let everyone in your organization who has a hand in the event know about the project (including the processes, roles, and deadlines) so that they can track progress and know who is responsible for what and when.

Asana includes a specialised event planning template that can be modified to keep track of tasks and milestones for event-related processes, whether you are working alone or with a large group. The technology may be linked to your existing platforms, such as Mail Chimp and Salesforce.

PROGRESS CHECK

1. What are the points need to keep in mind for organizing a successful event?
2. Write an essay on environmental, social, and economic aims of event management.
3. Briefly analyse SWOT for one cultural event planning.
4. Develop one event proposal for a marriage ceremony.
5. Explain the role of CRM in event organization.

MULTIPLE-CHOICE QUESTIONS

1. What is the purpose of an event proposal?
   (a) To list the event attendees
   (b) To present a detailed plan and concept for an event to potential clients or sponsors
   (c) To showcase event decorations
   (d) To summarize the event's entertainment programme
2. What information is typically included in an event proposal?
   (a) Event concept, budget, schedule, venue details, and proposed services
   (b) Event's guest list, dress code, and catering menu
   (c) Event promotions on social media
   (d) Event entertainment lineup only
3. What is an 'RFP' in the context of event proposals?
   (a) Rarely featured performer (b) Recommended food platters
   (c) Request for proposal (d) Reliable front-row placement
4. What does 'scope of work' refer to in an event proposal?
   (a) The length of the event
   (b) The budget allocation for event promotion
   (c) A detailed outline of the tasks and responsibilities for each aspect of the event
   (d) The event's dress code requirements
5. What is the primary purpose of including a budget breakdown in an event proposal?
   (a) To showcase the event's entertainment lineup
   (b) To provide transparency and show how funds will be allocated for different aspects of the event

(c) To list potential event sponsors
(d) To outline the event schedule

6. Why is it important to tailor an event proposal to the specific needs of the client or event?
(a) To save time and effort
(b) To showcase the event organizer's preferences
(c) To demonstrate a clear understanding of the client's objectives and how the event will meet them
(d) To highlight event decorations

7. What is the first step in organizing a successful event?
(a) Defining the event's objectives and purpose
(b) Booking a venue
(c) Designing event decorations
(d) Sending out invitations

8. What does 'target audience' refer to when organizing an event?
(a) The event›s entertainment line-up
(b) The specific group of people the event aims to attract and engage
(c) The event's budget
(d) The event's schedule

9. Which factor is crucial for selecting the right event date and time?
(a) The latest event trends
(b) The event's catering menu
(c) Considering the availability and preferences of the target audience
(d) The event's social media promotion plan

10. What role does effective communication play in event organization?
(a) It impacts the choice of event colours
(b) It ensures clear coordination among all involved parties and stakeholders
(c) It determines the event's dress code
(d) It influences the entertainment programme

11. How does creating a detailed event timeline contribute to success?
(a) It ensures the event's social media presence
(b) It determines the event's catering options
(c) It helps keep all tasks and activities organized and on schedule
(d) It showcases the event sponsors

12. What is the purpose of post-event evaluation when organizing an event?
(a) To finalize the event budget
(b) To assess the event's success, identify areas for improvement, and gather feedback for future events
(c) To select the best event decorations
(d) To showcase the event's entertainment programme

13. Threats are
    (a) Chances for unexpected favourable outcomes
    (b) Opportunities of the event
    (c) Strengths of the event
    (d) External factors that influence the event

Answers to Multiple-Choice Questions

1. (b)	2. (a)	3. (c)	4. (c)	5. (b)	6. (c)	7. (a)	8. (b)
9. (c)	10. (b)	11. (c)	12. (b)	13. (d)			

Chapter 11

Event Protocols, Staging and Staffing

Objectives

After going through this chapter the reader will be able to:

- Understand various event protocols.
- Know the staging of an event and analyse the role of stage manager.
- Work on staffing guide for event organization.
- Design the dress for event professionals as per event requirements.

11.1 INTRODUCTION

Formal procedures and etiquettes are encompassing event protocol. An event is a gathering of people for a specific purpose, such as a party, lecture, sales pitch, or family get-together. Whether it is a wedding, a festival, a private party, a sports event, a conference, or a meeting, successful event management is a potent combination of creative and technical talents necessary for the conception and execution of any live experience. The '5 Cs'cover almost every aspect of the event process. These five Cs are: concept, coordination, control, culmination, and close out. These are the stages of planning: preparation, execution, evaluation, and finalisation. While organising an event, 'protocol' is shorthand for the social norms that must be upheld while engaging with or hosting high-ranking government officials or representatives from other organizations. It may also include considerations of cultural etiquette. Staging means how to present one event or actual exaction on the event day with required facilities and adequate staff.

11.2 PROTOCOLS OF EVENT MANAGEMENT

11.2.1 Protocol

The word 'protocol' literally translates to 'first glue' in Greek. Protocol is the 'glue that keeps society's formal institutions functioning smoothly. When foreign dignitaries are brought together, it is extremely necessary to observe protocol as a sign of respect and concern for one another. There are certain rules on how to approach important people and how to present oneself at formal events. Protocol refers to the established norms and customs for interacting with and meeting new people. The proper way to fly a flag and where to place dinner guests are also covered.The purpose of a receiving line at an event is to allow attendees to greet and meet important individuals

11.2.2 Inviting Guests

It is acceptable to make first contact verbally and then confirm the invitation in writing at least three months before the event. In addition, make sure everything is in order by checking in a day or two beforehand. Talk to them about these things:

the reason for the visit;

the length of time allotted for the visit;

who will pay for travel, food, parking, and lodging; and

whether or not a meal will be provided for their spouse.

Do you have any dietary restrictions? Provisions, tools and suitable clothing or does the visitor need help about town or finding a place to stay?

11.2.3 Greetings

In both written and spoken greetings, the use of the honorific 'sir' is commonly accepted as an appropriate alternative to the formal address. It is appropriate to use 'Madam' or 'Ma'am' when addressing a woman. Religious leaders and those of noble birth are exempt from this regulation. In formal greetings, "Mr." is reserved for male recipients. Madam, Mrs., Miss, or Ms. are all acceptable alternatives for the female form of address. There is no hard and fast rule on when to use "Ms."; instead, you should always defer to the choice of the person being addressed.

11.2.4 Attire for Official Occasions

The invitation should include the dress code for the event. Dressing formally throughout the day may include wearing a suit and tie. Dress is black or white for the evening. Name badges are should be displayed on the right side of the chest. So that the name badge may be seen clearly when the hand is extended to shake.

11.2.5 Protocol for Speaker

The highest-ranking individual usually the first person to speak or be introduced in a formal event. A list of the visitors to be greeted, in order of importance, should be handed to the speakers ahead of time so that they may prepare appropriate greetings. Before the event, it is important to negotiate the time and duration of talks with the speakers and to canvass the chief.

11.2.6 Seating Protocol in an Official State Function

The host of an event is responsible for making sure the guests are seated appropriately for any formal meals or presentations. Families and foreign officials alike might be offended or feel insulted if they are treated unfairly regarding table precedence. Assigning seats at a table is as easy as deciding who is superior and then sitting them there.

11.2.7 Rules on Seating (Formal Dinner)

The host and hostess traditionally take seats on opposing ends of the table when there is only room for one.

1. When there are too many guests for a single table, the host and hostess may be seated at different locations.
2. It is customary to seat the host or hostess on the left of the guest of honour. To the right of the host is seated the wife of the highest ranked male or the highest ranking woman.
3. There were no tables with more than one person at each.
4. Couples that are married are not seated together, although engaged couples often are.

11.2.8 Dining Etiquette

Typically during designated moments, such as speeches or formal dinners it is appropriate to raise a toast during an event. Placement instructions: Sit at the table facing the placement, arms at your sides. Cut into small pieces and pile onto a fork. Do not overload your fork with food. Keep your lips shut and your meal chewed well before speaking. Do not make a fuss with your fork and knife when you are trying to eat. Avoid slurping while eating soup or other liquid foods. You may cool down the meal by blowing on it gently if it is too hot to eat. Think about the others who are there. Do not yell or yell too loudly. Do not light up when we are eating. Put down the phone and pay attention to your dinner companions.

11.2.9 Protocol of Flag Flying

The Flag Code of India, adopted in 2002, specifies the rules for flying and handling the flag.

(a) The national flag must be flown at an appropriate height and in a dignified manner at all occasions.

(b) The flag must always be displayed prominently and in a certain location whenever it is flown.

(c) Any public structure where it is customary to display a flag during daylight hours.

(d) The saffron band must be on top when the flag is flown horizontally or at an angle from a window or balcony.

(e) If the flag is being exhibited at a public meeting, the speaker should face the audience while the flag is to the right of the speaker.

(f) The flag is held in the right hand while being carried in a procession or demonstration.

(g) The national flag should be placed in the centre of a row of other flags.

(h) The national flag must always be flown at the highest possible position.

(i) At no point during the meeting is the flag to be used to adorn or cover the desk of the speaker.

(j) Never fly the national flag with the saffron band facing down.

(k) The flag must never touch the ground or be dragged through the water.

(l) No part of the flag's display or attachment should put it at risk of harm.

11.2.10 Wedding Protocols

Traditional wedding ceremony among the linden trees.The hostess or lady of the manor usually meets the bride and husband as they exit the castle. who, with a nod to the past, shows them the way to the stately linden promenade. Music plays as the newly weds exchange vows among the trees. The lady of the manor leads the couple through the ceremony by playing a lute or violin while they exchange vows, rings, and the marriage licence. Following the formal proceedings, the wedding party and guests form a double queue behind the wedding arch, signifying the beginning of a new chapter in their lives.

11.2.11 Guidelines for Meeting

Send invitations and share the agenda and any necessary background information with attendees well in advance of the scheduled meeting time. Notify your superiors when you require specialised employees. Make sure that any necessary preparations with outside resource people have been made in advance of the meeting. At the outset of the gathering, introduce the people who will be resources and the new attendees. Make sure the other participants are aware of their connections and the areas in which they excel. Include attendees in the meeting notice and minutes in alphabetical order. Show your appreciation to those who helped make the meeting a success, both within and outside of the organization.

When planning and carrying out a formal event, it is customary to adhere to a set of rules and regulations known as 'ceremonial protocol', which are based primarily on etiquette and precedent. Protocol is based on long-standing norms and traditions. In reality, a habit may evolve into a tradition, and the ensuing salutes and honours for dignitaries and the Royal Family can become institutionalised etiquette.

11.3 EVENT PLANNING DRESS CODES

For planners perspectives

- Do wear dark colours.
- Do not bring a change of clothes every time or middle of an event.
- Do wear comfortable shoes.
- Do not forget to layer.
- Do not carry extras.
- Do not use bags with shoulder straps, use backpack if required
- Do wear clothes that have pockets.

For client or customers perspectives

Depends on host, declaration, or specific protocols as per the event.

11.4 EVENT STAGING

Designing and arranging the physical elements of the event space is known as event staging. A diagram illustrating the layout of equipment, performers, and props on the stage is known as stage plot. Planning and rehearsing the movements and positions of performers on stage is considered a blocking of event staging. A rehearsal to test and fine-tune technical aspects such as lighting, sound, and visuals is considered a tech rehearsal before event staging.

1. Event staging
    - Examine the needs for event setup
    - Finding and negotiating with staging companies
    - Keep an eye on the rigging companies
2. Analyse event staging requirements: Things to think about when staging an event, conditions for staging- When choosing a location for an event, it is important to think about how it will affect everyone involved. First responders, caterers, performers, patrons, and customers.
3. Three primary factors should be considered when choosing a location for an event: the number of people expected to attend the event. Design of the venue and its appropriateness for the gathering, stadium, playing field or theatre, Movement and storage, Location close to lodging and tourist hotspots, Problems with supplies for businesses providing products and services, such as caterers help with technology and event planning.
4. The constraints of the location should be made clear upon examination. Consistency with the event's topic, attendee ease, audience viewability (sightlines), sound reproduction, ways in and out, space for performing (if applicable), space for storing, accessible tools, to take shelter against bad weather, guaranteed protection, allowing easy passage for rescue vehicles, and routes of evacuation.
5. Major stakeholders:
    - The Performers - they have special requirements that are crucial to their success, such as the degree of closeness with the audience (often the consequence of the distance from the audience) or the loudness of the sound.
    - The Audience - they also have requirements, the most basic of which is to be able to see the action.
    - The Planners.
6. The following six components may be included in a staging: landscape that is framed, landscape that bears weight, scenery that matches, gentle landscape, furnishings and other stage equipment, transforms, transports.
7. Telescopes, maxi-lifts or genie-type lifters, cherry pickers, mobile scaffolding, ladders and A-frames, and scissor lifts are all examples of equipment that might be utilised (subject to regulatory restrictions and licencing requirements).
8. To brief contractors and create specification papers for the following services, you must have this information: catering; venue or site services and set-ups; technical services;

entertainers; and transportation. Prerequisites and setup for registration, elements of nature, security, stories in the press, and precautionary measures.

9. Everything about the event, from the decorations to the lighting, to the music, to the special effects, must go in with the concept.
10. Colour, scenery, and setting are all forms of art that may help drive home a point. film/theatre/art/dance, humour, fantasy.
11. Décor entertainment: A variety of performances may be employed to complement an event's theme, and corporate gatherings in particular, often include engaging entertainers. Consists of a wide variety of elements, such as the paint and curtains, the furniture, and the flowers. The design of the event space is crucial to the success of the event.
12. Sound, lighting, and special effects: Nighttime activities provide the chance for more dramatic outcomes than their daytime counterparts due to the greater potential for stunning lighting effects. A song may completely alter your state of mind. All projected pictures, such as game highlights on giant screens and scoreboards, are considered part of the audience's "vision".
13. Set stage: Performances, award ceremonies, and other presentations are just some of the various uses for the stage. Everything you see onstage—props, flats, lecterns, staircases, curtains—is part of the set.
14. Field of play tenting: A tent's expanse allows for limitless possibilities in terms of lighting and decoration. The rules for each competition vary. Rehersal is the time for everyone to synchronise their actions.
15. Event services: Services of critical need, transport and traffic control, and communication.
16. Source and negotiate staging contractors: For both legal and practical reasons, it is crucial to provide contractors with thorough and detailed staging specifications that outline the exact needs based on an understanding of the product or service in question.
17. The organizer's aim: Locate and negotiate with suitable service providers for the occasion, Contractors should be given detailed briefings or specifications outlining their exact staging needs. Get accurate price estimates in a timely manner for the delivery of services. Consult with relevant parties to evaluate bids and make contractor selections. Get everything in writing, including the terms of your agreement with contractors and the price tag for their services.
18. The organiser is responsible for keeping tabs on how well the contract is being carried out by maintaining constant communication with the contractors and other parties involved. Determine what modifications are necessary, and then set them into motion; get them confirmed in writing. Make sure the event's quality and authenticity are preserved by negotiating the necessary changes. Examine the progress you have made in the light of the event's needs and deadlines, and take corrective measures if necessary.

19. Staging area is usually handled by certified experts because of the importance placed on safety and is needed to avoid physical harm or any unwanted tragedy.
20. Catering contractors: Typically, a catering company handles all aspects of event catering, including receiving orders, preparing the food, and staffing the event.
21. Common approaches to event catering: Table service with a predetermined menu buffet, snacks, and quick meals.
22. Accommodation providers: The inclusion of lodging is crucial. When organising a gathering, it is also important to consider food safety. Kitchen staff at events that need catering have a lot on their plates. drinks served during parties and banquets the handling of queues is a further factor.
23. Waste management specialist: Create, roll out, and oversee integrated waste management programmes that aim to cut down on trash while increasing recycling and reusing.
24. Cleaning contractors: They are responsible for cleaning the venue before and after the event, as well as ensuring that it remains spotless throughout.
25. Monitor staging contractors: You must keep an eye on the events leading up to the big day to make sure everything is on track and that all necessary preparations have been made; check in with vendors and participants to make sure everything is ready to go before the big day.
26. Green room: A room where speakers/participants prepare and relax before going to stage for performance.

The stage director assumes a significant role in the creation and execution cycle of event organization. In enormous theatres and scenes, they could likewise be in a chief position going with choices on organizing planned operations and managing the specialized methodology for occupant and visiting organizations in an extensive variety of fine arts. On the other end of the spectrum, they might work as company managers and technicians for a small touring company. The role will change based on the size, type, and scope of the organization hosting the event.

In all cases the stage director will have an administrative position, driving the group of creation agents and experts. This might incorporate the deputy stage manager (DSM), assistant stage manager (ASM), stage group and lighting and sound professionals. The stage administrator additionally guarantees clear correspondence between every one of the groups dealing with the show. We will examine the abilities and procedures required for pre-practice arranging, the practice and fit-up cycles and after creation for a stage manager.

11.4.1 Responsibilities of Stage Manager

The Stage Manager is a vital situation in any fruitful event. To oversee the coordination and execution of all stage-related aspects is the primary role of an event stage manager. The position has a remarkable capability since it serves the double capability of partner to the chief and creation staff during the practice time frame and afterward turns into the individual responsible for the event during the genuine presentation. The Stage Manager will face different and distinct requirements at each event. The obligations and obligations recorded here might act as a manual for assist with making an effective encounter.

(a) General: To meet live event necessities, the stage manager conveys stage intends to arrange team and scene the board. He arranges stage group exercises and helps with or regulates stage planning including dumping, arrangement and situating of show stage components, for example, instruments, gear, or foundation sets. On the off chance that he sees a wellbeing, security or coordinated operations issue, he works with the demonstration and scene the executives to change the plans. He also makes sure that an act gets everything they need for the backstage facilities, like specific food or drinks.

(b) Specialized: A stage manager likewise manages specialized matters. He audits show specialized necessities with different individuals engaged with arranging the presentation, like the demonstration, the demonstration's managers, and experts. During rehearsals or recordings, he watches the lighting, speakers, microphones, and other equipment. Before a show, he manages light, sound, fixing and other stage hardware tests. He additionally regulates show component testing, for example, fireworks tests, if relevant. During a presentation, he settles on specialized changes or decision prompts to a specialized team taking care of the hardware.

(c) Execution: The act is informed when it is time to enter the stage by the stage manager before the performance. Other than gear specialized signs, a phase chief likewise prompts other stage activities, for example, opening and shutting stage shades, if material, toward the beginning, recess, and end of the show. Subsequently, he oversees stage cleanup and evacuation, stacking and shipment of stage components given by the demonstration. If a demonstration stores stage components at the setting, he administers nearby vehicle and capacity.

(d) Other: Stage managers likewise survey crisis methodology and implement rules and guidelines intended to forestall security issues or well-being dangers. For instance, a stage manager frequently looks at behind the stage passes to prevent unapproved people from getting to the stage or act. They likewise keep swarms from shaping that could disturb the show or make a peril. Furthermore, if a stage manager needs a brief stage group to help, he normally makes the fundamental spending plan, enlists the team, manages their work, and keeps up with finance.

11.4.2 Stage Manager Duties: Live Events

The following is a list of common stage management responsibilities, even though they vary depending on the production and the institution. This is appropriate if there should be an occurrence of live events, for example, film shows, extraordinary broadcasts, live exercises and so on.

Pre-Production

- Review Institutional and Rules Regarding Production
- Create a Contact Sheet
- Create a Rehearsal Schedule w/ the Director
- Get the Ground Plan and Dimensions of the Performance Space
- Distribute Rehearsal Schedule
- Figure out Specific Needs of Production
- Assist Production Manager in Planning First Production Meeting
- Rehearsal Process
- Distribute Daily Rehearsal Calls
- Collect Emergency Contact Forms
- Call Breaks
- Call Meal Breaks, If Rehearsal is Longer Than 5 Hours
- Protect the Safety of the Cast
- Distribute Script
- Create Costume List
- Coordinate and Facilitate Communication within the Design Team
- Send Rehearsal Reports

Notes for EACH Technical Department (including additions and alterations)

- Scenic
- Props
- Lighting
- Sound
- Costumes
- Projection
- Hair/Makeup
- Upcoming Events
- Run-Throughs
- Visiting Guests
- Publicity

Technical Process

- Lead Rehearsals of the Show
- Light Cues
- Sound Cues
- Music
- Costumes
- Quick Changes

- Create and Maintain the Calling Script
- Begin Calling Cues
- Create and Distribute Preset Lists for Backstage Crew
- Create and Distribute Run Sheets for Backstage Crew
- Manage Backstage Crew
- Organize Backstage Traffic
- Find Solutions to Potential Safety Problems
- Continue Sending Rehearsal Reports

Performances

- Coordinate with front of house to open the house and begin the performance
- Call the show's cues, including
- Automated Scenery
- Lights
- Sounds
- Projection
- Orchestra
- Actors
- Maintain the artistic integrity (the director's vision) of the show
- Run rehearsals to assist show maintenance

Runs rehearsal for all understudies/replacements

- Update the calling script
- Update pre-set lists and run sheets

Send Performance Reports regarding with information including:

- Late Arrivals/Absences
- Illnesses/Injuries
- Run Length
- Audience Reaction
- Issues with Scenery or Props
- Issues with Costumes
- Issues with Light Instruments or Board
- Issues with Sound Equipment
- Dropped Lines/Missed Cues/Show Error
- Any Other Unusual Occurrences

The role of Stage Manager is one that is both complicated and time-consuming, and it requires calmness, tact, efficiency, and organization. The Stage Manager organizes and runs rehearsals, coordinates all aspects of the production during technical rehearsals and performances, and serves as the primary point of contact for the director, technical staff, and cast. The Stage Manager speaks with each branch of creation however works especially intimately with the chief, the planners, and the behind the stage team.

Stage Manager are liable for guaranteeing creations are finished by chiefs' desires, in time for the principal execution and kept up with all through the disagreement agreement with industry best practices. They are likewise the chief coordinator and communicator between imaginative staff, creation groups, front of house staff, and regulatory staff for their relegated creation.

11.5 EVENT STAFFING

Event staffing may take on as many forms as an event does. Enough employees are hired to manage the many responsibilities necessary for a successful event, and this number is based on the expected number of visitors.

Staffing includes roles such as waitresses, coat checks, drivers, drivers for the disabled, information desk workers, valet parkers, and ticket takers.

Employees may also be responsible for managing the flow of attendees, setting up and breaking down booths and exhibitors, monitoring nurseries, helping with guest speakers, supplying necessities throughout the event, and cleaning up any trash that accumulates.

In certain cases, the decorating committee may require extra help with setting up tables and chairs. Workers could also be expected to manage the workflow of subordinate workers or to manage the funds collected from ticket sales. Many of these tasks may be completed by event volunteers, by current firm workers, or by the caterer, equipment rental agency, or event site itself.

Staff duties are determined by the nature of the event and the range of services required to ensure attendees have a good time. While it is easy for event organisers to picture a great gathering, few of them really consider how many people will be needed to pull off all the little details. To alleviate issues brought on by a shortage of manpower, it is important to define every aspect of the event, from the entrance of visitors to the cleaning afterward.

Catering companies, rental companies for things like chairs and tables, flower shops, ticket booths, and event spaces often supply staff to run their operations. These could be part of the agreed-upon services, or they might be supplied as an optional extra. The identification of volunteers from within the ranks of the firm, membership rosters, or interested persons willing to fulfil these responsibilities may provide savings, provided there is guidance to coordinate personnel to carry out their assignments. It is usually a good idea for event planners to hire experts in these fields, since they will have the necessary resources (such as insurance and training) to carry out these tasks to the satisfaction of the event's sponsors.

PROGRESS CHECK

1. What are the various protocols one should follow in event management?
2. What are the duties and responsibilities of event stage manager?

3. Write a short note on event staffing.
4. What are the basic requirements of event staging?
5. How you will plan the dress code for event staffs?

MULTIPLE-CHOICE QUESTIONS

1. What does 'event protocol' encompass?
   (a) Event catering (b) Entertainment activities
   (c) Formal procedures and etiquette (d) Event decorations
2. Which element does event protocol often dictate?
   (a) Event budget (b) Dress code (c) Menu options (d) Event location
3. In a formal event, who is usually the first person to speak or be introduced?
   (a) The youngest attendee (b) The event organizer
   (c) The highest-ranking individual (d) A random volunteer
4. What is the purpose of a receiving line at an event?
   (a) To allow attendees to greet and meet important individuals
   (b) To showcase event sponsors
   (c) To serve refreshments
   (d) To display event merchandise
5. When is it appropriate to raise a toast during an event?
   (a) At any point during the event
   (b) Typically during designated moments, such as speeches or formal dinners
   (c) Only at the end of the event
   (d) When there is a lull in the entertainment programme
6. What does 'event staging' primarily refer to?
   (a) Setting up the guest list
   (b) Event promotion on social media
   (c) Designing and arranging the physical elements of the event space
   (d) Preparing the event budget
7. What is a 'stage plot' in the context of event staging?
   (a) A map of the event venue
   (b) A diagram illustrating the layout of equipment, performers, and props on the stage
   (c) A chart showing the event's schedule
   (d) A list of event sponsors
8. In event staging, what is the purpose of a 'green room'?
   (a) A room filled with plants for decoration
   (b) A room dedicated to environment-friendly initiatives
   (c) A space where performers or speakers can relax before going on stage
   (d) A room with green-themed event decorations

9. What is the primary role of an event stage manager?
   (a) To oversee the coordination and execution of all stage-related aspects
   (b) To manage event invitations and RSVPs
   (c) To design event graphics and promotional materials
   (d) To handle event catering arrangements
10. What does 'blocking' refer to in event staging?
   (a) Creating physical barriers around the event space
   (b) Setting up a ticketing booth
   (c) Planning and rehearsing the movements and positions of performers on stage
   (d) Assigning event tasks to different team members
11. What is the purpose of a 'tech rehearsal' in event staging?
   (a) A rehearsal involving only the technical crew
   (b) A rehearsal focused on event decorations
   (c) A rehearsal where performers showcase their talents
   (d) A rehearsal to test and fine-tune technical aspects such as lighting, sound, and visuals

Answers to Multiple-Choice Questions

1. (c) 2. (b) 3. (c) 4. (a) 5. (b) 6. (c) 7. (b) 8. (c)
9. (a) 10. (c) 11. (d)

Chapter 12

Leadership & Event Branding

Objectives

After going through this chapter the reader will be able to:

- Understand the leadership styles and qualities.
- Know the event branding and brand management.
- Chalk the advertising strategies.
- Promote the events.

12.1 INTRODUCTION

To put it simply, leadership is the ability to inspire a group of individuals to act in pursuit of a shared purpose. They are the group's undisputed leader because of their magnetic charisma and obvious aptitude for inspiring loyalty in others around them.Initiative includes the capacity to impact individuals to make moves towards finishing an objective. Event leaders are generally responsible to manage event logistics. Events contain various parts and an event administrator need to have dynamic authority abilities to address different difficulties. Branding is important for the success of any event and need to apply various tools accordingly.

12.2 LEADERSHIP STYLES

12.2.1 Leadership Styles based on Authority can be 4 Types

- Authoritarian Administration,

An autocratic leader possesses centralized power, making decisions without much input from others. They often a full control over their domain, limiting participatory decision making and individual freedom.

- Democratic or Participatory Administration

A democratic leader promotes inclusivity and shared decision making, valuing input from group members. They encourage open communication, collaboration, and respect for diverse opinions, fostering a sense of empowerment.

- Autonomous or Do-What-You-Want-To-Do-Leadership.

An autonomous leader delegates authority and responsibility to team members, allowing them to make decisions within their expertise. This empowers individuals, fosters innovation, and encourages self-sufficiency in the team.

- Leadership that acts like a parent.

A parent leader adopts a nurturing approach, guiding and supporting their team like a parent would. They prioritize mentorship, growth, and wellbeing, fostering a positive and familial work environment.

12.2.2 Leadership Process

Trait theoriesare the approaches to the study of leadership which emphasise the personality of the leader. In leadership process when people operate as leaders their role is not always clearly established and defined but it is a part and process to pick and act naturally. A detailed schedule of event activities refers to run of show in event leadership. A further confusion of the event chief's job originates from the multi-layered climate in which they work. At the centre of everyday tasks are the event office and the event group. A subsequent aspect is the intra-association, i.e., the parent association, client local area, and project workers. The third aspect is the between association, i.e., outer associations having a personal stake, or oversight expert in the event office. This perplexing climate presents a correspondence worldview unrivalled by some other management position. The event group is many times huge in number and comprises of a complex blend of multi-disciplinary, entomb hierarchical, topographically dispensed individuals, inside utilized work force, and revaluated or contract staff. Consequently, the event director should adapt to shaky lines of power and power and the event administrator should connect with numerous fluctuated gatherings and partners inside and beyond the utilizing association, frequently with clashing interests applicable to the current event. In this manner they force various administration challenges.

Obligation without power is one more test that the event administrator faces. At the point when colleagues have a double detailing structure the event supervisor might find it hard to apply impact over the colleagues. Direct power over work force will in general rest with the practical administrator while the event supervisor has minimal direct power over the event colleagues or their chiefs. In such powerful climate the event supervisor should accomplish the goal with administration styles arranged towards keeping up with efficiency and positive human relations.

It is generally acknowledged that authority is an affecting cycle among pioneers and supporters to accomplish hierarchical targets through change. Authority has additionally been characterized as finishing things through others. In event management, this implies that the event supervisor must accomplishes results through the event group. All in all, motivating individuals relegated to the event to fill in collectively to accomplish the event objective is fundamental part of event administration.

Summary of Leadership Process

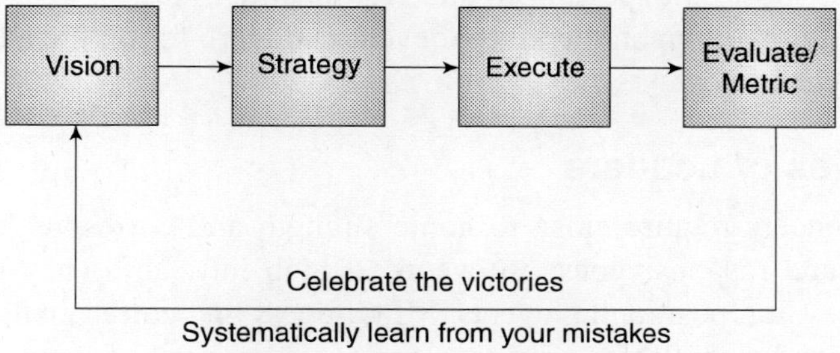

12.2.3 Leadership Skills

The abilities of the pioneer can be recognized to hard abilities and delicate abilities. Hard abilities demonstrate specialized or industry-explicit information and the capacity to discuss this information with the group and by delicate abilities meaning. Strong negotiation and sound communication are one of the major leaderships skills. In a worldwide event the human relations abilities, for example, group management and struggle, diverse capability might be the most applicable administration expertise in comprehension of various work styles and helps the event chief to address clashes.

The three central management abilities, specialized abilities, relational abilities and critical thinking abilities, are fundamental for any to succeed. Specialized abilities include the information and the capacity to utilize strategies, processes, procedures, instruments, and gear to play out an errand. These abilities are likewise here and there called business abilities. The specialized abilities are the simplest one's to create from the three management abilities, yet they can fluctuate more relying upon the gig. Understanding the office management plan, different gear is expected during the event and different parts of room format are important for specialized abilities. Effective event pioneers can utilize a frameworks approach for finishing jobs that satisfied presentation guidelines on time and inside arranged costs.

Relational abilities are likewise called relationship building abilities or delicate abilities. They are the capacity to comprehend, convey and function admirably with people and gatherings through creating viable connections. Pioneers required relational abilities, for example, arranging, spurring, independent direction, and critical thinking balance between the specialized and initiative parts of event management and states that the event's supervisor will likely form camaraderie and cultivate great working relations so everybody is anxious to pursue a shared objective.

Reasonable abilities depend on the capacity to comprehend difficulties of future, select activity intends to tackle issues and make the most of chances. It includes decisive reasoning, breaking down other options and endeavouring to boost positive result for the association. These abilities relate to different abilities like decisive reasoning and vital preparation.

One should take in to thought that the abilities required careful relying upon the degree of management. High level chiefs utilize for the most part relational and thinking abilities.

Centre level supervisors should adjust between every one of the three abilities and first-level chiefs utilize for the most part specialized and relational abilities. In event management the abilities required rely totally upon the kind of event and there for on the administration style expected in a particular event.

12.2.4 Qualities of Leaders

Effective event pioneers require close to home strength and correspondence in events of medium intricacy and responsiveness in events of high intricacy. They should have high persuasive capacities in repositioning events. Mindfulness and correspondence in discussion abilities and understanding collective vibes are vital to the progress of event pioneers. An event leader ensures successful stakeholder management by involving stakeholders in decision-making. A leader minimizes the potential issues in event risk management. By incorporating interactive elements and activities an event leader enhances attendee engagement.

These abilities are expected at different stages. While the capacity to oversee individuals are significant in the plan state, awareness is more significant in the charging stage, overseeing assets are most pivotal in all stages. Appropriate criticism and solid work culture is additionally expected at all phases of event management.

Enabling worker, for example, giving them a comprehensive point of view and set them up for testing jobs is a significant initiative ability. People need to demonstrate the way that they can achieve objectives and address difficulties and to that end it is fundamental to establish a workplace and culture that engages individuals so the event chief includes colleagues in choices and enables them to pursue choices inside their area of obligation.

Creating workers as a skill has a wide range of points of view of initiative. One portrayal is that creating is the reinforcing of others' capacities through criticism and direction. It is having faith in others potential and empowering them to take significantly more-requesting undertakings and jobs. Putting time and exertion in training colleagues and chipping away at basic criticism additionally offices in keeping up with group elements.

A compelling event supervisor is focused on the turn of events and preparing of the individuals from the event group and for that considers the event to be a chance to enhance colleague's insight.

Creating colleagues is profoundly connected to inspiration, since one method for accomplishing inspiration is by testing colleagues and giving them a change to foster themselves by developing their abilities and authority and so on. It has been shown that this effects work fulfilment and responsibility of the representatives and relate emphatically to event achievement. Creating at the event level is viewed as giving coaching, offering testing tasks and recognizing qualities and commitments of colleagues.

Scholarly authority: Basic examination and judgment helps the forerunner in the everyday appraisal and assessment of various sorts of data, significance containing logical abilities. As such, considering inward and outside elements and data and thinking of the most ideal answer for the given conditions.

Vision and creative mind connect with the rule to being imaginative and setting a dream for the event group to follow. All in all, being imaginative is one of the variables in progress of events.

An event chief for accomplishing achievement should lay out a sensation of reliability among his subordinates that can be accomplished by creating compatibility among him and his representatives. He should be an attentive person and should have the option to deal with tough spots. Moreover, a pioneer should decide on a discretionary component that will incorporate compromises on occasion for showing up at better open doors and accomplishing more prominent impact over workers. They should lay out a sensation of validity among various gatherings which will assist them with gaining appreciation of the representatives through sure exhibitions.

12.2.5 Ten Essential Leadership Traits and Characteristics Shared by all Successful Leaders

- Integrity
- Ability to delegate
- Communication
- Self-awareness
- Gratitude
- Learning agility
- Influence
- Empathy
- Courage
- Respect

Integrity

The value of honesty and honesty alone should be self-evident. Integrity is important for both the employee and the company; thus, it should be considered whenever possible. Executives at the helm, who are responsible for setting the company's direction and making many other crucial choices, cannot afford to overlook this issue. According to our findings, honesty may be a major blind spot for businesses. Ensure that executives at all levels of your organization are reminded of the value of honesty and transparency.

Ability to delegate

Effective delegation is essential for every leader, but it is not always easy to do. The point is not simply to give oneself more leeway; it is to assist others under you as well. That means empowering them to do their jobs, working well with others, making their own decisions, and developing themselves. Building trust with your team is essential if you want to delegate effectively.

Communication

There is a direct correlation between good leadership and clear communication. It is important to have a wide range of communication skills, from sharing facts to mentoring employees. Not only that, but you will need the interpersonal skills to talk to individuals of different occupations, socioeconomic classes, and more.

Self-awareness

Despite being an introspective trait, self-awareness is crucial for effective leadership. One's efficiency increases when one gains insight into oneself. Do you have any idea how you come across to others, or how you perform on the job?

Gratitude

You will become a more effective leader if you practise gratitude. Practising gratitude has been linked to several health benefits, including improved mood, less stress, and more restful nights. Even while most employees say they would go the extra mile for a manager who appreciates their efforts, few really take the time to express gratitude for their supervisors' efforts.

Learning agility

Knowing what to do when you do not know something is a sign of learning agility. You may already be learning agile if you are a "quick learner" or do well in novel situations. But with time, effort, and experience, everyone may develop their own learning agility.

Influence

Some individuals see "influence" as an insult. But part of being an inspirational, successful leader is having the ability to persuade others by rational, emotive, or collaborative arguments. Having influence is quite different from having power, and it must be used in a genuine and open manner. Emotional acuity and the ability to create trust are prerequisites.

Empathy

There is a link between empathy and success in the workplace. According to our findings, managers have a more favourable impression of employees who exhibit empathy for their subordinates. You may enhance your job and the work of people around you by developing your capacity for empathy, which is a skill you can acquire.

Courage

It might be difficult to raise your voice at work, whether you want to share an idea, give your direct report some criticism, or bring up an issue with your superior. This is why bravery is an essential trait of effective leaders. Leaders that exhibit bravery can take charge in difficult situations, rather than shying away from challenges or allowing disagreements to fester.

Respect

One of the most crucial things a leader can do is treat people with respect on a regular basis. It will decrease hostility and conflict, build trust, and boost efficiency. There are many various methods to demonstrate respect, and it is more than just the absence of disrespect.

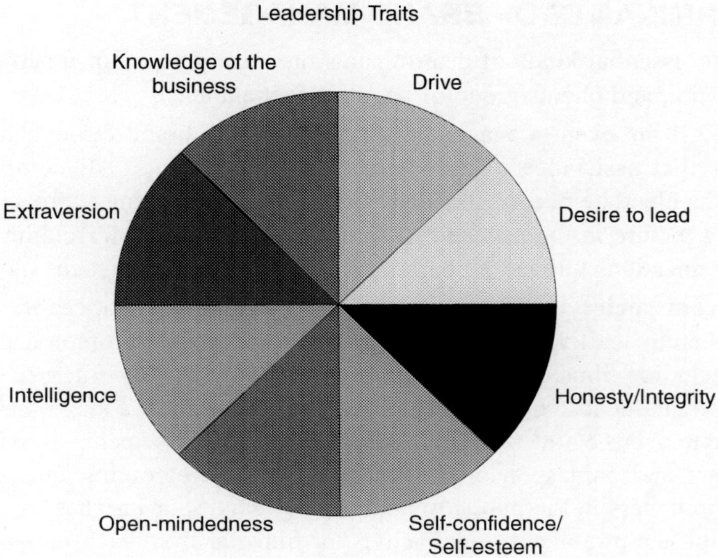

12.2.6 Leadership Image

There are several facets to a leader's public persona, including their official rank and physical appearance, as well as their personality, behaviour, body language, and speaking style. Your image is the general perception people have of you based on their interactions with you.

- Personality
- Behaviour
- Birth
- Social factor
- Body language
- Communication
- Physical appearance
- Formal status

Branding has become one of the main parts of business technique. Marketing strategies start with the incentive, i.e., the different kinds and measures of significant worth that the event management firm believes clients should get from the market offering. In advertising, the offer is some of the time alluded to as the situating proclamation. The brand is the item as it is capable and esteemed in ordinary public activity. The action word — to brand alludes to every one of the exercises that shape client insights, especially the association's exercises. Marking, then, at that point, is an administration viewpoint that spotlights on moulding the apparent worth of the item as tracked down in the public eye.

12.3 DETERMINANTS OF BRAND MANAGEMENT

Brands have four essential kinds of determinants-organizations, mainstream society, forces to be reckoned with, and clients/group of people-target audience.

(a) **Firms:** All the event management firm shapes the brand through its item related exercises that assistance to associate with the c clients. All components of the showcasing blend item, correspondence, channels, and valuing approaches are utilized to make a picture in the psyche of planned clients. fore. G for public level displays event organizations utilized all parts of limited time blend to focus on the clients.

(b) **Mainstream society:** Different kinds of events are a noticeable region of the planet wherein we live. As a result, they are frequently promoted in all forms of media, including films, television, books, magazines, and the internet. Brands can be significantly influenced by these representations. For almost a long time, organizations have tried to oversee how their brands are introduced in the media, through advertising endeavours and paid sponsorships. This includes welcoming famous people and strong forerunners in the public to address the brand. For instance, the event's brand ambassador is a prominent social activist or film star from each Indian state.

(c) **Clients:** Clients decide the adequacy of the brand culture as they consume the item. Also, are essential for event process as they cooperate with different partner during the occasion cycle, they make experience stories including the event which they frequently share with companions and all associated with the course of event. For instance, partaking in a game might prompt sharing of accomplishments and testing during the entire event process.

(d) **Influencers:** In numerous classifications, non-clients' perspectives are compelling. Consider exchange magazine audits, the suppositions presented by experts and authorities during work and recreation social events, and the assessments presented by retail sales reps. These sentiments make a situating of event management firm in the psyche of masses. Most of the public wide occasions are given exposure by different media firms which make a discernment about the event.

12.3.1 Components of Brand Value

(a) **Notoriety worth:** According to a financial perspective brand serves event firm notorieties. Event management includes unmistakable highlights, i.e., flights are on time, great nature of food, explicit items at the presentations. Clients face risk challenges they buy items, especially items that will be utilized into the future and items for which quality cannot be dependably assessed upon review before buy. The brand works as a flagging system to expand clients' certainty that the item will give incredible quality and dependability on significant capabilities. The item encounters the two triumphs and disappointments spread in stories and totals to shape a piece of the brand culture of the event firm.

(b) Relationship worth: Brands likewise convey that the firm delivering the item can be relied upon to go about as a drawn-out accomplice that will deftly answer future client needs. For some events, particularly if there should be an occurrence of celebrations or fairs client uses and needs cannot be completely expect thus incorporated into an agreement at the hour of procurement. Relationship esteem gathers as specific stories, pictures, and affiliations that circle around the item become traditional, underestimated.

(c) Brand societies: According to a mental point of view, the brand goes about as a perceptual edge that features specific advantages conveyed by going to a particular event. This outlining guides shoppers in picking events and furthermore shapes their item encounters. The heuristic worth of the brand gives for extensive reserve funds in search costs and in the need to consistently handle data to go with compelling decisions. Thus, event management firms frequently look to brand their items as especially viable in following through on a solitary advantage wanted by clients. An exemplary model comes from determined shows in the space of vehicles and schooling administrations which might give all data to the objective clients among the contenders.

(d) Representative worth: Express Qualities and Character Brands likewise go about as images that express qualities and personalities to act as substantial markers of values and characters. Specifically, brands have become strong markers to communicate situations with, governmental issues, and an assortment of optimistic social personalities, a design show by driving event Management Organization is one such model.

Most brand societies are comprised of a few, or even all, of these four parts. Notwithstanding, frequently one part will be the essential driver, representing the brand's prosperity versus rivals. The general significance of every part will change by society, item class, portion, and brand. While it is helpful to separate brand esteem into these four discrete parts for key purposes, clients seldom experience the brand along these lines. Rather, the parts are covering and related inductions that clients draw from the brand culture. The best brand societies, then, offer a solitary lucid story where the parts cooperate in a synergistic style so the entire is more prominent than the amount of the part.

12.3.2 Designing Brand Strategy

Brand strategy is a vital piece of the general showcasing strategy. Brand strategies follow through on business objectives by improving the brand culture. As e\ brands, business settings of event management organizations and corporate objectives fluctuate so a lot, there are no all-inclusive principles for planning brand strategies. Rather, a precise four-step interaction can be utilized to tailor strategies to answer fittingly to the particulars of the unique circumstance

Stage 1: Recognize objectives that branding can address: Brand strategies are suitable when the business objective can be accomplished by improving apparent item esteem. Since branding requires changing shared shows, it is essentially a drawn-out project. What is more, thus, branding is not typically a decent device to accomplish momentary deals objectives. Alternately, it is additionally critical to consider whether non branding strategies like bringing cost down to serve, seeking after cost separation with advancements have potentially negative results on branding of an event.

Stage 2: Guide the current brand culture: Assess the current brand culture across the four parts of brand esteem. This assessment requires planning and gathering statistical surveying that is receptive to the four distinct parts of brand culture. Subsequently study, criticism from the participants of the events, sponsorship association and explicit partner are expected to comprehend the degree of brand esteem.

Stage 3: Break down aggressive climate: Serious benchmarking is one the main driver of brand strategy is to convey unrivalled brand esteem versus essential contenders. Serious prevalence in brand esteem requires benchmarking against contenders' brands.

The main advances in brand esteem come from recognizing open doors in the climate like customers, innovation, framework, and so on that contenders have not yet followed up on and planning the brand strategy to make the most of these open doors. For instance, new kind of event plan, office management can give huge chances to upgrade notoriety, arising data and cycle advances, e.g., the Web, client relationship management can consider enhancements in relationship esteem, changing client inclinations can set out open doors for various experiential outlining, and changes in the public arena and culture set out open doors to convey new imagery.

Stage 4: Plan the strategy: A brand strategy portrays the development from the current to the ideal brand culture and the rationale for its following this way. A strategy report for an event management firm ought to plan the ongoing brand culture, frame the most encouraging chances to upgrade the brand culture considering both climate shifts and cutthroat benchmarking, lastly detail the ideal brand culture.

Execution: A brand strategy requires an activity plan that indicates which showcasing blend components will be utilized, how they will be utilized, and the way that they will be coordinated to accomplish a predictable branding effort. Each firm action that draws in imminent clients is a potential branding device. Branding is not restricted to interchanges. Rather, all components of the promoting blend add to branding. In this way, supervisors should constantly adjust branding targets against other advertising objectives.

12.3.3 Objectives and Responsibilities of Event Branding

The name, logo, colours, and other identifying features of an event are all part of its brand. Branding is the equivalent of a memorable face for event organisers. People are more likely to take notice if they recognise it. There is a formula for event branding that accounts for everything that goes into planning an event.

Smart event branding begins with clearly defining success. Examine this document for a summary of the most important goals in event brand management:

- **Increase awareness.** Promotion of event organisers, sponsors, and featured speakers is facilitated through event branding. Thereis a plethora of gatherings whose primary objective is to promote a brand, a new product, or a particular individual. It is well worth your time to raise people›s awareness by means of eye-catching décor, branded freebies, and a logo that serves to remind people of your aims.

- **Drive sales.** Branding during an event may represent the host organization to attendees and generate interest in their products. Events are a great place to get people to try out a client›s product or service and provide feedback on how well it performs. Branding them spreads awareness about the business and perhaps brings in new customers.
- **Build engagement.** Branding your event in a way that keeps people interested is more than just a means to greater brand loyalty. Whether via costumes or sweets, a brand›s memorableness increases when it is associated with a good time. Surprise your audience with a branded contest, a special visitor, or delicacies that are too pretty to eat. The decision is entirely yours.

What does event brand management include?

Let uslook at the fundamentals of managing the event's brand:

Event website. Marketing does not begin with the location. In the early phases of planning, it is important to consider how your event will be portrayed. The event website should effectively communicate the brand via the use of a unified logo, theme, colour scheme, and typeface. For many interested parties, this will be their first exposure to the gathering. We all know how important it is to make a good first impression.

Event app. A survey found that 40% of event organisers used event apps to improve attendee experiences. You may remind consumers of your identity and objectives by incorporating your brand into an event app.

Onsite event design. Any visuals shown at the event location must do so in the brand›s voice. Think about the different kinds of businesses you will be representing. Find out whether you need to be as pristine and organised as Apple, or if you should take inspiration from Airbnb's focus on the surrounding environment.

Booths. If you just have one booth to work with, it must be a great reflection of the brand. You may increase brand recognition by using digital billboards, branded laptops, and logo creation. Finally, freebies are essential. People will remember you longer if they carry your brand home with them.

Social walls. Use social media walls to show how people feel about the company. Reviews and testimonials from actual customers are a great way to highlight positive experiences with your company and its wares.

Banners. Banners from your childhood will never fail you. Pick up prominent spots throughout the arena to hang your customised banners and spread the word. However, remember to think about the long-term effects. The event business is becoming more environmentally conscious; therefore, guests may be offended if you promote the event using plastic. Instead, go for materials that can be recycled.

Swag. One of the most effective methods of raising brand recognition is to disseminate your brand's strength to individual families. If you want to transform event attendees into paying customers, make your brand the focus of the freebies you hand out.

Tips for event brand management

Logo, colours, typography, and design elements considered brand identity for an event. Slogan or tag line of event branding aims to convey the essence of the event in a few words. Consistency important in event brandingas it helps build a recognizable and cohesive image. Every brand event organiser is aware that just slapping a slogan or logo on a banner will not do anything to increase brand awareness. It is all about making a special outfit for the occasion. We have included some useful guidelines below to assist you in maintaining command of the most important operations.

Automate. Event branding, registration, and onsite activity management may all be handled by reputable event management solutions. This will assist in harmonising the operational procedures with the brand identity.

Have a plan for an onsite design. Make a rough plan of the event space and think of creative ways to include branding materials. Go through the final strategy with the customer and then get to work!

Leverage technology. A simple paper banner cannot compare to what technology can convey about your brand. Take use of social walls and event apps to create an effective method of contact with your event›s attendees.

Reward smartly. Engagement is essential for human beings. Keep your audience interested with on-site competitions and award campaigns, and hand out branded swag to the victors. Put two feathers into one nest!

12.4 EVENT ADVERTISING

Marketing during events is a great way to reach many people. When an event is being promoted, it is common practise for the name of the sponsor to appear in all promotional materials. The company's name is exposed to people both at the event and at home who are watching on television in certain circumstances, especially during sports events.

Strategies and measures

- Raise the excitement level of your event with the use of interactive engagement, icons, and live streaming.
- Find your niche by catering to people's sense of ease.
- Commit to complete submersion To Get Customers Interested in the Brand.
- To attract more interest, put a new spin on a well-known concept.
- Encourage attendance at your event by making people daydream.
- Introduce a New Audience by Pique Their Interest with Contests.
- To get people talking about your ads, try using wordplay.

- Reinforce your brand message by placing it in a high-traffic area and using an eye-catching visual motif.
- Promote the Big Event with a Pop-Up Workshop!
- Put on a costume to increase the party atmosphere and the number of social media shares.
- Use Flora and Fauna in Your Event Promotion to Expand Your Network.
- Promote your event to your fans by having a book signing or a celebrity meet and greet.
- Distribute Free Brand Samples.
- Make a stunning window display to draw people in and get them excited about the upcoming event.
- Make something real (and wow the press) with the help of technology.
- Use Important Events and Charitable Organizations to Gain Media Coverage.
- Use Hashtags to Bring People Together.
- Use social media at top speed to ensure timely updates.
- Connect with email marketing by adding a personal touch.
- Incentivizing the Preferred Behaviour using Reward Streaks and Statistical Charts.

12.5 EVENT PUBLICITY AND PUBLIC RELATION

The term "publicity" is used to describe the public relations activity of spreading word about a person, place, or object via various forms of mass communication. Public relations (PR) are a kind of advertising that helps keep a positive image for a business and its offerings in the public eye.

You may promote your business, customer, or goods and services to the public at large by holding a public relations event. The stakes are high when the press is present at a public relations event. You should try to look and act professionally and interesting.

Maintaining a good name in the eyes of the public is the goal of public relations (PR) efforts. Maintaining positive public relations with this method is a crucial part of any effective marketing strategy.

Publicity, on the other hand, is infotainment, or content that aims to educate and amuse audiences simultaneously. It gives the audience information that is both fascinating and contentious, increasing the likelihood that they will form a new opinion about the product or firm.

The public relation industry vs. the event planning industry. Public relations (PR) entails tending to one's name and image. A public relations specialist's job is to protect the good name of their clients and to help them connect with their target audiences. In contrast, event management is a kind of project management with the overarching goal of producing exceptional events.

PROGRESS CHECK

1. What are the various styles of leadership?
2. What are the qualities of a good leader?
3. Write as essay on event brand management.
4. Write a short note on leadership traits.
5. How event advertising helps to promote an event?

MULTIPLE-CHOICE QUESTIONS

1. What is the primary role of an event leader?
   (a) Designing event invitations
   (b) Managing event logistics
   (c) Performing on-stage entertainment
   (d) Handling post-event catering
2. Which skill is essential for effective event leadership?
   (a) Expertise in a specific event theme
   (b) Proficiency in social media marketing
   (c) Strong negotiation and communication skills
   (d) Fluency in multiple languages
3. How does an event leader ensure successful stakeholder management?
   (a) By ignoring stakeholder opinions
   (b) By prioritizing own preferences
   (c) By involving stakeholders in decision-making
   (d) By avoiding all stakeholder interactions
4. What is the importance of risk management in event leadership?
   (a) It increases the cost of event planning
   (b) It ensures that everything goes according to plan
   (c) It minimizes the impact of potential issues
   (d) It eliminates the need for contingency planning
5. How can an event leader enhance attendee engagement?
   (a) By limiting communication channels
   (b) By focusing solely on formal presentations
   (c) By incorporating interactive elements and activities
   (d) By discouraging networking among attendees
6. What does the term 'run of show' refer to in event leadership?
   (a) A list of event sponsors
   (b) A detailed schedule of event activities
   (c) A guide to selecting event venues
   (d) A summary of post-event feedback
7. What is the purpose of conducting a post-event debriefing?
   (a) To determine the event›s date and time
   (b) To identify areas for improvement and success

(c) To finalize the event budget
(d) To assign blame for any issues during the event

8. __________ is increasing leadership rapidly.
(a) Strategy (b) Command
(c) Control (d) Getting others to follow

9. Regarding leadership, which statement is false?
(a) Leadership does not necessarily take place within a hierarchical structure of an organization
(b) When people operate as leaders their role is always clearly established and defined
(c) Not every leader is a manager
(d) All of the above

10. __________ are the approaches to the study of leadership which emphasise the personality of the leader:
(a) Contingency theories (b) Group theories
(c) Trait theories (d) Inspirational theories

11. What is event branding?
(a) Printing tickets for an event
(b) Creating a consistent identity and message for an event
(c) Choosing a date for the event
(d) Hiring security personnel for the event

12. Which of the following is NOT a benefit of strong event branding?
(a) Increased recognition and credibility (b) Higher attendance rates
(c) Lower ticket prices (d) Enhanced audience engagement

13. What does a brand identity for an event include?
(a) Venue layout
(b) Ticket prices
(c) Logo, colours, typography, and design elements
(d) Local transportation options

14. Which element of event branding aims to convey the essence of the event in a few words?
(a) Event theme (b) Slogan or tagline (c) Event schedule (d) Social media posts

15. What role does event branding play in attracting sponsors?
(a) It does not affect sponsor interest
(b) It makes sponsors irrelevant
(c) It can make the event more appealing to potential sponsors
(d) Sponsors only care about the event date

16. Why is consistency important in event branding?
(a) It makes the event less memorable
(b) It confuses attendees and sponsors
(c) It helps build a recognizable and cohesive image
(d) It increases event costs

17. What is the purpose of an event branding style guide?
    (a) To dictate event attendees' behaviour
    (b) To provide guidelines for maintaining brand consistency
    (c) To create a list of prohibited items at the event
    (d) To determine the weather conditions during the event
18. How can social media be utilized for event branding?
    (a) By randomly posting unrelated content
    (b) By using a variety of colours and fonts
    (c) By consistently sharing content aligned with the brand's identity
    (d) By ignoring social media altogether
19. What is the 'target audience' in event branding?
    (a) The event organizers
    (b) The event sponsors
    (c) The group of people the event aims to attract and engage
    (d) The competitors of the event
20. What is the post-event phase of event branding?
    (a) It doesnot exist (b) Evaluating the success of the event
    (c) Rebranding the event completely (d) Sending out invitations
21. .... used the terms 'employee-centred' and 'production-centred' to describe leader behaviour
    (a) Blake and McCanse (b) Fiedler
    (c) McGregor (d) Likert
22. __________ is not a component of promotion mix.
    (a) Advertising (b) Publicity (c) Sales promotion (d) Market research
23. Advertising is a part of
    (a) Product mix (b) Place mix (c) Promotion mix (d) Price mix
24. Any paid form of nonpersonal presentation and promotion of ideas, goods, or services by an identified sponsor is called __________ .
    (a) Sales promotion (b) Direct marketing (c) Advertising (d) Public relations
25. Advertising __________ define the task that advertising must accomplish with a specific target audience during a specific period of time
    (a) Objectives (b) Budgets (c) Strategies (d) Campaigns
26. Compared to other marketing communications tools, PR is the
    (a) Worst for generating trust and confidence
    (b) Average for generating trust and confidence
    (c) Excellent at closing sales
    (d) Best for generating trust and confidence
27. Public relations require the purchase of media
    (a) True (b) False

28. The main PR activities are
    (a) Publicity and event management
    (b) Sponsorship and publicity
    (c) Lobbying and literature
    (d) Exhibitions and publicity
29. Which of the following is best in dealing with the media to publicise the event
    (a) Only the event director should deal with the media
    (b) Anyone on the organising committee can deal with the media
    (c) Event sponsors should deal with the media
    (d) The event team should have a media liaison officer appointed

Answers to Multiple-Choice Questions

1. (b)	2. (c)	3. (c)	4. (c)	5. (c)	6. (b)	7. (b)	8. (d)
9. (b)	10. (c)	11. (b)	12. (c)	13. (c)	14. (b)	15. (c)	16. (c)
17. (b)	18. (c)	19. (c)	20. (b)	21. (d)	22. (d)	23. (c)	24. (c)
25. (a)	26. (d)	27. (b)	28. (a)	29. (d)			

Chapter 13

MICE

Objectives

After going through this chapter the reader will be able to:

- Know the growth and evolution of MICE industry.
- Plan MICE.
- Understand The technologies involved in MICE.
- Recognize how this is important for hospitality and events.

13.1 INTRODUCTION

The tourist sector known as MICE stands for meetings, incentives, conferences, and exhibitions. Therefore, this sector is business-oriented and involves required (or non-discretionary) travel. The incentives part of MICE is the odd one out – though it is related to business, as it is usually provided to the employees or dealers/distributors as a reward, it tends to be leisure based.

According to the Oxford Dictionary, a meeting is a gathering of people, a seminar is a professional conference, a workshop is a location or gathering for coordinated action, and a conference is a gathering for debate. They all seem to be expressing the same idea, which is that of people coming together for a cause, in a very distant way.

13.2 EVOLUTION OF MICE INDUSTRY

The events industry has experienced unprecedented growth over the last 20 years with destination and international businesses looking to events to build reputation and develop marketing communications. The MICE industry has developed into a crucial communication tool for global company development and a driving force behind significant regeneration projects everywhere.

As per different sources MICE market is worth around $30 billion a year worldwide. . Some nations substantially rely on the MICE sector; for example, MICE accounts for 30% of Singapore's tourism earnings, while Malaysia specifically targets the MICE market with programmes like the Meet and Experience campaign, worldwide at least 50 million trips are taken each year for MICE purpose. The focus on knowledge sharing in conferences and showcasing products in exhibitions is a common difference between these two.

13.2.1 M = Meetings

Meetings bring people together in one location for the exchange of information, discussion, and problem-solving. Meeting attendance can range from ten to thousands of people. Food and drinks are frequently provided during meetings. Meeting times vary depending on the meeting type. Meetings typically relate to corporate gatherings that businesses hold in the following ways:

- Board meetings are the regularly scheduled annual meetings of a corporation's board of directors.
- Management Meetings: When necessary, managers from several locations of a firm come together to make choices that will affect the entire organization.
- Quarterly shareholder meetings are held for shareholders of a corporation.
- Training Seminars: A company conducts these to train employees when needed.
- Meetings with clients, suppliers, and partners: A get-together to negotiate business agreements that typically takes place with minimal advance notice.

Product introductions usually, when new products are released onto the market, there are a meeting with customers, the public, and media representatives.

- Strategic planning: Meetings between managers and staff to discuss the direction of the business.
- Retreats: The entire personnel of the organization spend one to two days together engaging in team-building exercises, training sessions, and strategic planning meetings.

The Meeting sector in India is flourishing in today's thriving global economy. Online conferencing and booking systems; multimedia and presentation software; touch displays that boost competitiveness considering current industry trends all contribute to the technical setting. Most of the individuals who travel for business purposes to attend these meetings have advanced degrees and work in fields such as management, company ownership, corporate and exhibition representation, sports, the arts, the media, the government, and politics. The event planner coordinates with hotels and convention centres to ensure the success of all events.

13.2.2 I = Incentives

A management strategy known as incentive travel is used to reward and inspire/ motivate sales representatives, dealers, distributors, production workers, support staff, and even customers. When sales personnel surpass their goals, the corporation compensates them by taking them on excursions. The incentive trip typically includes hotel accommodations, tour packages, and organized events like meals, parties, and games. Travel packages and rewards is a common incentive in MICE programme.

Decision-making factors for incentive travel

Budget incentive economy:

- How robust is the economy of the nation where the sponsoring organization is based?
- The following factors should be taken into consideration when choosing a travel destination: Buying power;
- Political climate;
- Travel alerts for places with political unrest;
- Safety and Security; Terrorist Alert Levels Following the 9/11 Incident; Value;
- How do facilities and services compare.

A strong team is the backbone of a successful company, and a team-building event is a terrific way to instil the appropriate mentality in the workforce. Increasing workers' output is the goal. Trust, connections, and morale are bolstered by these efforts. In your role as event organiser, one of your primary concerns should be selecting activities for the team-building session that would excite the client's staff. It might be challenging to get people excited enough to join in a team-building activity. If you are looking for a way to get out of the office while also fostering a sense of community among your staff, consider planning an activity that mixes productive work with the pleasures of a beautiful day outside. Therefore, there must be special measures made for these kinds of events.

13.2.3 C = Conferences/Conventions

Conferences and/or conventions are like meetings in that they bring individuals together for the purpose of discussing issues that are important to the group. Every year, an organization, typically an association will host a convention with a theme pertaining to the organization's subject. The association charges a registration fee that covers all the convention's seminars, panel discussions, meals, and site visits. Conventions, specifically, are made up of a range of events, such as congresses (large-scale regular trade gatherings), conferences (small-scale gatherings intended for information sharing), convenes (conferences with a small exhibition attached), and one-to-one events (premium networking). Conventions can be categorized into international, national, and regional levels. Smaller group discussions or workshops is the purpose of a "breakout session" in a conference within the MICE framework.

Meetings and conventions differ significantly in that a convention:

- is a large event often lasting for several days and involving a social programme;
- is organized by associations;
  - Professional and trade associations, e.g., the Dentist Association
  - Voluntary associations and societies
  - Charities
  - Political parties
- usually conducted once a year;
- generates income for the association; and
- quite a bit of work was spent choosing the convention's location.

13.2.3.1 Conference Types

Types of Conferences

- Planning Meeting/Corporate Retreat, with the Goal of Future Success.
- Workshop for Staff Training and Improvement, to Improve Knowledge and Performance.
- Sales/Product Meeting, whereby Novel Product Details Are Disseminated to The Staff. Gathering of the Association to Discuss Past Performance and Plan Future Course of Action.
- Event to commemorate and honour the team's efforts and success.

Information and instruction on methods, goods, and more are the goals of many types of seminars, conferences, and workshops. Information is often presented by speakers over the course of a few hours to a full day.

Specialist conference centres, resorts, hotels, and motels are just some of the various options for hosting a conference. It is important to consider the event's structure when choosing a location. This includes things like the number of guests expected and their availability, the size of the venue, and the sorts of function rooms that will be needed.

13.2.3.2 Planning Areas

The following criteria must be considered by an event manager:

- Preferred and possible alternative dates for the event.
- Information about the guest.
- How long people may anticipate the event to go for. Estimated participant turnout. Details on what should be included in the package (meals, lodging, venue rental, etc.).
- What kind of lodging (private or shared) you are looking for and how much you are willing to spend.
- Information about how to get in touch with notable members.

13.2.3.3 Things to Consider for International Conferences

The following are important considerations for global gatherings:

- **Venue:** The chosen location must be big enough to hold all the attendees, as well as have designated spaces for the various activities (talks, workshops, displays, and so on).
- Many hotels are equipped to host conventions, so they may provide both hotel rooms and common areas for attendees at reduced rates. Think about a conference centre with adjacent hotels if your group is too big for a hotel. When booking for a big party, most hotels will give a special deal.
- **Food:** It is usually a good idea to set up a hospitality room in the conference area or a suite of rooms. To encourage networking and socialising late into the night, provide finger appetisers and non-alcoholic beverages in a relaxed, casual atmosphere.
- **Translators:** Translators are essential for a global team. While the venue's multilingual personnel will be able to assist guests, it is still the event's responsibility to provide interpreters in any meeting rooms where guests will be gathered.
- **Agenda:** The success of an event depends on the planning that goes into its scheduling and flow. It does not matter where you put things on the calendar if they are happening at the same time, but if they are happening one after the other, space them out as little as possible. Because people's interests vary, a varied and staggered timetable is preferable.
- **Day-long events:** In the case of a full-day event, the schedule should be divided into three parts: a morning session with a break in the middle, a lunch break, and an afternoon session with a break in the middle.
- **Equipment:** Most gatherings of this kind will need the use of a plethora of electronic devices, including those used for audio and visual purposes, as well as for lighting, computer workstations, and television displays. Conversations are important. There must be no loss of clarity from the rear of the room to the front, and visitors should be able to communicate easily at any point.

- **Transportation:** Group discounts on airline tickets are common. A seasoned travel agent may be able to do more than just negotiate a bargain; they may also be able to provide valuable references and helpful trip planning advice. It is also important to think about going about town. Guests may be responsible for arranging their own ground transportation, or a limo service may be provided, with the option for the visitor to prepay in advance or pay per ride. There are hotels that will transport you to local hotspots for free.
- **Entertainment:** If there is going to be a dinner, a little of imagination may go a long way. Do everything you can to plan an event that will be remembered. The walls of the subterranean eating areas at Sea World in Orlando, for instance, are glass windows onto enormous tanks. A dinner cruise is another great option, as is a restaurant with a breathtaking view.
- **Supplies:** When going on a vacation, everyone forgets something. Provide writing implements, notepaper, fasteners, and clipboards.

Conference attendees often have a variety of goals in mind, including participation, education, networking, and debate. However, they will not come back to another badly run event. The details that set an event apart from others are the ones that the host has put the most thought and effort into organising for comfort, function, and purpose.

13.2.4 E = Exhibitions

Exhibitions are events planned to organize trade shows and display new goods, services, and knowledge to interested parties, such as prospective consumers or buyers. Typically, the exhibitor, or business showcasing new products, leases space from the organizer and constructs a booth to interact with possible customers. The **buyers** or the public need an invitation or a ticket to be allowed into the exhibition.

13.2.4.1 Purpose

- Get sales leads
- New product introduction
- Build a network for influential contacts
- Gather latest information about the competitors
- Build the company's image

13.2.4.2 Categories of Exhibitions and Fairs

The many types of trade shows and conventions include:

- Targeted commercial event"
- Displays for commercial purposes
- Private displays

Specialized trade fair: In most circumstances, a specialised trade fair will take place at the same venue on a recurring basis; however, there may be exceptions when the event is held elsewhere yet still sponsored by the same entity. Fairs for the industry are often referred to as Industry Fairs to differentiate them from Consumer Fairs. The former is closed to anybody except industry experts, while the latter welcomes all members of the public. The scope of the trade show is defined by the location and scale of its target market.

Commercial exhibition: They usually denote an event that has been planned by a collection of businesses for a certain subset of their customers. Rather than being a regular occurrence, these meetings are often called into being on an as-needed basis to meet the unique marketing and manufacturing goals of individual businesses.

Private exhibition: To introducing a new product or establishing the supplier's position in a new market region, for example, a supplier may hold a private exhibition to showcase their goods and services to a chosen clientele. A Buyers' Fair, like a commercial exhibition, is an event organised to promote businesses and facilitate contacts between suppliers of a similar range of products (such as processed food, clothing, etc.) and invited buyers (such as distributors and buying offices of department store chains).

(a) **Trade mart:** The term "trade mart" is often used to refer to a large, permanent commercial building that has several retail showrooms showcasing the goods and services of a variety of sectors.

(b) **Conference fairs:** Meetings whose primary purpose is to host conferences and seminars sometimes have smaller trade shows known as "conference fairs," which feature displays of a limited selection of items.

13.2.4.3 Factors in Organizing Exhibitions

The success and longevity of trade fairs depend on factors such as proximity to international trade hubs, the influence of market forces on demand, the development of a domestic industry that attracts interest from overseas buyers, and, of course, the professionalism and marketing savvy of the event's organisers. There are further considerations that may be made, such as:

- The demands of the market must be reflected in the development of an exhibition.
- The allure of involvement is based on the health of the local industry.
- Since exhibition sponsors' interests and areas of focus often vary, it is important for shows to be able to sustain themselves financially in the long term.
- Reliable infrastructures and facilities, as well as the safe and attractive environment of the hosting nation, play a vital part in creating a positive impression of the exhibition and the industry.

A fair price to attend an exhibition is one that reflects the value of the experience for both the organisers and the attendees. Experts from the nation holding the trade show as well as visitors from other countries are the ones who matter most. Although it is probable that all categories will be present at the trade show, it is still useful to have a complete list of potential attendees in mind so that you can decide which groups will be prioritised depending on the show's emphasis and your marketing goals. Institutions, Press, Other Media, Technical Cooperation Agencies, Press, Manufacturers, Traders, Agents, Suppliers of Industrial Inputs, Components, Accessories, Services, Research and Training Institutions, Professional Associations, Trade Promotion Organizations, Press, Other Media

13.2.4.4 Exhibition Design

The art of communicating ideas via setting and narrative. Architecture, interior design, graphic design, experience and interaction design, multimedia and technology, lighting, and audio are just few of the many fields that may be included into this integrative, interdisciplinary approach. Museums, tourist centres, historical parks, themed entertainment venues, trade exhibitions, corporate settings, expositions, and retail spaces are just a few examples of the many places where exhibition design may be use. Using elements of visual narrative and architectural design, it facilitates interaction between users and their surroundings.

Exhibit design may be as simple as a single installation or as complex as a whole building. As more and more technologies become available to the public, exhibition design has become more media-driven, social, and democratic, with material created not just by designers and curators, but also by users themselves.

The exhibition sector is thriving across the Asian, Asia Pacific, Middle Eastern, and African areas. The release of both new shows and localised adaptations of existing performances signals the need for state-of-the-art performance spaces. This strategy is being implemented at the same time as more and more convention centres are being built and new shows are being launched in these areas. By Expo 2020, we expect these areas to have grown this industry enough to contribute significantly to global GDP. The promotion of tourist locations and the construction of cutting-edge infrastructure are two factors that will help the countries in these areas become global leaders with robust economies.

MICE are the new buzzword in the international travel market and relates to varied GITs and FITs. One of the fastest-growing segments of the global business tourism market is MICE tourism, an innovative business enterprise. It meets a variety of corporate demands through conferences, international conferences and conventions, meetings, and exhibitions, and it is gradually but steadily catching the attention of every major hotelier. The significance of the MICE industry rests in the fact that it turns the annual business conventions and conferences into an opulent occasion that rewards the delegates and attendees. MICE business tourism is a must for most events, whether it is a meeting to bring together all delegates from one's company or from a wider range, a conference with 1,000 delegates from around the world, a party to celebrate a new product, or an exhibition.

It is crucial to use off-site workdays to motivate staff to increase their production significantly and acquire quality inside the corporate environment. When regional dealer conferences, incentive trips, and targeted business conferences are planned in exotic places that provide them leisure, recreation, and shopping options, corporate companies are also experiencing the commercial benefits.

13.3 PLANNING

MICE are an acronym for the Meetings, Incentives, Conferences and Exhibitions tourism segment. Therefore, this sector is business-oriented and involves required (or non-discretionary) travel. The odd one out in MICE is the incentive component. Although it is tied to business because it is typically given to employees, dealers, or distributors as a reward, it is typically more leisure-based.

13.3.1 Planning MICE: General Considerations

A session where all attendees gather for a common presentation or discussion known as plenary session of MICE event. MICE planning is fundamentally different from other types of planning because it necessitates an understanding of the environment in which it develops and functions.

Capacity and location are one of important factor for venue selection. Visiting and evaluating potential event venuesis part of venue inspection. Both domestic and international meeting, conference and convention tourism including small meetings, training courses, seminars, and workshops as well as large conferences and conventions is a very special type of tourism throughout the world. Conference, convention, meetings, or exhibition facilities that are specifically committed to this type of tourism have been established by numerous nations, regions, towns, resorts, and individual hotels. The Trade and Convention Centre in Vancouver, Canada, and the conference centre in Manila, Philippines, are two international examples of this.

These centres are major investment projects and are internationally recognized for the kind of facilities that they offer. In our country, New Delhi has a major exhibition centre at the Pragati Maidan, a hosting ground for one of our largest domestic fairs – the India International Trade Fair. One of our top meeting venues is the SITA Resort at Manesar, which is close to Delhi. By collaborating with airlines and conference centres that may provide discounted rates for business travellers, our nation can likewise entice MICE tourists. Day tours and sightseeing may also be provided as additional incentives to MICE travellers so they would return as repeat customers. A lot of countries have in fact developed MICE as their primary activity of tourism interest. Countries like Singapore, Thailand, South Korea, South Africa, Malaysia, New Zealand, Australia, Spain and even Nepal, etc., are all attempting to advertise their destinations as MICE locations. In a similar manner, cities like Dubai are positioning themselves as important exhibition and event hubs.

13.3.2 Infrastructure for MICE

There is need for

- Determining the sufficiency of support services
- Identifying any barriers to the growth of MICE
- Determining the level of usage of the venues
- Forecasting expected future demand for the venues
- Determining the adequacy of existing venues to fulfil the expected demand
- Outlining any serious flaws with existing venues

Additionally, we must keep in mind that building MICE infrastructure requires large capital expenditures. Hence, it should also generate economic gains for the host society or else investments from the public sector would be difficult and hence the issue of planning arises.

13.4 PLANNING FOR MICE

MICE planning needs a lot of collaboration, possibly more than tourism planning in general. Although there are many people involved in preparing for tourism, MICE planning is more difficult. Below mentioned are the areas that require a special set of planning as far as MICE components are concerned.

Venue

- Taking stock of existing capacity of the ventures for meetings, conferences, and exhibitions
- Forecasting the extent of use of the venues
- Calculating future demands for the venues
- Determining the adequacy and inadequacy of existing venues to meet their expected demand.

Transport

One of the main issues the industry has identified is transportation, which includes both ground and air transportation. Other issues that require attention during the planning stage in this regard include choosing the right type of coaches for road transportation, trained drivers, escorts, etc. Typically, tourism transporters are hired to provide these services.

Accommodations

As a result, accommodation becomes a crucial factor. MICE travellers typically seek lodging options close to the locations of their meetings, conferences, and exhibitions. Additionally, these lodging units must be furnished to handle their operational needs, i.e., they must be able to accommodate visitors. For this kind of work, you will need things like fax machines, laptop supplies, internet connections, telex, etc.

Additional support services to get the most out of the developing MICE scenario, a number of limitations, such as catering, shopping, entertainment, and others, need to be planned. For the sector to become a MICE destination, learning and comprehension must happen quickly. Giving information to foreign MICE travellers on the local weather, clothing codes, language, tipping, behaviour, etc., will help them as well.

13.5 ECONOMIC AND SOCIAL SIGNIFICANCE OF MICE

Destinations for MICE tourists are influenced by safety and security. Although they must be deemed politically safe for travel, there is a strong desire to see new places.

Some of the preferred MICE destinations are:

- Vienna, Austria
- Paris, France
- Singapore
- Barcelona, Spain
- Berlin, Germany
- New York, USA

For the incentives sector, however, up-market resort locations in destinations in Asia are popular.

Additionally, it is claimed that a MICE traveller will spend at least twice as much money as a leisure traveller. Conventions and meetings provide a high return on investment for delegates and also have the added benefit of advancing international relations. Players have more than enough motivation to get involved in the lucrative MICE industry because of this. It also impacts employment and hence creates a ripple effect for the tourism business and leads to socio-economic improvements in the community. The MICE industry in India, according to a senior executive from a reputed travel agency, is accidental. When compared to the often-chosen locations in the Americas, Europe, or Oceania, enormous savings are offered on offerings in India, which is the main reason this occurs. The mere thrill to discover a developing country makes India a safe bet, and it is better than Pakistan, Afghanistan, Nepal and China. In addition, MICE tourism, which generates five to ten per cent of tour operators' overall revenue, has suffered the most during this crisis. Companies in the fast-moving consumer goods, insurance and entertainment sectors offer the highest number of MICE trips to employees and sales dealers.

The MICE sector, like tourism in general, is susceptible to a variety of factors, including economic, political, and social climates; security and terrorism challenges; as well as, health concerns. Large-scale events or exhibitions have a multiplier effect on tourism. An exhibition is a tool for promotion and there are buyers and sellers, both local and international. International buyers and sellers frequently go to Indonesia with their partners or other family members, who visit tourist spots and spend money on meals, souvenirs, etc. When deals are inked during an exhibition, the domestic sellers, for example, furniture or handicraft home industries, get orders and make more products, which means employment. So, the multiplier effect is very strong. The MICE industry has begun to pick up again as a promising business. The sector has high potential to grow given the increasing demand for meetings, seminars and exhibitions from local private firms, governmental offices as well as international parties. The players and all pertinent parties must be conscious of the necessity to constantly improve services.

India, the fastest-growing segment of the global tourism sector is a hot MICE destination for the new type of business travel. It accommodates many kinds of corporate gatherings, international conferences and conventions, events, and exhibitions, and it is gradually but surely catching the interest of every major hotelier. India is heavily involved in the industry and is a popular tourist destination. In the race to become the ultimate MICE destination, India is quickly gaining ground on hotspots like Hong Kong, Malaysia, and Dubai. The aim appears to be within reach thanks to the cutting-edge facilities and technology, warm hospitality, and individualized services, as well as the abundance of scenic natural beauty and culturally rich heritage. The term 'MICE tourism' has become popular in the global tourism industry and refers to a variety of businesses.

The annual business meetings and conferences are a spectacular and exciting event for the delegates and attendees, thanks to the MICE industry. MICE tourism finds itself to be unavoidable in all the situations, whether it is a meeting to bring people together from within one company or from a wider spectrum, an international conference of 100 delegates, a product launch party, or an exhibition.

13.6 IMPORTANCE OF MICE FOR HOSPITALITY/HOTELS

For many hotels, MICE is a significant source of business. First, exhibitors and attendees fill many rooms at properties with meeting facilities or close to convention centres. Second, a recent study from Hong Kong found that on an MICE guests pay 17.5% more than leisure guests.

Third is partly because having large events in town leads to high demand and the chance to charge premium room rates. Hotels that provide on-site meeting or conference space may provide organizers with significantly reduced pricing. However, they can generate more money by offering conference and F&B packages.

Finally, MICE may be a dependable source of ongoing income. The frequency of conferences and trade exhibits means that hotels must factor them into their annual budgets.

13.7 LEADING MICE TECHNOLOGY

The MICE industry has advanced significantly in recent years. Some of the most well-known and influential examples from the industry are provided here.

13.7.1 MICE Technology for Event Organizing and Planning

Proposal management

Modern proposal management systems allow one to automate proposal creation. Additionally, they allowed us to create interactive micro sites, which are simpler for clients to navigate than large PDFs.

Supplier networks

Venues can be listed on the basis of these networks, best example being the Covent Supplier Network and get notifications when an organizer posts a request for an event proposal (RFP). The advantage for event venues is that they have access to international planners and can respond rapidly to new RFPs.

Event diagramming tools

They allow organizers to carefully plan their venues setup and floor plan. It is possible to include and map out every chair, table, booth, and hand sanitizer station. This is crucial to ensure that events adhere to all local safety laws, especially in the backdrop of COVID-19.

Room block management

Tools like Cvent Passkey makes it easier for hotels to manage event room blocks, all without endless room spreadsheets. They allow properties to provide organizers with a private booking link that feeds attendee bookings directly into the hotels' reservation system.

13.7.2 MICE Technology at the Event

Facial recognition

On the first day of the event, this technology can be utilized to admit registered guests. Additionally, since visitors may just have their faces scanned to get entry, IDs and tickets are no longer required.

Augmented, mixed and virtual reality

As these technologies evolve, they create new chances for more immersive and engaging events. AR and VR are opening countless new possibilities in the MICE sector, particularly for product demonstrations, presentations, and entertainment.

Internet of Things

Web-based access control (example, digital keys), thermostats, speakers and lighting controlled via the Internet. All of this is made possible by the Internet of Things, which also gives venues new methods to cater to services to the demands of their patrons.

Virtual event platforms

The increased demand for hybrid and virtual events created the need for sophisticated virtual platforms. Event Virtual Attendee Hub addresses that by offering an online space where organizers and attendees can network, engage, and interact.

13.8 CAREER PROSPECTS AND OPPORTUNITIES IN MICE FIELD

As a fresh graduate looking to enter the hospitality and MICE industry, one must be willing to keep an open mind and embrace trends. This will be beneficial for the candidate to align to current industry needs. Career progression is possible as hotels, event management companies and attractions are continually upgrading their workforce to be nimble and agile, valuing talent who can work across various functions.

Change management, revenue management, customer engagement, data analytics and digital marketing roles are also exciting options for those in the hospitality and MICE industry, who continue to keep themselves at the forefront of consumer and business trends. Human resource specialists will also be in demand as job redesign spreads throughout the hospitality and MICE industries.

The MICE industry is likely to step up efforts in creating engaging hybrid events. Digital events managers – individuals with both event management and digital skills will be in high demand.

Given below are the career/ jobs of MICE at hotel level, event location and large companies.

MICE jobs at hotel level

Many of the MICE-related organizational responsibilities are handled by the sales and marketing teams at the hotel level. To achieve the clients' vision for their event, they respond to incoming inquiries, develop offers, and collaborate with other departments.

Banquet managers look after the operational side of things. They plan setup and tear down, schedule the staff and work with suppliers to ensure everything runs smoothly on the day.

MICE jobs at event location

At a concert hall or convention centre, account and event managers look after a group of clients to assist them in organizing their events. They make calls to suppliers, request quotes, and take part in the planning of every aspect. They might show up to make sure everything goes smoothly, depending on the event.

MICE jobs with large companies

Large companies who host events regularly often have an in-house events team. They take care of all the organizational tasks like outlining and planning events and communicating with the venues.

They are also responsible for sending out invitations and organizing the entertainment, though they may enlist outside assistance with the latter task. Of course, they will be present on thesite throughout the event to monitor the flow of things.

Relevant qualifications/skills

- A degree in tourism and hospitality management, or related disciplines
- Passion for travel and service, with an interest to build a career in the sector
- Strong communication, interpersonal and persuasion skills
- Resourcefulness and agility, with the ability to learn quickly on the job

What recruiters look for

- Digital literacy, with the ability to embrace and learn new technologies
- Familiarity with travel, business, and consumer trends
- Strong organizational and project management skills
- Ability to work under pressure and manage complexity

Typical roles for fresh graduates

- Management associate or trainee
- Marketing executive
- Business development executive
- Account servicing executive

13.9 TRENDS IN MICE INDUSTRY

Events today are exciting, creative, and innovative because of evolving MICE industry trends. The best event planners are those who are thinking are out of the box as because they are paying attention to what's happening, stays updated on current trends, from technology to novel ideas there is always something fresh and interesting in the MICE industry.

Some of the major trends that must be known to an event planner are as follows:

13.9.1 Sustainability

Even if hosting eco-friendly events is not a new trend, it is now more common than ever. There are many ways one can incorporate sustainability into the event. Few of them are as follows:

- Serving vegetarian food, organic food
- Using of seasonal flowers for decoration
- Using of online booking system to save paper
- Choosing a venue close to guests location to reduce transport

- Encouraging of car sharing, cycling, and using public transport
- Setting up of recycling and compost bins alongside waste bins
- Choosing to host the event in a venue with a LEED certification
- Encouraging attendees to bring their own water bottles and have filling stations

13.9.2 Social Media

One of the most well-liked MICE industry developments for the past a few years has been the integration of social media into events. Social media is crucial for events because it promotes involvement and interaction. Making social media a part of the event encourages the attendees to create user-generated content. This also makes the attendees feel involved and can be used to the advantage for those hosting the event before, during or after the events

13.9.3 Personalization

Events are becoming more personalized for each attendee. This is one of the few MICE industry trends that make it a priority to view events from the attendee point of view. It makes our goal to improve how guests experience our events in the best possible ways.

Personalization has several different applications and can be made possible more easily by collecting data. For this first, we need to understand what people want so that we can tailor aspects of the event to suit them.

By creating full personalized events, we can make each event more memorable and attendees more engaged. We will also able to plan more interactive experiences and customize communications.

13.9.4 Digital Attendance

Digital attendance is opening the doors to much added event exposure. That is why it is one of our favourite MICE industry trend.

This adds possibilities for different applications. It might entail live-streaming an event on Facebook or Instagram or digitally presenting a speaker from another location via video chat. It could also look like using digital hangouts for networking, or creating VR content that will make people feel like they are right there in the room with us.

13.9.5 AR and VR

Augmented reality and (virtual reality) are two of the biggest buzzwords right now. Although this technology isnot brand new, it is only recently developing to the point where it is becoming more accessible for a range of applications.

Augmented and virtual reality is often used interchangeably, but they are different. Virtual reality can transport a person into a completely different world using an immersive headset. Augmented reality often uses only a smartphone and creates a digital overlay on the real world, as seen in Snapchat filters.

As augmented reality and virtual reality technology make it simpler for guests to enjoy it without physically being present, this trend strongly relates to digital attendance. Apart from this it is also used to give the attendees an immersive experience during the event.

13.9.6 Gamification

Gamification is a huge trend in the event planning industry. It refers to taking the competitive nature and structure of gaming and applying it to our event. It can be a powerful way to encourage the audience to engage in the event proactively.

Because it is based on the concept of rewards, gamification is extremely successful.

13.9.7 Mindfulness

A growing number of event organizers are finding that scheduling too many sessions back-to-back prevents attendees from having enough time to assimilate what they have seen and learnt. So, creating areas for mindfulness within the event itself is currently one of the hottest trends. Allowing for these mental pauses will assist conference attendees experience less stress and increased levels of creativity.

13.9.8 Event Apps

It can be much simpler for participants to interact and engage if our event has a smartphone app. The use of event applications is now so commonplace that it is expected, particularly at important conventions, shows, and festivals.

13.10 CHALLENGES IN THE MICE INDUSTRY

One of the major forces behind the tourist sector is the MICE. (meetings, incentive, conferences and exhibitions) - sector, which has experienced significant expansion in recent years. The future of the MICE industry is promising as demand for meetings, incentives, conferences, and exhibitions rises. However, as things grow, challenges arise. Example: For MICE hotels, one of the greatest challenges is retaining a share in the increasingly competitive marketplace and this competitiveness poses issues on every sector of the MICE industry. Some of the biggest challenges are as follows.

Virtual meetings vs. destination meetings

The fast meal versions of destination meetings are virtual meetings. Although the latter are more valuable since they provide engagement opportunities with pertinent topics without any distractions.Virtual meetings are appealing because they allow us to attend without having to book a hotel room, get on a plane or leave the workplace. Since they donot involve booking rooms and buying plane tickets, virtual meetings are often cheaper than destination meetings. At the end of the day, there is value in both. Sometimes we cannott miss out on the huge networking opportunities during an event and choose to go there in person, other times we are just interested in a topic and attend a virtual conference. However, planning for both and trying to appeal to both types of attendees is something the MICE industry will have to work on and it will notbe an easy task.

Keeping up with technology

Technology is developing quickly, and as a result, event goers' expectations are rising. They want to be able to book hotel rooms, plane tickets, event access with minimum hassle, at the time of their convenience and on the device they are using.

On the other side, to minimize duplication and minimize errors, hotels must stay up with technological advancements and enhance their systems for meeting planners and hotel broker organizations.

Managing accommodation contracts

Old participants in the industry are extremely familiar with this. However, negotiating a contract with a hotel or venue can be challenging for individuals who are new to the business event industry. Hotel chains provide a variety of contracts, and signing one without fully comprehending what each and every clause implies might lead to disastrous results. The PCOs and anybody else signing venue contracts should thoroughly studies them, if they have any questions, consulting an attorney before signing important. Also, they should establish their own clauses.

Following are some excellent practices for handling contracts for accommodation:

- Thoroughly read and understand contract terms.
- Be careful with the expected numbers, as over-inflation is not going to do anyone any good while underestimating the number of rooms may force to find additional spaces elsewhere.
- Make sure that room rate protection is included so that one can have competitive rates.
- Include all financial liabilities in the contract.
- Maintain a constant communication with all parties involved.

13.11 STEPS TO RESTART MICE BUSINESS POST-COVID-19

To restart MICE business post-pandemic, being an event planner we have to follow the following steps:

Prepare for hybrid events

It is likely that future events will be a blend of in-person and virtual attendance. For the hybrid event to be successful, the event manager must keep in mind the following factors:

- Sufficient audio-visual capabilities
- Engaging formats for both in-person and digital attendees
- Great communication with planners

Prioritize health and safety

Event planners have to source venues that meet stringent cleanliness and sanitation requirements.

Shifting to smaller, local events

Due to air travel restrictions and other associated risks, the event planner should focus on local events as well.

Social distancing to be considered

Use of collaborative diagramming tools and virtual tours helps the event planners in constructing a safe, engaging event space.

Reconsider food and beverage

Buffets likely will not be a viable option for quite some time. The event planner should consider cost effective alternatives and train staff in food sanitation.

PROGRESS CHECK

1. What does the acronym MICE stand for in the tourism sector?
2. How is the incentives part of the MICE sector different from the other components?
3. How has the MICE industry evolved over the last two decades?
4. What is the approximate global worth of the MICE market each year and predicted future?
5. Which countries rely heavily on the MICE sector for their tourism earnings?
6. How do meetings, conferences, and seminars differ in their purposes?
7. What is the purpose of incentive travel in the MICE industry?
8. How do conventions differ from meetings in terms of scale and organization?
9. What is the purpose of exhibitions in the MICE industry?
10. Why is the MICE industry significant for business tourism?

MULTIPLE-CHOICE QUESTIONS

1. What does the 'M' in MICE stand for?
   (a) Management (b) Meeting (c) Marketing (d) Modernization
2. Which element is typically a part of the 'I' in MICE?
   (a) Music (b) Menu (c) Incentive (d) Mood
3. What is the primary goal of the 'C' in MICE?
   (a) Creating (b) Celebrating (c) Conferencing (d) Coordinating
4. In the context of MICE, what does 'Exhibition' refer to?
   (a) Excursion activities (b) Trade shows and displays
   (c) Entertainment events (d) Event catering
5. Which aspect is often emphasized during the 'Incentive' part of MICE?
   (a) Industry trends (b) Motivating and rewarding attendees
   (c) Networking opportunities (d) Certification programmes

6. What is a 'plenary session' in the context of MICE events?
   (a) A session where all attendees gather for a common presentation or discussion
   (b) A session focused on event catering
   (c) A session reserved for VIPs only
   (d) A session dedicated to recreational activities
7. Which type of event typically involves a large gathering for sharing information and knowledge?
   (a) Expedition (b) Extravaganza (c) Conference (d) Concert
8. What is the purpose of a 'breakout session' in a conference within the MICE framework?
   (a) To end the conference on a high note
   (b) To facilitate smaller group discussions or workshops
   (c) To showcase exhibition booths
   (d) To provide entertainment activities
9. Which factor is often considered when selecting a venue for a MICE event?
   (a) Weather conditions (b) Number of restrooms
   (c) Capacity and location (d) Availability of Wi-Fi
10. What is the significance of a 'site inspection' in the context of MICE?
    (a) Conducting a food tasting session
    (b) Performing a security check
    (c) Visiting and evaluating potential event venues
    (d) Reviewing event marketing materials
11. Which element is a common incentive in MICE programmes?
    (a) Awards for best-dressed attendees (b) Travel packages and rewards
    (c) Event merchandise sales (d) Availability of free parking
12. What is the primary difference between a conference and an exhibition in the MICE context?
    (a) The length of the event
    (b) The focus on knowledge sharing in conferences and showcasing products in exhibitions
    (c) The number of attendees
    (d) The type of cuisine served

Answers to Multiple-Choice Questions

1. (b) 2. (c) 3. (c) 4. (b) 5. (b) 6. (a) 7. (c) 8. (b)
9. (c) 10. (c) 11. (b) 12. (b)

Chapter 14

Theme Events and Decoration

Objectives

After going through this chapter the reader will be able to:

- Understand various theme events/parties organized by various organization.
- Recognise the role of hospitality and housekeeping to set things properly.
- Get the idea of various world-renowned theme events.
- Organize successful theme events.

14.1 INTRODUCTION

Theme parties are unique events normally merry for specific capabilities and ought to attempt to draw out the soul and climate of a specific event or area at that specific time or night. The primary purpose of theme event is entertainment. Decoration is an important part and sets the tone for a theme event. Theme decoration transform spaces with specific concepts creating immersive environments that align with events, enhancing ambience and guest experiences. The lodgings might have their own tasks of local moves of India, outfits of India, food celebrations of various pieces of India and of the world.

14.2 POINTS TO CONSIDER FOR THEME EVENTS

The accompanying focuses are thought of:

- The determination and decision of a catchy name for the area.
- How much cash to be spent for the capability, the spending plan accessible.
- Choice of the site/place where the party is to be held.
- A decent theme ought to be thought of and chosen and embellishments ought to be done in light of the theme. The effect ought to be on each of the five feelings of any visitor/individual entering and partaking in it.
- The design of the whole region should be appealing, enchanting, noticeable agreeable and engaging to the visitors.

- The guest plans and eating courses of action ought to likewise be just about as agreeable as could be expected.
- The smell and scent of the room ought to likewise be reasonable with the appropriate sort of blossoms utilized alongside the food fragrance.
- The actual food should be painstakingly arranged by the theme and be served in appropriate way according to the standards.
- Staff who serve or look out for such events ought to likewise dress according to the theme and stylistic layout set for the event.
- The ambient sound playing must likewise be appropriate to the event.

The theme parties are generally held to acquire some benefit for the lodging as they are publicized ahead of time and tickets are sold especially to individuals/outsiders who love to go to such capabilities mirroring the customs and culture of the country.

Benefits can be made provided that the lodging has figured out how to fulfil their visitors in all regard. To accomplish this the staff should cause the visitor to feel good, protected, cheerful, all around engaged, pressure free climate, and so on he ought to likewise be content that he has got his/her best possible value. The compare/masters of ceremonies should be the main entertainer by adding humour, information, and harmonies in his/her discourse.

The don'ts:

- Try not to aggravate the visitors.
- Food ought to be served on time and hot.
- Diversion shouldnot get exhausted.
- The smorgasbord ought to be parted in a crisscross structure so the visitors doesnot need to follow the other.
- Staff should be available behind the smorgasbord to help the visitors during serving, assuming they have any inquiries.

Extraordinary arrangement of work goes in the creation of theme parties by every one of the various branches of the hotels/hospitality sectors especially the F&B, itchen and confectionary, Housekeeping, and the designing divisions. When the party is ready to move on is the work/obligation of the housekeeping to eliminate every one of the embellishing impacts and store them or return them to the project worker. The whole region is clean completely before selling again the following day is open.

14.3 OCCASIONS FOR SPECIAL DECORATION

For the most part, to create more income, hotels organize unique festivals for celebrations. This changes as per the area. Vintagetheme event celebrates a specific historical era. Design is a fundamental component in making a right air for such merriments. Seasonal theme event celebrates a specific holiday or festive occasion.

Certain materials are customary for specific events. A few normal celebrations celebrated in hotels are given below.

14.3.1 Christmas

- A Christmas tree finished with lights and merry style.
- A den scene.
- A ginger bread house.
- Glitter and paper adornments.
- Christmas stockings are in many cases furnished in the rooms with chocolates inside.

Given

14.3.2 New Year

- Balloons and decorations with a few glitter and paper enhancements are customary.
- Guests generally get a sack with a paper cap, a whistle, and decorations inside.
- Show of firecrackers at 12 PM.
- A 'black-tie' dress code suggests formal attire.

14.3.3 Deity Feasts

- Pictures of the divinity.
- Decorative layouts in the customary way.

14.3.4 Easter

- Easter chickens produced using chocolate and marzipan.
- Chocolate rabbits and eggs loaded down with desserts and shocks.
- Unique breads with eggs prepared inside.

14.3.5 Deepawali

- Lighting and decoration.
- Crackers.
- Idol and pujas.
- Sweet.
- Festival of light.

14.4 5-R CONCEPT

The standard materials utilized for making any embellishments are paper, paint, foil, poly styrene shapes, blossoms, leaves, lights, yet the creative mind can be given free rule. For unique events a few hotels make an air, for example, makes a café seem to be pixie land, or a tent, or no big deal either way. This is exorbitant and one ordinarily gets the necessities from an external party.

Since eating is by and large a piece of any party, buffets are frequently utilized and these can be brightened with containers of blossoms, polystyrene pictures, ice of margarine/fat carvings, and so on.

One generally puts buffet skirtings, and the skirtings can be effectively embellished.

The conservation of verifiable milestones and the reclamation of old structures present new difficulties to the expert maid who should figure out how to reestablish, clean, and keep up with transitory old decorations and to keep a wonderful patina on them. For example, the Waldolf-Astoria in New York city, the fantastic lodging in Michigan, the Broadmoor in Colorado Springs, has had an exhaustive occupation of reclamation.

Rebuilding implies reestablishing a property to its precise.

Remodel implies making new and, from an overall perspective, reestablishing a property to its previous state.

- Recovery implies making a property helpful and reestablishing it to its previous condition.
- Redesigning implies changing the construction.
- Repairing implies sprucing up, reestablishing an outside precisely and redesigning the goods so they are near genuine, however not definite; a region might be rebuilt and a few rooms may basically be renovated.
- Many rehab projects today include all the R's, i.e.:
- Restoration
- Renovation
- Remodelling
- Refurbishment
- Rehabilitation

The critical path of restoration/renovations

For the management

(1) Define the task, for example, list the quantity of visitor rooms and public region to be revamped.

(2) Have the administration explain the rate structure comparative with the reviewing of the rooms and public regions (how much cash to be spent will be in relation to the room rates and the expenses of dinners and beverages).

(3) Establish a timetable for culmination, for example, due dates of augmentations.

(4) Prepare staffing diagrams of the faculty important to set up the areas for remodel.

(5) Prepare a detailing component of the work cost task.

(6) Prepare an authoritative construction. The undertaking chief will be accountable for every one of the exercises, that individual might be the modeler or the associate trough or even the executive housekeeper.

(7) Identify the assets accessible in-house: budget, staff, equipment.

(8) List the assets to be gained.

For the housekeeping

(1) Report the construction and extent of the undertaking and put it on a PC.

(2) Outline the nature of the items to be reestablished and the attitude of disposed of goods.

(3) Prepare designs to stay away from issues, yet get ready for any crisis.

(4) Build an initiative group and select a task boss.

(5) Arrange security for the recovery regions.

(6) Check the conveyance plans for new things and sort out for extra room until establishment.

(7) Prepare a cleaning timetable to limit the bother and the dirt for bordering regions.

(8) Keep the regions as appealing as conceivable during the recovery.

(9) Work intimately with the architects and installers.

(10) Suggest the request for the work to be finished to be finished all together that the establishment be finished:

- Clean the vents.
- Paint the walls and the woodwork.
- Introduce the backdrop.
- Lay the rug cushion and tack strip.
- Lay the rug and vacuum.
- Introduce the furnishings, apparatuses, and merchandise in the room.
- Wash the windows.
- Hang the shades and curtains.
- 'Stage the room' that is polish off the room with every one of the decorations and extras situated precisely according to plan, make up the bed, put the cover, residue unsettles on, etc.
- Residue and once again vacuum.
- Add the conveniences and the showcasing helps.
- Examine and address any blunders, then, at that point, report that the room is fit to be sold.

Jobs that are carried out during renovation/ re-decoration

(1) The room/s are procrastinated on for the necessary measure of time.

(2) This work is anticipated the leeway time of the year is done floor by floor or part of a story at a time, depending on the shape and number of rooms on a story.

(3) It is constantly wanted to cause as little bother as conceivable to the guests.

(4) Re-adornment obviously is likewise conveyed in open regions as well, then eateries are shut and in entryways the work is just finished around evening time, cleaning away everything before sun-up. A few evenings might be expected to finish the work.

(5) Basically, the work engaged with re-enrichment is repainting, in the event that a wall is utilized this is likewise supplanted. Furniture is repolished, if necessary, as well, and after this work a full upkeep work and general clearing is done.

(6) Many hotels utilizing clean and talented experts deal with this work without eliminating the rug yet dust sheets are set ready to move on and not look back for security.

(7) Dust sheets are by and large old sheets fixed and coloured an alternate tone for simple distinguishing proof.

To prepare a room for re-decoration

(1) Remove linen from beds and bathrooms; send all to the laundry including bed spreads and blankets.

(2) Remove all supplies and store in the maid's service room.

(3) Remove the curtains and send for cleaning. Save the hooks in an envelope marked with the room no. and place in the maid's service room.

(4) If sufficient space is there in the service room, then place the lamps and other fixtures as well, if no space available then cover the room using dust sheets.

(5) If the whole floor is taken for re-decoration, then the furniture can be shifted to another place, if not then all the furniture can be shifted to the centre of the room and covered with a dust sheet.

(6) Now re-decoration takes place.

(7) Next the maintenance does a complete overhaul. A snagging list is prepared by the housekeeping or the maintenance department.

(8) After the maintenance department completes checking, the housekeeping takes over and prepares the room for sale again.

To prepare the room after re-decoration:

(1) Remove all dust sheets, ship off the laundry.

(2) The bathroom walls and all apparatuses and fittings and floor are scrubbed.

(3) Vacuum tidying up of the room is finished.

(4) Scrub the gallery, porch and things that can be washed.

(5) Polish or clean all the furnishings, inside as well as outside.

(6) Replace the draperies, bed cloth, bathroom towel, and so forth.

(7) Arrange all furniture accurately.

(8) Replace all provisions in the room and the bathroom.

(9) Re-fix the lights and other electrical fittings.

(10) Put in the little ice chest.

(11) Shampoo the rug when dry, or vacuum clean whenever required.

(12) Check for any positions scattered, if no then discharge the room to the front work area to sell.

Refurbishing a guest room

(1) Refurbishing includes re-decoration yet another way.

(2) Refurbishing can be fractional or complete for example everything can be supplanted like shades, floor coverings, furniture and so on.

(3) If it is fractional, it may not include rugs or furniture evolving, for example, just beds might be supplanted or certain furniture parts. Nonetheless, in some cases, it incorporates evolving draperies, bedspreads, and upholstery.

(4) Refurbishment is typically completed during the day as it includes clamour It is finished in the slackest season. It may be done each room in turn.

(5) It incorporates evacuation of bed and shower material, cover if conceivable, bathroom fittings and so on.

(6) Renewing is finished by eliminating the old and supplanting it with new and present-day plans.

(7) Once revamping is finished then the electricals are checked and adjusted.

(8) The new furniture is introduced and all wiring finished, that is, essential, for example, mirrors, pictures and so on are introduced.

(9) Then housekeeping tells the truth of the whole region which has been revamped.

(10) The room is taken back to a similar state as it was before with the couple of changes that were completed during revamping.

(11) The prepared room is reviewed at long last and delivered to the front work area available to be purchased.

(12) Revamping happens generally every 5-7 years, albeit a few hotels might do it rather slowly, for example, bathroom and floor coverings one year, furniture one more year, and so forth much relies on how occupied a lodging is and the kind of customer base it gets. It is a significant capital speculation however on the off chance that a lodging isnot kept up to the standards it will free its ordinary clients and the income, thus it is important over the long haul.

14.5 POPULAR CORPORATE EVENT THEMES

Arranging a corporate event that everybody on staff will appreciate is a seriously difficult task.

The key to take it-out-the-recreation area corporate gatherings begin with picking the right subject. It should be a proper thing for the corporate culture, as well as being comprehensive of various characters, ages, and wellness levels. In addition, you will have to adhere to the spending plan you have been given.

Assuming that sounds like an unthinkable assignment, dread not! We bring you 22 corporate event subjects that make certain to give you the perfect thought for you.

Assuming you arre prepared to toss the corporate slam of the year, read on for thoughts to fuel your corporate event arranging virtuoso.

1. Back to the 1980s

For a corporate party subject that stones, make a stride back to the 1980s with large hair, shoulder braces, and OTT eyeliner.

Go retro with stylistic theme roused by Walkman's, Rubik 3D shapes, and monster band banners. Complete the night with a live 1980s band who will pack the dance floor with tunes from 80s groups like Dexy's 12 PM Sprinters, Spandau Expressive dance, or Bon Jovi. It is continuing to survive by chance alone playing in everyone's mind for long. Charity gala theme event usually supports social justice.

To reproduce an all-out 1980s rave, all you want to add is lumo. Deck out visitors with sparkle headbands, wristbands, and pieces of jewellery to finish the look. Very much like the 1980s is a remarkable period, your back to the 1980s event will be extraordinary as well!

2. Un-awards

Collaborators who snicker together, remain together. Is not that so? For a pleasant evening of letting down hair, holding, and some real appreciation, have an Un-Awards evening.

Before the time, draw up a rundown of awards that are totally facetious. Allow colleagues to decide in favour of one another to make the awards more private. Choose things like:

- Probably going to be five minutes late for a gathering.
- Neatest working space.
- Most chaotic working spaces.
- Most intense, office-shaking chuckle.
- Bounteous espresso shopper.

Book out a steakhouse or a dark tie scene, go super tasteful with the stylistic layout. Think honorary pathway, sensational hanging, and white material napkins. Provide food for an elegant celebration supper, and serve champagne, mixed drinks, or wine.

Have testaments made and toss in a few tomfoolery prizes for a decent snicker as well. You can distribute a modest bunch of certified awards for those who have blown away in their work, or confronted and beat individual battles.

3. German beer festival

On the off chance that you are searching for a cheerful great time, a German Lager Celebration subject is a cherry on top. Nothing beats the foot-tapping, lager chugging state of mind made by a true live Oompah band.

Go straightforward with snacks by whipping out brew and pretzels. For a somewhat one-of-a-kind flavour, get in a special mix. For a plunk down supper, sauerkraut and bratwurst will supplement the German subject.

Between the band and the brew, the temperament will be perfect for drinking games.

For style, hang merry blue and white banting, with hints of yellow sprinkled through the remainder of the room. Broaden the temperament and energy by giving out suspenders and snowcapped caps to the party attendees.

4. Under the sea

Take your event profound under the waves into a captivating watery hidden world. Make the wizardry unmistakable by making a phony coral and kelp curve for visitors to stroll through.

Utilize blue uplighting for an undulating submerged feel. Light bar regions in sparkling blue or lime green. Hang bubble inflatables or jellyfish light fixtures to drench your visitors in your submerged miracle world. Shells or coral make ravishing table style, blended with starfish or vivid exotic fish (counterfeit ones, obviously).

To finish the arrangement, lay on a rich fish buffet, with mixed drinks the shades of remote ocean animals.

5. Hollywood

Hollywood glamourmight feature costumes from famous movies and TV shows. All are adoring motion pictures. Recruit a cinema, or a spectacular corridor, and present a royal welcome. To cause your visitors to feel like genuine stars, recruit a gathering of lease a-swarm paparazzi to invite them as they show up.

Introduce the following Brilliant Age by designing with gold and silver stylistic layout. Make the clothing standard gold, silver, and dark, and recruit a swing band to finish the festival. Cater with shrimp and steak and lobster, joined by a lot of effervescent champagne to go around.

For additional tomfoolery, set divisions in opposition to one another (or tables if you might want to advance between departmental blending) in a film test fight. Consolidate this multitude of components and you will have an event that will be discussed over the copier for a long time.

6. Carnival

Who can fail to remember powerful summer evenings, encompassed by the clamour of over-invigorated amusement park participants with shining eyes? Reproducing a festival will permeate your event with the same amount of elation while inclining towards a blustery relaxed event.

On the off chance that you cannot track down a major top tent to recruit, make similar climate by utilizing brilliant varieties, designs roused by a bazaar tent, and strings of bulb lights.

Set up a couple of basic outdated game stations, for example, a ring throw. Furnish a photograph corner with a lot of tomfoolery props to browse. Enlist a balloon craftsman or a performer to wander the group and keep individuals entertained.

Ifyou are searching for a bonus vital, enlist a flexible performer or a fire artist to excite the group.

Exemplary fair food fits right in with the amusement park subject. Serve channel cakes, wieners and palmiers (elephant ears). Serve soft drinks, cider, or beer.

7. Winter wonderland

Traditional holiday parties are a superb method for wrapping a time of really buckling down together. Take out the conventional wear, dust off the moving shoes and celebrate to the merry hints of a Christmas band.

Deck out the corridor in soft white with decorations of silver. Hang shimmering snowflakes and clear balloons loaded up with sparkle. Blue uplighting will make a twilight impact that can very entrance.

Ifyou would lean toward a hotter range, choose fire tones, light the chimney, and proposition visitors knee covers.

Fill the menu with a flavourful cluster of soul-fulfilling food sources like dish chicken, tenderloin, or salmon. Barbecued portobellos make an incredible vegan elective.

Avert the colder time of year chill with hot drinks, red wine, cranberry-imbued martinis, and sherry.

Reflection is great toward the year's end, so find opportunity to remember the highs. After that hand over to the band and dance the night away.

8. Grand masked ball

If you are searching for a reason to spruce up, this is all there is to it! Have a stupendous covered ball to draw out the tail suits, ballgowns and wonderfully made veils. Improve with painted Venetian settings, Italian busts, and Roman points of support.

Book a setting with water elements or wellsprings as a rich dash of debauchery. Ensure you enlist an authority picture taker to catch everybody looking their best.

Permit the lavishness of the event to reflect in the menu. Pick food, for example, crab puffs, stuffed mushrooms, and connoisseur cheeses. Offer a spread of completely debauched small sweets that offer visitors the chance to test the assortment on offer.

9. Festival

Mirroring the wizardry of an open-air live event is one of the most mind-blowing relaxed corporate party thoughts you can make appear out of nowhere.

Find an open-air scene that fits a phase being set up. Enlist a non-mainstream band for a definitive melodic experience, and your diversion is good to go.

Scour good cause looks for old sheets, splash-colour them in varied varieties and balance them as style. Mats, covers, and toss pads are all you want for seating.

Pack outing crates for bites and drinks and prepare for a night under the stars of gaining melodic experiences.

10. Enchanted forest

Take away for a mysterious evening of charming polish. Make backwoods like setting with live plants that will take the visitor's breath away as they step inside. Dab in the middle between plants for a genuinely supernatural feel.

Enliven feasting tables with green materials, candles, gold-touched foliage, and ivy with a smudge of pixie dust for shimmer.

Make the bar region to be settled in the woods and utilize a smoke machine for added impact. Intriguing mixed drinks are called for, suggestive of elven nectar that would magically give long life.

Waitron staff can dress as timberland sprites or naughty forest mythical people and serve visitors at their tables.

Take the strain to partake off your visitors by recruiting a multi-discipline performing bunch who can convey the night's diversion.

11. Office olympics

One of the most well-known corporate event diversion thoughts is to have an in-office interdepartmental Olympics day. Toss for entertainment only games, for example:

Office Chair Obstacle Course

Plan a racecourse through your office utilizing tape or chalk. Dump obstructions in the manner, for example, boxes of printer paper or waste paper canisters. Join and let one partner sit on a wheeled office seat, while different pushes them through the course. Once more, they trade over and go, all while being planned.

Any contact with a snag adds a five-second punishment. The group with the briefest time wins.

I.D. Badge Toss

Reflecting the wizardry of an outside live event is one of the most stunning loosened up corporate party considerations you can make show up suddenly.

Find an outside scene that fits a stage being set up. Enrol a non-standard band for a conclusive melodic encounter, and your redirection is all set.

Scour great objective searches for old sheets, sprinkle them in shifted assortments and equilibrium them as style. Mats, covers, and throw cushions are all you need for seating.

Pack outing boxes for nibbles and beverages and get ready for a night under the stars of acquiring melodic encounters.

12. African safari

For a genuinely wild event, take your visitors on safari to the African Bushveld. Deck out you are setting in creature print, African safeguards, and Djembe drums. Welcome your visitors with credible Zulu artists or creature brace walkers.

With a clothing standard of safari guide or creature print, your visitors will submerge themselves in the safari experience. Fill the setting with the spirit mixing music from The Lion Lord.

For a group breaking action, run a test on perceiving the hints of African natural life. The victor can be delegated Lord of the Bushveld for the evening.

Catering can be potjiekos and pap, an African stew customarily cooked in a three-legged pot over a fire, presented with maize dinner.

13. Peaky blinders

Dive deep underground with a highly classified Peaky Blinders event. Join the beguile of the 1920s with the coarse disobedience of hoodlums and you host an ideal get-together topic.

Recruit a setting that feels concealed with a mysterious passage prompting the entry. Remember a secret key for the challenge to add to the show of the event.

Visitors who effectively go through the entryway will step into lavishness suggestive of the denial age. With a 1920s band playing live, a private, cryptic moving bar is standing by.

Enriched in a Workmanship Deco style with Tiffany lights loaning outdated appeal, visitors will be brought into the secret of a former period. Utilize dull furnishings, keep the lights low with candles and ceiling fixtures to the secretive feel of the event.

A gin bar gives fluid reward, with canapes and other finger food sources close by for eating.

14. Western country chic

Dial down to a rural subject that checks all the extravagance boxes. Employ an old horse shelter and deck it out with roughage bundles, tropical storm lights and sections of land of delicate hanging. With live succulents for table settings, the scene will be set for an enchanted evening.

Keep the dance floor open for a customary stable dance or line moving. For both of those choices, enlist a prescribed guest to give your visitors the best insight and the best time.

Visitors can come shrewd easy-going, prepared to move in pants, really look at shirts, handkerchiefs, and boots. Women can adhere to the boots and trade out the pants for a rolling dress with a skirt that fits moving.

15. 1950s American diner

Black and white checks with red trim style sings 1950s stronger than Jerry Lee Lewis could belt out a tune. Flues, slicked-back hair, and blue softened cowhide shoes get the folks looking like it. Women move to shake the night away in wide-trimmed swing dresses to the hints of a 50s rock 'n' roll band.

Get a wild dance teacher to get everybody's feet going in the correct bearing, then let the band play!

With burgers, French fries, and milkshakes on the menu, you will lay the right foundation for a great night of returning to the brilliant time of Bluff Richard, The Shadows, and Elvis.

16. Back to school

Return to the past and neglect being an adult for a night. Tossing a class kick-off corporate event allows your visitors to embrace the light-hearted days of their teen years for a couple of hours.

School garbs and haircuts are the expected clothing regulation. Serve food buffet-style from a school cafeteria setup. Do not bother adhering to dry sandwiches and tired lunchmeat however, you can update the menu to a flavourful spread to suit your spending plan.

With a 1990s band to set the state of mind, open the dance floor to get the party cooking. You will not require a lot of additional diversion, yet for chuckles, you can open the mic for courageous people to relate their most humiliating school minutes. Can we just be real, being a youngster has forever been testing.

17. Outer space

Set your sights past the stars for an event topic that is mind boggling, in a real sense. An outer space topic offers bunches of chances for inventive style, cooking, and diversion.

Book out laser tag and have a scaled down in the middle between courses. Laser tag is easy to play and requires no specialized ability, however will get visitors chuckling. A dancefloor encompassed by laser lights adds a layer of changed reality.

For inside, pick a dim variety range and sprinkle sparkling lights like stars. Black star material will add profundity to the dimness. Finish with planets, Ufo's, and stars. Wrap astounding green and purple sparkle textures where fitting. A smoke machine is fundamental!

For the tables, pick black decorative liners matched with smaller than expected moon highlights. Get however much sparkle in obscurity treats that you can lay your hands on.

Mixed drinks that burst into flames or smoke will add to the outsider feel of the night. As will hold up dried frozen yogurt for dessert! Serve food in partitioned food platters for an additional hint of life on a spaceship.

18. Speakeasy

Time trips your visitors back to the 1920s for a one-of-a-kind hoedown that will get their feet tapping. To make the electric energy so inseparable from that time, get a 1920s swing band.

Dissimilar to Peaky Blinder which inclines to the clouded side of the 1920's, Speakeasy is refinement and class.

For the women, this implies glossy silk or kid's gloves, matched with long quill boas. Shimmery sequined textures, flapper headbands and long pearl necklaces. The men can deck themselves out in derby caps or fedoras and tuxedos.

Present customary Speakeasy food varieties, for example, hor de oeuvres, blended nuts, spiced eggs, and platters of olives. Cheddar platters and shrimp mixed drinks were likewise a hit in those days and will be at your event as well.

Take a drink time trip back as well. Bring back the 1920 beverages of the day, for example, champagne, gin rickey, bath punch, home brew, gin bubble, mint julep, and grower's punch.

19. Murder mystery party

Murder Mystery Party suitable for a 'mystery masquerade theme event.For a no-sweat event that will go down as one of the most engaging evenings of the year, have a Homicide Secret Get-together.

Will it be feasible to Do-It-Yourself this one, you will love employing a homicide secret organization. They will give all that to keep the visitors occupied all night long. If you have a decision, utilize their setting. That saves you from setting up or tidying up subsequently.

There will be subjects that you can look over, or a few organizations will engineer a customized secret around the time span or area that you give them.

Go through the night in a phony personality employing props, tackling a non-existent homicide secret in the extraordinary organization of entertainers.

Match your food to the subject you pick, however a cheddar and wine spread is an ideal other option. Present with subject proper mocktails and mixed drinks for a lethally decent night of diversion.

20. Bond 007 - Casino royale

The name is Bond, James Bond. For a notorious night of smooth suits and smooth dresses, you cannot turn out badly with a Bond 007 topic.

An Electric String Group of four gives music to lift the night to a soiree of top-notch food, extraordinary organization, and remarkable class. Provide food for elegant, multi-course, plunk down supper. Martinis are the beverage of decision, shaken, not blended, is evident Bond style.

Relegate monikers to add a layer of interest to the government operative component of the evening. The large supervisor will be M, obviously.

Recruit roulette and blackjack tables with croupiers for high-moving tomfoolery. For low pressure, book an arrangement that accompanies 'fun cash' so visitors can play unreservedly without consuming openings in their pockets.

PROGRESS CHECK

1. What is the purpose of a theme party?
2. How should a catchy name for a theme party be selected?
3. What aspects should be considered when planning the budget for a theme party?
4. How does the choice of site or place impact the success of a theme party?
5. What are some important factors to consider when designing the decorations for a theme party?
6. How can staff contribute to the success of a theme party?
7. What role does entertainment play in a theme party?
8. What are some key factors that contribute to making a theme party profitable for a hotel?
9. How can the various departments of a hotel collaborate to create a successful theme party?
10. What all the points you will consider before organizing a theme event?
11. Write an essay on various theme events celebrated in Indian hotels.

MULTIPLE-CHOICE QUESTIONS

1. What is the primary purpose of a theme event?
   (a) Entertainment (b) Networking (c) Education (d) Fundraising
2. Which element sets the tone for a theme event?
   (a) Venue (b) Food (c) Decorations (d) Invitations
3. Which type of theme event celebrates a specific historical era?
   (a) Fantasy (b) Vintage (c) Sci-fi (d) Cultural
4. What aspect of a theme event focuses on the visual appeal and atmosphere?
   (a) Guest list (b) Entertainment (c) Dress code (d) Decoration
5. A 'black-tie' dress code suggests:
   (a) Casual attire (b) Semi-formal attire (c) Formal attire (d) Sporty attire
6. What kind of theme event might feature costumes from famous movies and TV shows?
   (a) Masquerade ball (b) Hollywood glamour
   (c) Around the world (d) Casino night
7. Which factor is crucial when selecting a theme for a corporate event?
   (a) Personal preferences (b) Budget constraints
   (c) Trendy themes (d) Colour schemes
8. What does a 'destination' theme event typically incorporate?
   (a) Interactive games (b) International cuisine
   (c) Comedy performances (d) Art exhibitions
9. A theme event centred around "retro arcade" might appeal to fans of
   (a) Literature (b) Science fiction (c) Video games (d) Gardening

10. What does a 'charity gala' theme event usually support?
    (a) Creative arts
    (b) Environmental causes
    (c) Social justice
    (d) Competitive sports
11. Which type of theme event celebrates a specific holiday or festive occasion?
    (a) Cultural festival
    (b) Seasonal
    (c) Wellness retreat
    (d) Business conference
12. What type of entertainment might be suitable for a 'mystery masquerade' theme event?
    (a) Live music concert
    (b) Dance competition
    (c) Murder mystery game
    (d) Cooking demonstration
13. What is the deciding factor for selecting a theme for an event
    (a) Budget
    (b) Venue
    (c) The target audience
    (d) Security

Answers to Multiple-Choice Questions

1. (a)	2. (c)	3. (b)	4. (d)	5. (c)	6. (b)	7. (b)	8. (b)
9. (c)	10. (c)	11. (b)	12. (c)	13. (c)			

Chapter 15

Virtual Events

Objectives

After going through this chapter the reader will be able to:

- Understand the concept and types of virtual events.
- Know the growth and history of virtual events.
- Distinguish between hybrid and virtual events.
- Explore the new possibilities to get online.

15.1 INTRODUCTION

The term virtual means not physically existing as such but made by software, use of the Internet to appear to do so and virtual event refers to any event that brings the people digitally together when the event is ongoing. These events happen via live over video on various digital platforms like Zoom, Microsoft Teams, Cisco WebEx, Facebook Live, etc, and range from a small group conversation to a panel, fireside chat, direct video live stream lecture, demonstration, or class. Virtual reality (VR) is useful in conducting virtual events. These virtual events are highly interactive and aim to create a similar experience as far as possible to their physical counterparts.

Virtual events have gained popularity across various industries, serving as platforms for a wide range of purposes. They are utilized for virtual trade shows, webinar, exhibition, job fairs, conferences, sales meetings, college open days, and company-wide gatherings. Different organizations, such as associations, meeting organizers, executives, marketing and product management teams, and human resource departments, take the lead in hosting these events. They leverage virtual events to deliver presentations, training sessions, job fairs, expos, internal meetings, and more.

Virtual events have been widely held due to the COVID-19 pandemics, during which in-person gatherings have faced restrictions, prohibitions, or concerns related to safety and health.

15.2 TYPES OF VIRTUAL EVENTS

Virtual events, after the pandemic have become the new normal. It made life easy during the tough times of the pandemic because through virtual events each and everybody was able to get connected digitally.

A few types of virtual events are listed down below.

15.2.1 Virtual Conference

Virtual conference helps a business to increase its brand awareness, helps the business to generate leads, and helps the business to build relationships and it is more than a simple virtual meeting. These conferences are hosted over a small number of days and generally include keynotes, panel discussions, training, educational sessions, etc. If a person desires to bring people together from several locations that share the same interest and wants to learn more about a particular industry, a virtual conference is the right platform.

15.2.2 Webinar

It is one of the most popular virtual events whose requirement is to have little audience participation and one or two of a particular company shares knowledge and advice related to a particular topic. This event reaches a wide range of audiences as audiences can connect as per their wish without having to participate. Webinars usually last from 30 minutes to a couple of hours.

15.2.3 Online Workshop

This virtual event is ideal for a business that looks forward to giving skill-based training without having to meet face-to-face. One major factor of a successful online workshop is keeping the attendees engaged by involving audience participation to test their newly learnt knowledge. It works best with few attendees, thereby providing everyone a chance to engage with each other and ask questions if they are not able to understand.

15.2.4 Online Trade Shows and Exhibitions

It is equivalent to running a face-to-face trade event right down to the entrance of the exhibition hall. The organization creates the same experience for the audience to mimic their being there. These online exhibitions can offer webinars which lead to the audience visiting their online store a lot quicker than if they were physically there, thus creating more engagement and maximizing profit.

15.2.5 Live Streaming

Live streaming generally happens when a streamed video is sent over the Internet in real time and is not pre-recorded. It is generally done over Facebook. Although live streaming was used before the pandemic, it has become increasingly popular at the time of the pandemic. It is an excellent way to connect with potential customers through social media and helps to communicate the message of a particular brand.

15.2.6 Virtual Career Fairs

To find the best employees a virtual career fair generally hosts one-to-one video chats, job boards, video assessment tools, and much more for potential employees. This not only helps to improve the quality of the applicants of a business but also provides the scope for the business to meet them virtually.

15.2.7 Health and Well-being Sessions

With the closure of fitness training centres and gyms majority of the individuals have taken part in yoga and strength classes virtually to keep themselves mentally good during the tough times.

15.2.8 Virtual Networking

Virtual networking is an event that allows a person to meet with like-minded individuals to discuss and share ideas about the business and it is a great marketing tool. Networking is usually a part of a conference or webinar and is an opportunity for colleagues to let them relax while talking through different ideas.

15.3 HISTORY AND ORIGIN OF VIRTUAL EVENTS

In April 1993, Alan Saperstein, and Randy Selman, representing Visual Data Corporation (now known as on-stream media), introduced a concept called "Convention View" during an investor presentation at the Waldorf Astoria hotel in New York City. This innovative approach involved videotaping trade show exhibitor booths and incorporating the videos into HTML floor maps. While Convention View experienced initial positive reception, the company eventually discontinued the project. However, they later re-entered the market in November 2010 with a new multimedia virtual trade show platform named MarketPlace365.

The development of virtual events started in the middle of the 1990s with numerous software applications that enabled users to share their screens.

Virtual events became increasingly popular during the late 2000s recession as they offered an economically and environmentally effective way to bring thousands of attendees to an event around the globe. Hybrid events have emerged as a new trend where traditional physical events are accompanied by a virtual component.

This integration of virtual environments has become a significant element in marketing strategies. Virtual events offer marketers a valuable opportunity to gather extensive marketing data by tracking and evaluating the activities of participants.

A virtual engagement index serves as a metric to assess both the quantity and quality of interaction among participants. This is a very useful tool for salespeople who then know the quality of the lead they are pursuing, however not all providers offer this feature yet. Virtual events can offer several ways for participants to connect and communicate. Virtual booths, forums, and designated meeting places allow participants to connect with event staff, exhibitors and sponsors, or fellow attendees using online chat, video, and voice.

Attendees can utilize their social connections within an event to create groups based on shared interests or connect with individuals who share similar mindsets. Moreover, they can easily share their experiences and discoveries with their online communities, often leading to increased visibility and popularity for the event.

Virtual events have been under exploration by companies since the 1990s, but their adoption significantly surged during the COVID-19 pandemic when many in-person events had to be cancelled or altered. Not only have corporations implemented virtual events, but events that would normally take place at an onsite venue with live audiences have also transitioned to virtual events.

At the onset of the COVID-19 pandemic, scientific associations scrambled to convert their normally on-site events into virtual ones to share all the scientific research needed to combat the pandemic. The Genetics Society of America (GSA) was one of the early successes when they were able to convert The Allied Genetics Conference (TACC) event (only held every four years) into a virtual event in April 2020. A different industry example took place on 29 November, 2020 when Miss Earth 2020 was held virtually for the first time in history. Eighty-four international delegates participated. The utilization of virtual platforms has brought significant advantages and financial gains for virtual corporate emcees.

Amid the COVID-19 pandemic, the National Speakers Association observed a noteworthy increase in the importance of MC/facilitation as a revenue source for its members. In 2020, 14% of members reported it as their primary income stream, compared to just 3% in 2016. Considering the escalating expenses associated with travel and the scarcity of time for individuals balancing hectic lifestyles, attending numerous job fairs, or visiting potential employers can be challenging.

However, the solution to these predicaments may lie in a few simple keystrokes on a computer. Virtual job fairs are gaining popularity due to several reasons. Job seekers can conveniently participate from their own homes, even while currently employed. Similarly, employers find that virtual job fairs enable them to attract candidates from around the world and efficiently connect with a larger pool of job seekers in less time.

15.3.1 Virtual Job Fair

"A virtual job fair is just like a regular job fair, with different employer booths and a chance to talk to employers about jobs," says Don Best, director of marketing for Unisfair in Menlo Park, Calif. "You still give an employer a resume and anything else you think might help you get the job, but you are doing the whole thing while sitting at a computer."

More employers are using virtual events, whether it is a job fair, marketing event, sales training, or even award ceremonies because they can use technology to cut costs associated with such events and attract attendees worldwide, Best says for job fairs, the virtual aspect allows hiring managers to streamline a process that often can be onerous at a time when companies are under pressure to move faster to compete.

The following steps need to be followed to host a job fair:

15.3.1.1 Choosing a Proper Platform

Before selecting the platform for conducting the job fair, in-depth research must be done by the host, as the basic features that most virtual job platforms comprise are live streaming, chat rooms, branded booths, and provisions for audio-video presentations. Chat and messaging tools enable participants to interact in realtime during virtual events. Synchronous sessionis presented in realtime and can be attended by participants from different locations.

As the host of a virtual job fair, one must take into consideration if the online job fair platform could be optimized for smartphone users and if the platform allows access to candidate resumes. Also, the host must take into consideration the target crowd for whom the job fair will be conducted.

15.3.1.2 Developing a Proper Strategy

Diverse and engaging content is a consideration when planning virtual event content. Thorough planning is required for the success of the virtual job fair. A detailed list of all the requirements must be created by the host along with an exhaustive plan to be followed for the success of the virtual job fair. Some of the crucial aspects that the host needs to consider during this are:

- Number of attendees identified from virtual event registration
- Additional software requirements
- Cost of the virtual job fair platform
- Recruitment firms or companies that the host wishes to partner with
- The kind of job fair the host plans to organize

15.3.1.3 Planning of the Budget

After chalking out the requirements, the host needs to plan and prepare the budget in the following steps. Although the virtual job fair might be less expensive than the offline job fair, these virtual fairs may include some expenses in the form of software requirements. Although most of the software can be downloaded for free of cost, there is certain software that needs to be purchased.

15.3.1.4 Advertising of the Event

Job portals, social media platforms, and email services offer powerful marketing channels for promoting and advertising the virtual job fair. The best possible way to spread the word about the event is through recruiters and companies who are participating in the event.

15.4 HYBRID VS VIRTUAL TRADE SHOW

A hybrid trade show is defined as a dynamic event that offers an exquisite virtual experience to the virtual attendees and a memorable one to the physical attendees. It acts as a link between the online and the offline by ensuring that the trade show is accessible to all kinds of people coming from various parts of the world.

A virtual trade show is an online environment with a three-dimensional setup incorporated with certain event engagement tools that recreate the concept of a physical trade show. Question and answer sessions are important tool to engage audience in virtual events. This allows visitors and exhibitors to connect and interact through any virtual event platform. On-demand recording is useful to view the events at later stages; however, limited accessibility is one of the potential challenges for virtual events.

Recently, the popularity of hybrid trade shows is largely increasing. Approximately 34% of event organizers anticipate increasing their investments in hybrid events in the coming years. This strategic move is driven by the recognition that hybrid events offer an ideal solution to overcome the persistent challenges faced by physical and virtual events when conducted separately.

15.4.1 Advantages of Organizing a Hybrid Trade Show

Increased attendance capability

The topmost advantage of organizing a hybrid trade show is an increase in the attendance percentage and easy to connect with global audience. When an event is accessible online, it enables those people to attend the event who might otherwise not be able to attend because of reasons like travel, costs, and time as well as venue size constraints. Also in many cases, 50% of the virtual attendees have never attended the physical version of the conference or meeting. Incorporating an online component into a hybrid event enables the host to reach out to inactive employees, members, and customers associated with the organization.

Eco-friendly

Reducing the need for travel indicates reduced environmental impacts. When the host plans to include a virtual environment, the biggest and added advantage is that eco-friendly events can be enjoyed which was not possible previously.

Here, one will be interacting with zero-waste. The virtual portion of the event produces only 1% of the carbon emissions that in-person events produce. Hybrid events offer a sustainable and environment-friendly solution by eliminating the need for excessive construction and minimizing waste generation.

Powerful sponsor opportunities

About 72% of corporate sponsors are highly interested in participating in a hybrid event. These events are of incredible value to sponsors. The topmost reason is the increased reach. The second reason for the powerful sponsor opportunity is that sponsors can easily communicate 1:1 with interested parties and this can be done by interacting with online virtual attendees.

Higher audience engagement

When it comes to higher audience engagement, adding a virtual element to the live element is the key. This expands the range of engagement possibilities beyond those offered by a purely live event. This is because the virtual audience is actively participating from their cell phone or desktop computers or laptop, indicating the fact that they can talk, share, like, comment, and perform many more online functions. Apart from this, a question-answer session can be conducted with a speaker at the live event. During a live-streamed presentation, online viewers can submit their questions in real time and receive immediate answers along with the in-person audience.

To facilitate this interaction, a moderator or a screen can be set up for the presenter to view the online questions. Additionally, both offline and online attendees can engage in networking activities. Attendees can search user profiles, allowing them to identify potential prospects for either inperson or virtual meetings.

Valuable data

Hybrid events offer a significant advantage in terms of the valuable data they generate, which provides valuable insights. The exact participation number is known to the host, and the host also knows how they engaged and when they dropped out of the session. The host also gains information about the attendee's interests with the help of matchmaking data and session participation.

15.5 IDEAS TO MAKE THE VIRTUAL TRADE SHOW A SUCCESS

15.5.1 Choose the Appropriate Virtual Trade Show Platform

The first thought that drives the entire trade show is which platform will be best for the show. To be more honest, this is the primary step that holds the responsibility for the ins and outs of the hybrid trade show.

The host must have planned out the venue and accommodation for an offline audience. But it also becomes crucial to choose the best virtual event platform compatible with all the objectives that the trade show is organized for. Therefore, comprehensive thinking is a must before choosing the platform that offers all the solutions to power up the hybrid trade show. Create a comprehensive plan outlining the essential features required for the virtual audience of the hybrid trade show. Subsequently, identify suitable providers capable of offering the necessary solutions to meet our requirements.

15.5.2 Decide what to Incorporate into the Virtual Trade Show

Examine all aspects of the hybrid trade show to ensure a smooth and effortless experience, determining the essential features that should be included.

All the integrations should align with the idea of the hybrid trade show. The saying that the first impression is the last makes it important to rethink and re-evaluate the features of the hybrid trade show.

Here are some of the crucial features that the host must incorporate in the hybrid trade show:

- Showcasing branding elements and comprehensive brand information on both physical and virtual booths.
- Establishing a seamless connection between online and offline participants and exhibitors through videoconferencing.
- Enabling attendees to directly provide their contact information to exhibitors.
- Presenting digital brochures, videos, and other multimedia content adjacent to exhibitor booths, both in person and virtually.
- Exhibiting a Social Wall at the trade show location and on the virtual event platform to foster engagement and interaction.

15.5.3 Customize the Exhibitor's Booths

Unlike traditional trade shows, capturing the attention of attendees at hybrid trade shows can be challenging due to the diverse nature of the audience. To address this, event organizers can provide exhibitors with customized booths, allowing them to design unique and eye-catching displays. This customization enables exhibitors to effectively engage both physical and virtual attendees.

Additionally, exhibitors can allocate a dedicated team to cater specifically to the virtual audience. Through their booths, exhibitors can showcase branding elements, such as logos and social media walls, as well as deliver high-quality audio and video content, sponsored materials, creative commercials, coupon slides, announcements, and more. They can also incorporate designs that align with their brand colours and effectively represent their products or services.

15.5.4 Work on Sponsorship Opportunities

Self-funding cannot fulfil the revenue requirements of the hybrid trade show. Sponsorships play a crucial role in generating revenue and setting the stage for a successful event.

To create a platform that connects sponsors with the hybrid trade show audience effectively, organizers can offer a Social Wall. This feature enables companies seeking to engage with the audience to partner with the event host and seize sponsorship opportunities. By leveraging these opportunities, the hybrid trade show can reach new heights of success and attract a larger audience.

We must not forget that sponsors need some spotlight and the more exposure they will get, the more doors will open for the host to expand the hybrid trade show.

15.5.5 Provide Technical Support

Furthermore, it is essential for us to maintain round-the-clock availability to offer comprehensive technical support for the hybrid trade show. Our commitment extends beyond the event itself, as we ensure dedicated teams are in place to cater to the needs of both our online and offline audiences.

Helping the exhibitors with designing their booth, providing those tools to engage the attendees, helping them bridge the communication gap between the physical and virtual audience, resolving any connection errors between the attendees and the exhibitors, and much more. Ensure that your contact information is visible to all the attendees, and the exhibitors so that they can get their issues resolved immediately.

15.6 BEST PRACTICES TO ORGANIZE A HYBRID TRADE SHOW

15.6.1 Facilitate Live Chat for Better Interactivity

The audience plays a crucial role in defining the essence of any event, and the hybrid trade show aims to cater to both virtual and physical attendees. However, managing these diverse audiences has added complexity to the task of organizing trade shows, particularly when it comes to attracting attendees to individual booths. The absence of in-person interaction between the online and offline participants further intensifies the challenge of engaging attendees.

Consequently, extra efforts must be invested to facilitate interactions between attendees and exhibitors. An effective solution involves implementing live chat features for the online audience, allowing attendees to have their questions about products and services answered in real time, while also enabling exhibitors to generate more leads. Additionally, the introduction of a dedicated event app can enhance the attendee experience by facilitating interaction among participants, regardless of whether they are attending virtually or physically.

15.6.2 Organize Live Webinars to Educate Your Audience

Your hybrid trade show will have the global audience in one place at one time; make sure that each one of your physical show exhibitors has a virtual booth for the virtual audience to attend. They can have extra staff that manages the virtual audience.

Host interactive live sessions to educate your audience about the brand's products, services, or other relevant topics in line with the concept of a trade show. Engage industry specialists or guest speakers to deliver valuable information and insights to the event attendees through webinars.

Optimize attendance by scheduling the webinars strategically, and encourage active participation by incorporating a questionnaire round to enhance engagement from the attendees.

15.6.3 Provide Opportunities for Immediate Sales using e-commerce Platforms

Expand your hybrid trade show experience beyond just product and service showcases and transform it into a convenient on-site shopping destination for attendees. Utilize this opportunity to enhance engagement and drive immediate sales. Consider setting up a physical exhibition of your products at the trade show venue or provide QR codes that attendees can scan. These QR codes will redirect them to your e-commerce store on the virtual event platform, enabling them to make purchases on the spot. By integrating an online shop into your event, you can effectively convert potential customers from around the world into valuable revenue generators. Offering attendees, a real-time purchasing platform will significantly boost conversion rates for your hybrid trade show.

15.6.4 Display Social Walls to Enhance Engagement

Social Wall or the Wall of Engagement is no less than the game changer of your hybrid trade show. Integrating your online and offline audience presents a valuable chance to foster a sense of unity.

By incorporating social media into your hybrid trade show, you can create a distinctive and effective method to engage attendees. The social wall will captivate your trade show audience by showcasing a variety of content such as social media updates, user-generated posts, branded materials, event announcements, key moments, exclusive deals, promotional offers, customized messages, sponsor highlights, and more.

With Tag Box display, you can create a unique and exquisite Social Wall for your virtual trade show platform, and can even be customized and personalized as per the objectives of the brand and trade show.

These social walls can be displayed anywhere in your virtual trade show platform and on the screens installed at the offline venue. Your exhibitors can display it on the booth desk, besides their booth on the info display, on the chat pages, in the webinars, on the registration desk, and much more.

This powerful tool effectively draws in a greater number of visitors to your booth, capturing their attention with your brand, and evoking their curiosity and enthusiasm.

15.6.5 Access Real-time Data to Measure Hybrid Event's Success

Throughout history, we have been encouraged to learn from our mistakes to achieve greater success. Applying this principle to the year 2022 would greatly benefit event marketers, especially when it comes to organizing hybrid trade shows.

These events offer organizers the valuable opportunity to receive comprehensive progress reports, enabling them to track the event's performance and identify areas for improvement. Therefore, accessing real-time progress reports becomes essential for measuring the success of a hybrid trade show and formulating effective strategies for future events.

15.6.6 Hold the Audience for a Long with Innovative Gamification

If you are feeling stressed about the decreasing number of attendees at your hybrid trade show or the drop-out rate during webinars and conferences, it is crucial to find ways to engage and captivate your audience.

This is especially important when a significant portion of your attendees are participating virtually. Incorporating gamification into your hybrid trade show can be a highly effective strategy to encourage participation from both online and offline attendees, bridging the communication gap between the two groups and motivating them to actively engage.

By organizing captivating contests, interactive games, Q&A sessions, polls, and other engaging activities, event organizers can increase attendee retention and encourage them to stay involved for longer durations.

15.7 BEST TOOLS FOR HYBRID TRADE SHOW

To successfully plan a hybrid trade show, it is essential to carefully select a diverse range of tools. These tools encompass virtual event platforms, social media integration, engagement features, live streaming capabilities, analytics solutions, and more.

It is crucial to consider factors such as the size of the audience, the trade show's objectives, the planned activities, and the desired features when choosing the appropriate tools. It is also important to ensure that the integrated tools align with the overall aesthetics of the hybrid trade show and effectively address any challenges that may arise.

Virtual trade show platforms: V Fairs, Dreamcast, 6 Connex, etc.

Social media wall tool: Tag box

Virtual trade show engagement tool: Tag box, Virtual Booth

Live streaming tools: Zoom, Instagram Live, Facebook Live, YouTube Live

Analytics tool: Tag box

15.8 MANAGE AND EXECUTE HYBRID TRADE SHOW SEAMLESS WITH THIS QUICK

- Utilize attractive teasers and compelling social media promotions to attract exhibitors and attendees.
- Develop a well-organized follow-up plan for the hybrid trade show.
- Select suitable tools and employ them strategically to maximize promotion and engagement.
- Seize sponsorship opportunities and ensure effective integration into the event.
- Schedule interactive networking sessions to facilitate connections between exhibitors and attendees.
- Implement social walls to create an engaging experience for both attendees and exhibitors.
- Provide seamless technical support throughout the event.
- Collect and analyze valuable insights to measure the performance and success of the hybrid trade show.
- Send a personalized email to all participants, expressing gratitude for their participation.
- Incorporate virtual events alongside webinars to adapt to changing industry trends and leverage new event marketing and management technology.

The meetings and events industry has undergone a significant transformation in recent months, with a growing number of event planners opting for virtual solutions.

According to a survey conducted by PCMA, approximately 79% of event planners have embraced virtual alternatives, including virtual meetings and conferences. This shift towards virtual platforms signifies the industry's willingness to adopt innovative event marketing and management technology.

With this new reality come new challenges and solutions. As a virtual event strategy is being built, there is a lot to consider. The right virtual event platform, the right type of content, and the best virtual engagement strategies – are all crucial components in crafting an effective (and enjoyable) virtual event.

15.9 TO MAKE A VIRTUAL EVENT ENGAGING, THE FOLLOWING POINTS NEED TO BE CONSIDERED

1. Create quizzes and questionnaires

Help the virtual audience to get more information about the topics and speakers letting them ask and answer the questions before, during, and after the event. The workshop enables a person to choose and show the most interesting questions and topics. During the activity, individuals can express their opinions and preferences regarding the questions being discussed. Encouraging the audience to be creative and rewarding the audience if they did an excellent job with the question-answer will make the event a lot more engaging.

2. Encourage voting during virtual events

The audience needs to get involved by creating fun live polls. Live polls are one of the funniest ways to boost attention. Allowing the participants to vote via workshop and displaying the result on a diagram in realtime. Polls regarding different aspects of the evening, like speakers' topics and graphics or ratings of different subjects and opinions can be asked of the audience.

3. Create a fun learning experience

Besides live polls, questionnaires, and ratings, it is always fun to learn through texts and pictures. The best way to make the event an engaging one is to give the audience to solve something and present results effectively in real-time on the screen.

4. Create memories with an interactive virtual events platform

The best way to create memories is to create some souvenirs from the event and make the crowd have more fun. Worksop can be used and the guests can be requested to take pictures of them. If the audience is playful, some props can be given to make the event more engaging.

5. Communication

Enable real-time chat between attendees and organizers. There might be a lot of questions that the guests would like to ask. Worksop makes this practice easier. Encourage the audience to organize online meet-ups and to share similar interests with others like-minded people. Attendees can chat directly with the organizers in the conference app. For instance, attendees can share ideas about the event or other requests there. Also, workshop enables us to share a link to share the live results.

6. Networking at interactive virtual events

Networking is becoming more and more important for every event industry. The conference app allows attendees to communicate directly with the organizers, providing a platform where they can freely share ideas about the event or make various requests. Furthermore, if we enable a virtual networking feature, the guests can create profiles and organize meetings and share ideas.

7. Virtual tour

Because of shelter-in-place and social distancing, many event planners are now relegated to their homes. However, they are still busy sourcing events for later this year and next year too, according to the latest Event Supplier Network data.

Assisting event planners in digitally exploring your venue is crucial for securing their future business. Fortunately, with the availability of online tools like Social Tables diagramming, you have the tability to showcase the advantages of your venue. This includes providing detailed visuals of each room's distinctive layout and presenting a comprehensive campus map, allowing planners to visualize how the rooms seamlessly connect with each other.

While you might have an unwelcome visitor on your video conference call – in the form of your adorable pup – you can still accomplish everything you need to with 3D diagrams, including answering planners' questions, showing them how their event will fit, and even building a relationship with them (Fido might even help with that!). Here we will explore how you can continue closing contracts during these uncertain times as best as possible using virtual site visit tours online.

15.10 EXPERIENCE THE ULTIMATE ONLINE SITE VISITS WITH AN IMMERSIVE VIRTUAL VENUE TOUR

Customize the virtual tour before your video call.

(a) Identify the decision maker

Closing an event can be challenging if the key decision maker is not present during the video chat. It is crucial to identify the individual with the final authority and make sure they confirm their attendance through a calendar invite. To facilitate this, it is advisable to establish communication with the event planner, who may sometimes delay the contract process while arranging the event. By collaborating with the planner, you can proactively involve the decision maker and align all stakeholders from the beginning, ensuring a smooth and efficient progression of tasks.

(b) Send the invite

Please send a calendar invitation for a video call meeting, and attach the relevant video conferencing details (Zoom, Google Hangouts, etc.) to the invite. In the invitation, please include the agenda for the site visit, including a dedicated time slot for the planner to ask questions. Additionally, kindly send email reminders one hour and 15 minutes before the meeting to ensure everyone is reminded to attend.

(c) Send a questionnaire

Based on responses to our site visit report, planners prefer venues that ask for event specifics before you arrive. Venue reps should already be familiar with their event needs and how they can accommodate themeven if they have to get a little creative to do so.

So, in addition to the agenda, send a short list of five questions, so you can drill into what their unique event is. That way you can cater your presentation ahead of time. Based on their RFP you probably already know details such as the type of event, the expected number of attendees, the programme agenda, and the estimated budget. Use your questions to dig deeper. Consider asking these survey questions:

- What are the event's goals?
- Will you need a wheelchair accessible floor plan?
- Is the event open to children?
- Would you be willing to send a programme agenda?

(d) Create sales deck

While you might need other hotel sales collateral throughout the process, the key asset you need to create right now is a sales deck. When conducting a site visit, it is important to anticipate the questions that planners may have and address all aspects of their concerns.

To ensure a comprehensive presentation, we have prepared a few slides covering the following inquiries:

1. Event timings: What is the latest permissible time for events to run?
2. Room capacities: What is the maximum capacity for each room?
3. Permit requirements: What permits are necessary for hosting events at the venue?
4. Functional areas: Are there designated spaces for storage, green rooms, and back-of-house operations?
5. Branding opportunities: What branding possibilities exist both inside and outside of the venue?

Additionally, based on the responses from the planner's survey, we have customized the presentation to address specific considerations relevant to their needs.

Furthermore, we would like to highlight our venue's exceptional features and capabilities in meeting planner requirements during the site inspection:

1. Accommodating event timings: Our venue offers flexible event timings, ensuring planners have the freedom to extend their events as needed while adhering to local regulations.
2. Versatile room capacities: Each room in our venue is equipped with adjustable layouts and seating arrangements, accommodating various event sizes and formats.
3. Permit assistance: We provide comprehensive support in obtaining the necessary permits for events, guiding planners through the process, and ensuring compliance with all regulations.
4. Functional space allocation: Our venue includes dedicated areas for storage, green rooms, and back-of-house operations, ensuring smooth event logistics and seamless coordination.
5. Extensive branding opportunities: We offer a range of branding options both inside and outside the venue, allowing planners to showcase their event's branding elements effectively and create a memorable experience for attendees.

By addressing these specific planner considerations and showcasing our venue's standout features, we aim to provide a comprehensive and tailored presentation during the site visit.

(e) Pre-customized diagram

According to the findings of our site visit report, event planners have a strong preference for venues that offer comprehensive access to precise and up-to-date floor plans, accurately represented to scale.

To cater to this requirement, I suggest utilizing virtual tour software like Social Tables to create a customized diagram showcasing the ideal room for their event. Drawing inspiration from successful past events, I will incorporate a layout that has proven effective, while adhering to best practices for floor plans. Furthermore, I will personalize the diagram by incorporating the client's logo and incorporating specific details aligned with their vision, such as microphone placement and room colours.

Plus, be sure to create two other layout examples (using saved ones for this is fine too!), so you can have them ready from the start in case the client wants more space between tables, and so on.

(f) Lock event elements in place on the drawing

Lock specific objects in place if they must not be moved: You have the option to keep certain elements unchanged in your design by utilizing the lock feature. By simply highlighting and clicking the lock button in the edit panel, you can ensure that the stage, permanent fixtures, columns, and doorways remain in their original positions.

This enables you to freely adjust other elements without affecting the layout of these fixed objects. Additionally, you can group together objects that need to maintain their specific arrangement, allowing clients to move, adjust, and rotate the group without altering its size or spacing.

This will be important for your video call!

(g) Guide the planner through your virtual tour

Kick off the video call by building a relationship. Try to find something you have in common. It could be as simple as how stressed you both are and how much trouble you are having adjusting to working from home.

(h) Reiterate what the planner is looking for

Retrieve the personalized presentation prepared for the client, incorporating their logo into the sales deck. Begin the call by acknowledging the planner's key priorities, emphasizing the three aspects they value most. Elaborate on how our venue can assist them in achieving their event objectives. Inquire if they have any immediate queries or apprehensions, ensuring that we can promptly address them.

(i) Present pre-built diagram customized to them

Utilize the screen sharing feature in our video call programme to visually present your computer screen. Display the Social Tables 3D diagram of our venue, allowing the client to visualize the space and its offerings. Guide them through each area, pointing out important aspects related to their event program. Explain how our staff can efficiently arrange the room and emphasize any distinctive benefits, such as outstanding sound quality, well-designed lighting, convenient proximity to restrooms, and more. Ask the planner what they like and dislike about the layout.

(j) Listen to the client as per the shared diagram

Listen to the client's requests and understand what the client is asking for before responding. Strong communication requires active listening rather than anticipating and reacting to an assumed need. To practise active listening:

- Show you are engaged by making eye contact, nodding, and using positive body language.
- Listen and consider the request of the client before responding rather than preparing your response while the client speaks.

- Don't interrupt; save your comments for a natural pause. This is important on a remote call because it can be hard to hear anything when two people are talking at the same time.
- Ask questions and repeat the client's concerns back to them to ensure you understand.

We strive to deliver, but we cannot always do it all. Always explain your ˜no' and back it up with examples and expertise and offer solutions based on what the client has communicated rather than what you think they want. Difficult clients respond better with effective communication methods.

(k) Have a backup ready

Being proactive and prepared in your design process is essential when it comes to client satisfaction. If a client expresses dissatisfaction with a particular design, it is advantageous to have alternative options readily available. This demonstrates your professionalism and ability to adapt to unexpected circumstances.

To achieve this, it is beneficial to keep previous layouts accessible, enabling you to present quick examples as needed. Additionally, consider creating additional layout templates for each client, allowing you to easily swap layouts between floor plans if necessary. By offering alternate plans, you exhibit your readiness to accommodate factors like unfavourable weather conditions, changes in venue room availability, or sudden adjustments that may arise at short notice.

Remember, having backup options on hand showcases your flexibility and dedication to meeting your client's needs, ultimately strengthening your reputation as a reliable and competent professional.

(l) Make adjustments together

After gaining a better understanding of the client's vision, you can collaborate on making changes to the diagram. To involve the client, you have the option to grant them edit access to the diagram. They will receive an email with a link to open the diagram on their own computer. Alternatively, you can rearrange objects on the diagram while the client observes, using a simple drag-and-drop method.

Feel free to adjust the number of rounds and add as many chairs as necessary—whatever suits their needs. As you analyze the diagram, it is important to proactively communicate any issues you identify, such as insufficient electrical outlets, displays obstructing wheelchair access, or potential violations of the fire code. Together, you can explore alternative solutions to address these challenges. And you can talk through how to bring safe meetings to life, by working through spacing issues.

(m) Keep previous versions of the layout for backtrack

You can also use the diagram version history to keep track of changes you and the client make together to the layout. Floor plans evolve constantly in the run-up to the event. Toggle between options to show the client the possibilities before making significant changes to the layout, or switch back to an early plan if the client decides they want the extra seating after all.

(n) Share your A/V capabilities

Another important factor (one of the top five!) for planners identified in our site visit report as they are looking for venues that do not overpromise. When your chosen venue is unable to accommodate specific requests for food, beverages, or equipment availability, it is essential to be honest and transparent about these limitations.

However, it is equally important to offer alternative options that are available. For instance, if the venue has on-site A/V equipment, it should be communicated to the event planners. Conversely, if the venue lacks such equipment, clients should be advised to bring in their own A/V providers during the site visit. Enlisting the expertise of A/V professionals can help identify any potential issues and discover exciting opportunities for an exceptional A/V experience.

(o) Share your F&B capabilities

Please inform event planners about the distinctive features of our catering options for their upcoming events. Additionally, highlight how they can optimize their budget by taking advantage of our weekly meal specials. Utilize Social Tables' attendee manager, which allows planners to assign tags to each guest based on their RSVP, ensuring accurate delivery of meals to the designated tables.

(p) Run through last minute changes by acting a scenario out

Because we all know the details of events change non-stop, show how your diagram and guest lists can update in real-time by playing through a scenario.

Have you ever experienced a situation where a significant guest had to cancel their attendance unexpectedly? For instance, imagine if your keynote speaker's flight was cancelled, and she could not make it to the event. Although we had initially reserved prime seating for her at the front of the room, there is no need to worry because we can make good use of it. We can swiftly update the seating chart, ensuring that all our staff members are informed. Witness how easily we can change the seating arrangement by removing her and assigning someone else to that seat.

(q) Use comments for easy reference

Please provide questions and comments directly on the diagram as you go along. This will allow for easy reference and clarification without the need to search for them in separate text or email exchanges.

(r) Identify the competition

You should always, ask the planner which other venues they are considering. It is important to get a sense of the competition to better communicate what sets your venue apart. This will help you tailor your follow-up materials.

(s) Do not forget to include the wow factor

When conducting a virtual site visit, it is important to make a good impression on the planner, just as you would during an in-person visit. According to our site visit survey, one of the top five factors that planners value in venue selection is a personalized and customized experience. While you may not be able to offer extravagant gestures like a luxurious ride on a putting green or customized napkins in their brand colour, there are still ways to enhance their visit virtually.

For instance, you could consider sending them a Starbucks or Amazon gift card or arranging for food delivery through services such as Caviar or Door Dash, to be enjoyed either before or after your meeting. This can help show the planner your superior commitment to service, as well as your attention to detail.

(t) After the virtual tour follow up right away

Please ensure that all relevant materials are promptly sent to the planner within the next 30 minutes after the call. These materials will assist in selecting your venue and obtaining approval from all relevant parties involved. When you give the planner everything they need upfront without them having to make the ask, you make it easier to select your venue.

(u) Send the planner the diagram design

Send the planner the web link for the diagram, so they can see it on their computer. Do not worry; they will not be able to make changes without you. Let the planner know that the design is changeable, and encourage them to share it with any other stakeholders.

(v) Includes photographs and videos

Consider including visual content such as event photos or video walk-throughs in your follow-up. However, keep in mind that these files can be large and may trigger spam filters when attached to emails. Instead of attaching them directly, you have a few alternative options. One approach is to incorporate them into your sales presentation deck. Another option is to create a web page where you can host the photos and videos, and then include the URL in your email.

Additionally, you can share the visual assets through Social Tables by uploading them to the corresponding event and storing them alongside the event diagram you created. By utilizing these strategies, you can effectively showcase the event space without encountering file size or spam-related issues.

(w) Set them on a virtual call with another planner

Send over the contact information of another planner who held an event in your venue and would recommend you, and encourage the planner to get in touch with any questions or concerns. That way, the planner can ensure you can meet their needs. Sometimes an unbiased third-party opinion is just what they need!

(x) Give the planner a checklist

Planners love checklists! Planners often bring checklists to site visits, but the checklist really should not stop there. Create a checklist that guides the planner through negotiation timelines, and contract timelines, as well as coordinate on all the details to work with your venue to bring their event to life. Even if you do not have time to make your own, there are plenty of templates available online for free event planning checklists that you can provide to the planner. Either way, you are giving the planner a clear path forward and showing you are a very organized partner.

(y) Be clear about pricing

Another top five factors reported by planners in evaluating venues is that they want a venue to be honest about hidden costs or availability. Planners want to know pricing options and fees upfront. To provide a pricing estimate in your follow-up materials. By emphasizing the anticipated high demand during the specified period, we can leverage scarcity to encourage the planner to take prompt action. It is crucial to note that we can offer a specific price for a limited time, after which it will inevitably increase without the possibility of reverting to the previous rate.

(z) Be proactive

Ask if there are any more questions the planner needs answered to pick you up. If they had any specific questions your set did not answer, add slides for them. And include a copy of the deck.

(zz) Conclude with a clear ask

Ask the planner to get back to you with any questions about the project or a signed contract by a certain date so the work can be started. Let the planner know the next steps by creating a shortlist and the concerned person responsible for acting on them.

(zzz) Follow up consistently

Things can be very hectic for planners. Set yourself calendar reminders in your sales and catering system to follow up. Try to provide value to the planner with every reminder. You can send information about possible upgrades for their event, news or articles, or new photos of your space. You could let them know you have heard from several planners this week, or keep them updated about availability. Or you could ask questions to keep the conversation going such as asking if anything about their event requirements has changed, or when they are hoping to decide.

Learn more about hotel virtual tours

How do I create a virtual tour?

Use Social Tables to create a diagram. Just drag and drop objects to bring your hotel rooms to life.

Are virtual tours worth it?

A virtual tour is worth it because it helps planners get a better feel for the space. It can show them what words cannot describe.

Win business with a virtual site visit to your venue.

Now that you have created a stunning virtual visit, use these sales closing techniques to bring group business to your venue. Up next, learn more about upselling.

PROGRESS CHECK

1. What are the virtual events?
2. What are some popular uses of virtual events?
3. Who leads virtual events?
4. Why have virtual events become popular?
5. Which digital platforms are commonly used for virtual events?

MULTIPLE-CHOICE QUESTIONS

1. What is a virtual event?
   (a) An in-person gathering (b) An event conducted over the Internet
   (c) An event with no attendees (d) A phone call
2. Which of the following is NOT a type of virtual event?
   (a) Webinar (b) Conference (c) Concert (d) Exhibition
3. Which technology is commonly used for hosting virtual events?
   (a) Telepathy (b) Virtual reality (VR)
   (c) Smoke signals (d) Augmented reality (AR)
4. What is an advantage of virtual events over physical events?
   (a) Limited reach (b) High costs
   (c) No interactivity (d) Global audience reach
5. What is a platform used for hosting virtual events called?
   (a) Stage (b) Venue (c) Studio (d) Platform
6. Which of the following is a common engagement tool in virtual events?
   (a) Face painting (b) Balloon animals (c) Q & A sessions (d) Rock climbing
7. What is the purpose of a virtual event registration process?
   (a) To collect phone numbers (b) To deter attendees
   (c) To gather attendee information (d) To promote physical events
8. Which of the following is a consideration when planning virtual event content?
   (a) Ignoring audience interests (b) Limited content variety
   (c) One-size-fits-all approach (d) Diverse and engaging content
9. What technology enables participants to interact in real-time during virtual events?
   (a) Snail mail (b) Social media
   (c) Smoke signals (d) Chat and messaging tools
10. What is the term for a virtual event session that is presented in real-time and can be attended by participants from different locations?
    (a) Synchronous session (b) Asynchronous session
    (c) Stationary session (d) Immersive session

11. What aspect of virtual events focuses on creating an environment that mimics real-world experiences?
    (a) Virtual unreality (b) Virtual mimicry
    (c) Virtual reality (d) Virtual eengagement
12. Which of the following is NOT a benefit of virtual events for event planners?
    (a) Reduced logistical complexity (b) Limited data and analytics
    (c) Access to a global audience (d) Increased reach and scalability
13. What is the term for the practice of recording a virtual event session and making it available for later viewing?
    (a) Simulcasting (b) Archiving (c) Live streaming (d) On-demand
14. Which of the following is a potential challenge of virtual events?
    (a) Limited accessibility options (b) High travel costs for attendees
    (c) Unpredictable weather conditions (d) Ease of networking
15. Which of the following is the most disastrous and makes it virtually impossible to run an event
    (a) Event director resigns (b) Major sponsor pulls out
    (c) The cost of the event goes over budget (d) No venue for the event available

Answers to Multiple-Choice Questions

1. (b)	2. (c)	3. (b)	4. (d)	5. (b)	6. (c)	7. (c)	8. (d)
9. (d)	10. (a)	11. (c)	12. (b)	13. (d)	14. (a)	15. (d)	

Chapter 16

Event Sponsorship and Trends

Objectives

After going through this chapter the reader will be able to:

- Understand the benefits of event sponsorship.
- Know various types of sponsorship packages.
- Analyse various event trends.
- Apply AI in event management.

16.1 INTRODUCTION

Events are amazing opportunities to put the brand in front of potential customers. Finding the appropriate events to sponsor is crucial when it comes to achieving marketing success. By financially supporting or sponsoring an event, brands can effectively advertise their products or services and gain exposure to a highly engaged audience. Special events may attract sponsors if they have target markets in common. Sponsorship is an effective tool for promotion of products or services for businesses, and they may get an opportunity to be exposed in the media. Private foundation grants for continuing projects and initiatives: Companies can enhance their brand exposure by sponsoring an event. Funding from private foundations can be utilized to support on-going initiatives.

16.2 EVENT SPONSORSHIP

Event sponsorship, allows brands to promote their brand in exchange for valuable brand exposure and connect with target audience. It is important to carefully select the right events to sponsor to ensure that the targeted audience aligns with the brand's objectives and to maximize the impact of the sponsorship.

16.2.1 Sponsorship Development Plan

Step 1. Brainstorm: Make a large list of companies or groups that would be a good fit for the event as you brainstorm. Include those who may have financial resources and are frequently very active in community activities.

Step 2. Determine purpose: There are two ways to work with sponsors.

(a) Sponsor provides a monetary contribution to the event.

(b) Sponsor and organizer agree upon at revalue.

An example of this would be a media sponsor running ads for the event through their outlets and the organizer would provide credit to that sponsor by including their logo on advertisements, social media mentions, event announcements, etc.

Step 3. Outreach: Once the list of potential sponsors is finalized it is time to start outreach.

It is important to be prepared for the conversation of what an event manager may expect from the sponsor and the benefits that they meant.

Step 4. Agreement: The event planner and the sponsor should draft and sign some form of agreement. This agreement should include the terms discussed during outreach.

Engaging sponsors: Once an event planner has secured a sponsor then it is important to stay in touch with the sponsors throughout planning execution, and wrap up the event. Company contribution is the main source of funding for sponsored events.

During the pre-event phase the event planner needs to consider the terms in the sponsorship agreement. This could include things like going inclusion on marketing materials or social media mentions. Acquisition stage of event planning involves identifying potential sponsors?

Not all sponsors choose to be present during the event, but if they would like to be included, here are some options for the event planner such as providing a tent area where guests of the sponsor could congregate, hang signage (usually provided by the sponsor) prominently throughout the event area, and provide them the chance to distribute free promotional materials. Sponsorship can be sought in different ways as the rare contacting agencies working to match sponsors with causes in need of sponsoring, and bodies related to trade and business whose aim is to endorse commercial organizations in their relationships to seekers of sponsorship or benefaction. An agreement that ensures benefits for both parties, stating the objectives, people responsible, marketing statements, and budget, as well as an evaluation part for measuring the outcome and impacts of the event is needed.

With the budgeted revenue and costs prepared in detail and approved by both clients identify any deviations from the organizing management, serious preparations can start. A strong control mechanism should be created to address any deviations from the norm.

16.3 BENEFITS OF SPONSORING AN EVENT

1. Increase return on investment

Though they usually require some financial commitment, sponsorships provide businesses with excellent exposure, which typically results in a great return on investment (ROI). Sponsorship roles are usually negotiable, which gives the company the level of exposure one is hoping for.

Before the event, one should determine what goals have to be achieved, and can then choose an effective metric to measure the success and decide if that specific sponsorship is worth doing again.

2. Build business relationships

Sponsoring an event or trade show can help the company make connections with non-competing businesses, giving us opportunities for collaboration in the future. Aside from having a strategy for engaging new customers, one should also prepare a plan to introduce themselves and the company to other sponsors and professionals in attendance.

3. Gain valuable insights

One can learn a lot from sponsoring an event, including the:

- Newest industry trends or business ideas.
- Unique selling proposition (USP) of other companies.
- Strategies other businesses use to attract new customers.

4. Expand its content strategy

Sponsorships can provide a great source of new material for a company's content strategy. By promoting one's involvement in an event or activity, one can drive traffic from the event and increase engagement. A great way to do this is by creating content themes and hashtags. Additionally, one can also connect with the host on social media and find new target audiences.

5. Foster a positive reputation

Perhaps one of the biggest benefits of event sponsorship is that it can strengthen the company's image. People typically enjoy supporting brands that invest in their community and spread positive messages.

By sponsoring an important cause, one can attract media attention, set their company apart from larger brands, and inspire brand loyalty by only determining what the target audience cares about, and choosing causes that align with these values in some way.

6. Generate leads

Brand loyalty is largely dependent on emotional connections. By sponsoring events, one can gain exposure to prospective customers and highlight the human side of the company. Additionally, when a representative of the company attends the events that are sponsored, one can learn valuable information about the customers, develop a mailing list and promote the services or products.

Event hosts can usually provide us with information about the attendees beforehand, such as attendance rates. If we conduct research in advance, we can develop a strategy for creating as many leads as possible.

7. Reach sales goals

Aside from gathering leads, we can also generate immediate sales at a consumer event, by looking for events that have high attendance rates and a limited number of direct competitors. In some cases, we can ensure that we are the only vendor in a particular market category by paying an additional fee.

8. Benefit from association

We can often grow the company's positive reputation through branded event marketing. When a company sponsors events or organizations, people often assume that it is reputable and reliable. As a result, consumers have a higher likelihood of purchasing services or products associated with the brands sponsoring high-profile events.

9. Boost brand visibility

Sponsorships can increase brand recognition before, during, and after the actual event by giving the company exposure to new audiences. This often happens through mentions in the press or social media and event advertising, like radio spots, signs, and featured ads. We can take advantage of this exposure by offering attendees free branded materials through promotional giveaways.

10. Engage niche markets

By choosing events that attract the target audience of a particular company, one can ensure that they are connecting with high-quality leads that are interested in our solutions or products.

11. Showcase a service or product

Events provide a great setting for launching feature updates or new products. We can increase our traffic by promoting launches and other incentives, like giveaways on social media before the event.

12. Gain a competitive advantage

When we sponsor an event, we automatically gain an advantage over our absent direct competitors.

13. Interact with prospects

In-person interactions can help us develop a connection between the company and its target audience. One can engage with prospective customers by providing demos or branded merchandise.

14. Establish its authority

As a sponsor, we can position our brand as a credible authority in its niche industry.

16.4 WHY ARE EVENT SPONSORSHIPS VALUABLE TO EVENT PLANNERS?

Event planners know what sponsors gain from event sponsorships, but they spend time and energy creating attractive sponsorship packages and then contact companies they think will align with their events for three main reasons. They are as follows:

16.4.1 Budget

Creating a memorable event can be expensive. The goal of event planners is to attract many people by keeping ticket sales affordable. However, often ticket revenue will not be enough to break even for the event. Getting sponsors for the event is one of the most effective ways of making it financially viable.

16.4.2 Sponsors Lend Credibility

If a person can attend two events that are being organized by the same company, featuring the same speakers, and focusing on the same topic, but one event is sponsored by Microsoft. Now the question arises which event would the person consider more credible?

The answer to this is despite the challenge of partnering with a top brand such as Microsoft, securing recognized and respected brands in a specific industry will give instant credibility to the event.

16.4.3 Bonus Perks

Often, partnering with sponsors results in bonus perks. Depending on whether a local restaurant has agreed to sponsor the event, they may not only provide the food but also allow us to host the event in their space, thereby reducing the event costs significantly.

Additionally, sponsors often provide increased exposure to an event. We can expect our sponsor partner to announce a local event on social media after they sponsor it. Anyone can sign up following their announcement. The benefit of free marketing cannot be overstated.

16.5 WHAT ARE THE TYPES OF EVENT SPONSORSHIP PACKAGES?

Organizers often offer a variety of event sponsorship packages depending on factors such as venue size and type, event type, on–the–day agenda, and break frequency. Most event organizers are very flexible when it comes to putting together a package that suits the needs and goals, but here are a few examples to help one get started.

16.5.1 Financial Sponsors

Sponsors who provide direct financial support to an event are referred to as financial or cash sponsors. This type of event sponsorship agreement involves a company or individual offering money in exchange for promotional or other benefits.

In the case of large-scale events, one can offer individual sponsorship packages to those who agree to contribute. Title sponsorship is a type of event sponsorship which involves the sponsor's name in the event's title.

For an event to reach its full potential, defining the sponsorship level is the first step. Realistic but ambitious goals need to be established. Following this, one can determine which businesses and organizations to tap and what levels of sponsorship to offer.

16.5.2 In-kind Sponsors

In-kind sponsors provide goods and services to an event rather than investing money.

Venue partner

For an event to be successful, choosing the right venue partner is crucial and in this case the sponsor will pay the amount only for displaying their names in the venue. In a survey report by Underback, 82% of event attendees said the location plays a significant role in their decision to attend an event. In addition to planning, we also need to make sure the venue matches the organization's brand and caters to the right audience.

Prize sponsors

Prize sponsors often distribute items branded with their logos to participants for the event. These are a great way to boost brand visibility during an event. Prizes can be awarded based on attendees' level of participation. One must be sure to customize those to fit the company's needs.

Food sponsors

An event is not complete without food. Delicious meals can indeed enhance the experience of attendees. Offering free food is yet another way to motivate attendees.

Catering is more expensive due to higher manpower. Therefore, it is crucial to find a food sponsor for the next big event. This can facilitate mingling between participants and increase event networking.

Digital sponsors

During tech-related events, one will usually find digital sponsors. The company offers an app for the event, poll questions, media walls, or live tweets. With the recent technology change, digital sponsors are becoming more popular in the event planning industry.

People enjoy fast response time and personalization. It is a growing trend to build digital event spaces in the world's most tech-cities, which can benefit venues.

In-kind sponsorships are not only limited to these four examples. The right ones that bring value to both the sponsor and the organization can be found in a variety of ways.

16.5.3 Media Sponsors

Social media likes are common metric used to measure the success of event sponsorship. Media sponsors secure advertising for an event. Event organizers benefit by expanding the media coverage of the event and saving money on marketing, while media sponsors get an extra promotion, improve brand recognition, and create an association with the event.

Often when media companies sponsor an event, they publish articles about the event and share them on social media. They may also post any other type of content according to the agreement.

16.5.4 Promotional Sponsors

Media sponsors are like promotional partners, but the difference between them is that in most, promotional sponsors are individuals, whereas media sponsors are companies and organizations. In most cases, these individuals are well-known social media influencers with a devoted online audience who follow them and trust their opinion.

Companies typically receive recognition during sponsored events by logos on promotional materials, banners, and stages. The popularity of promotional sponsorship is rising steadily and may soon surpass that of media sponsorship. There are several reasons for that. The first reason is that people prefer social media over TV and radio. Secondly, the event promotion made by influencers looks more personal, so followers are more likely to believe it. Overall, personal promotions are more likely to deliver better results and attract a broader audience.

16.5.5 Merchandise Sponsors

It is no secret that everyone likes merchandise, especially when it is useful or unexpected. Providing branded merchandise in the form of tools that attendees may need at the event, like lanyards, pens, or water bottles, is a classic sponsorship opportunity. With virtual events, attendees can receive merchandise delivered directly to their door, giving sponsors a chance to reach their customers in their own homes.

16.6 WHAT DO YOU NEED TO KNOW BEFORE BECOMING AN EVENT SPONSOR?

In activation stage a sponsor leveraging their association with an event to promote their products or services. Potential risk may occur with negative publicity from event controversies. Experiential sponsorship is a type of event sponsorship allows sponsors to create their own branded activities or zones within the event. To be strategic with the choice of events to sponsor and get the most value out of the investment, here are a few questions given below that need to be covered with the event organizer.

16.6.1 Event Theme and Content

The sponsors have to assess the following information to check for relevance with the brand objectives.

- What is the event about? When and where?
- What is the vision, inspiration, and purpose of the event?
- What subjects will the event cover?
- Who are the key personalities featured at the event?
- What are the unique highlights and features that will set it apart from other events?
- Who should attend?
- What are the key benefits of attending?

16.6.2 Event Success Metrics

The following data must be asked for to assess how the organizer's events performed in the past:

- The total number of attendees at the event vs registrants.
- The number of leads and/or meetings each sponsor received.
- The number of attendees for sponsored sessions or workshops.
- The number of in-app impressions (mobile event app).
- The number of social media impressions on the days leading up to, during, and after the event.
- Attendee testimonials and reviews.
- Sponsor testimonials and reviews.

16.6.3 Attendee Profile

Checking for the attendee profile of the event has to be assessed to know how they match the target market.

- What are the demographics – occupation, socioeconomic status, age, gender, etc?
- What are their key interests and aspirations?
- What industries, affiliations, etc., are being represented by the attendees?

16.6.4 Sponsor Package

Below mentioned are a few basic points for determining the value of the event sponsorship package and comparing these with what one would normally spend on traditional advertising.

- Cost of the physical brand exposure.
- Cost of the online brand exposure including reach and frequency.
- The estimated number of audiences that will be exposed to our brand.
- The estimated cost of customer impacts. The event features like sessions, announcements, demonstrations, video showcases, and moments at the event where attendees are confronted with our brand message.
- The estimated cost of media exposure that the event sponsors will receive.

16.7 BIGGEST EVENT TRENDS HAPPENING NOW

The past few years have brought some exciting developments in the events industry and some of these event trends are here to stay. These trends are as follows:

16.7.1 Sustainability

The world is healing up, both figuratively and literally. Concerns around climate change have been one of the major themes of the past decade as an increasing number of individuals and corporations commit to lessen their impact on the environment.

This eco–friendly approach has spilled over into the world of events, which traditionally has been a fairly wasteful industry, thinking about all the plastic water bottles and catering waste along with the merchandise and freebies that often get thrown away as soon as the event is over.

Now the tide is turning and sustainable events are becoming the more popular option.

So, to make an event a sustainable event there are many opportunities from switching to digital ticketing systems to replacing plastic bottles and cutlery with biodegradable alternatives, using seasonal, local produce in catering, and donating leftover food to local charities.

However, travel contributes majorly to the carbon footprint of an event. Event planners can reduce this impact by planning more localized events and even ditching physical events entirely in favour of online events.

As consumers demand brands to develop more sustainable practices, they will also expect events to be planned in a way that will have a minimal environmental impact. Organizations failing to follow this trend may well find that their audience votes with their feet and finds another, greener event to attend next year, keeping in mind that the event is a representation of a brand.

16.7.2 Mindfulness and Wellness

One has to say goodbye to a culture of hustle and grind. Working long hours and putting work over personal life is becoming increasingly unpopular with today's millennial workforce.

The workers of the coming year and beyond favour a more balanced approach – working smarter rather than harder, with more importance placed on the value of mental health and general wellness.

Keeping this in connection with events, all will agree that back-to-back workshops and seminars turns into an exhausting schedule and are an outdated approach.

Over the coming years, expectations to see more events incorporating mindfulness and wellness activities will increase whatever the industry is. This may include meditation and yoga workshops, dedicated brain breaks designed to inspire creativity, unplugged tech–- door activities, massage stations, and other sessions designed around wellness.

Sales forces annual event, dream force has taken this trend to heart by partnering with mindfulness organizations to provide guided meditations and mindfulness sessions during the four-day conference, as well as running yoga sessions and fun runs.

16.7.3 Hybrid Events

Hybrid events allow for the flexibility of a virtual event, but the connection and engagement of an in-person option.

As time passes, hybrid events are being refined and it does not look like they are going away any time soon. A few interesting statistics regarding hybrid events are mentioned below:

- Searches for hybrid events have increased by 237% in the last five years.
- 97% of event marketers believe that the number of hybrid events will increase over the next few years.
- 59% of event marketers believe that hybrid events will be crucial for their event marketing strategy moving forward.

Hybrid events can be any configuration or breakdown of virtual to in-person. Tread lightly though, because more reach and flexibility do not equate to ease of planning.

One must be sure to do extensive research before deciding if this could be the right route for the next event.

16.7.4 Smaller, More Intimate Events

Running a big flashy corporate event may be seen as a badge of success by many companies, but demand is growing for simpler, smaller events with authentic opportunities to meet face to face.

One must stop thinking of events purely as a marketing opportunity and must consider them more as a chance to engage better with the audience and build trust. Consumers are increasingly demanding authenticity from brands and becoming distrustful of big business. Creating more opportunities to speak with individual customers on a one-on-one basis makes a brand feel more personal and less like a faceless corporation.

Smaller events also open the possibility of using more unique boutique event spaces that are more appealing to attendees.

Networking opportunities are a big attraction for many event attendees, aside from the event itself, so one mustmake sure to schedule plenty of free social time and provide casual spaces that promote interaction.

16.7.5 Non-traditional Venues Gain Popularity

90% of research finding state that the event planners agree that events are more likely to be booked in a non-traditional venue than five years ago.

Thinking out of the box, when it comes to the event venue comes with advantages. Choosing a visually appealing venue is more engaging for attendees and encourages them to post images of the event on social media.

Some examples of venues that are becoming more popular for hosting events areinclude warehouses, barns, gardens, museums, art galleries, and co-working spaces.

This doesnot mean that hotels are out completely though. In line with this trend, more hotels are thinking about how they can meet this need for more inspiring surroundings with non-traditional spaces such as rooftops and outdoor venues, or simply offering more options when it comes to event design and styling.

If the weather conditions are good at an outdoor venue, the attendees will appreciate the fresh air and vitamin D that outdoor spaces provide.

Additionally, the growth of ride-sharing apps have made it more practical to host events outside of the typical downtown venues. More accessible and affordable transportation means that organizations can now take advantage of more varied locations and lower-cost event venues.

As more event planners are seeking out new venues for events, this has not gone unnoticed. There is now a new breed of venue-sourcing software available that makes it easier for event planners to find an ideal venue based on several different criteria.

16.7.6 Experience First Events

This should be a no-brainer, as because an event already is an experience. What one should think about is how the script of a work conference can be flipped to prevent it from being boring and just for work.

The homebodies are still out there and some even prefer hybrid events or virtual conferences still. Now the question arises of how to make the in-person event worthwhile.

Some elements of events are inherently experiential so those might come more naturally. Food trucks and swag bags, VIP sections, and photo opportunities.

Other parts of an event could be spiced up a bit. If networking is the only pull to have someone attend live rather than online, then the host must think harder.

Also, digital elements, such as photo booths with fun props can be added or even a hashtag-based photo contest can be conducted. The results must be shared immediately via a QR code or turning the photos into a social wall to display in break spaces or between speakers.

16.7.7 Enhanced Personalization

Advancements in technology mean that consumers are now expecting more personalization in their communications with brands, and this is going beyond digital marketing channels to become a key part of events too.

Big Data and AI are creating more personalization opportunities such as the ability to create a unique event schedule for each attendee, or even just to provide a personalized map of the venue location with nearby points of interest.

Companies using events for marketing can also use data collected about event attendee behaviour to create personalized follow-ups and more highly targeted and optimized marketing messages after event. This practice is commonplace in all the big and popular digital marketing conferences today.

16.7.8 Augmented Reality

Augmented and virtual reality technology solutions are becoming more commonplace and affordable. There are many potential uses for them in events for several different industries.

As per forecasts, the AR and VR industries are forecasted to grow by over 25% over the years, with AR leading the pack.

While VR has already been a bit of an event trend over the last few years, AR is taking over as the most popular technology, mainly because it is more accessible and offers more flexibility in the real world.

VR can certainly help to engage the event attendees and enhance their experience, but it is still seen as somewhat of a novelty. VR can transport event attendees to another world and can be useful for virtual tours and games, but its applications are limited.

While virtual reality creates a completely virtual world, augmented reality adds digital elements to the real-world environment.

AR technology is a more attractive and practical option for many event organizers because the technology is more affordable and accessible and it offers a huge range of possibilities.

AR can be used for interactive product demonstrations, to help attendees learn more about each other and network, to create interactive venue maps, to provide entertainment and opportunities for engagement, and more.

16.8 USE OF AI IN EVENT ORGANIZATION AND ANALYSIS

Another emerging technology seen in the event industry is artificial intelligence.

Event planners can use AI in several different ways from event planning to during the event and for post-event analysis.

Just as e–commerce sites use AI to power their recommendation engines, event planning software has started using AI to assist planners by finding potential attendees, speakers, influencers, and topics and suggesting optimal times and venue locations.

AI-powered Chatbots can be used for pre-event marketing and customer service to answer common questions, automate ticketing and follow-up leads.

Facial recognition is another highly useful application of AI that can be used in events for everything from security and streamlining registration to personalizing experiences.

PROGRESS CHECK

1. Why is finding the appropriate events to sponsor crucial for achieving marketing success?
2. How does event sponsorship allow brands to effectively advertise their products or services?
3. What factors do event organizers consider when offering different event sponsorship packages?
4. Why is it important for brands to carefully select the right events to sponsor?
5. How can brands maximize the impact of event sponsorship on their targeted audience?
6. What do you need to know before becoming an event sponsor?
7. How can we make an event successful?
8. What are the event trends happening now?

MULTIPLE-CHOICE QUESTIONS

1. What is event sponsorship?
   (a) Selling event tickets
   (b) Promoting a company's products
   (c) Financial support from companies for events
   (d) Event planning services

2. Which of the following is a benefit of event sponsorship for companies?
   (a) Increased event planning responsibilities
   (b) Decreased brand visibility
   (c) Limited audience engagement
   (d) Enhanced brand exposure
3. Why do companies engage in event sponsorship?
   (a) To reduce their marketing budget
   (b) To solely support non-profit organizations
   (c) To connect with target audiences and boost brand awareness
   (d) To avoid competition with other companies
4. What is the main source of funding for sponsored events?
   (a) Government grants (b) Individual donations
   (c) Company contributions (d) Ticket sales
5. Which type of event sponsorship involves the sponsor's name in the event's title?
   (a) Venue sponsorship (b) Media sponsorship
   (c) Title sponsorship (d) Product sponsorship
6. Which stage of event planning involves identifying potential sponsors?
   (a) Promotion (b) Execution (c) Evaluation (d) Acquisition
7. What is the primary goal of a company when sponsoring an event?
   (a) Decreasing brand visibility (b) Generating immediate sales
   (c) Building brand recognition and loyalty (d) Restricting customer interaction
8. What is a common metric used to measure the success of event sponsorship?
   (a) Social media likes (b) Event duration
   (c) Revenue from ticket sales (d) Number of event planners
9. In what ways do companies typically receive recognition during sponsored events?
   (a) No recognition is given to sponsors
   (b) Sponsors are mentioned only in private materials
   (c) Logos on promotional materials, banners, and stages
   (d) Sponsors are recognized after the event is over
10. What potential risk might sponsors face when associated with an event?
    (a) Decreased brand visibility
    (b) Enhanced positive brand perception
    (c) Negative publicity from event controversies
    (d) No impact on brand image
11. Which of the following is NOT a common objective of event sponsorship?
    (a) Brand awareness (b) Revenue generation
    (c) Employee training (d) Building relationships with customers
12. Event sponsorship is limited to providing financial support only.
    (a) True (b) False

13. Which type of event sponsorship involves the sponsor's name and logo being prominently displayed at the event venue?
    (a) Title sponsorship (b) Venue sponsorship
    (c) Product sponsorship (d) Community sponsorship
14. What is the primary benefit for sponsors in event sponsorship?
    (a) Cost reduction for the event organizers (b) Tax deductions
    (c) Exposure to a target audience (d) Exclusive access to event entertainment
15. Which stage of the event sponsorship process involves negotiating terms and benefits between the event organizer and the potential sponsor?
    (a) Activation (b) Evaluation (c) Negotiation (d) Post-event
16. What term refers to the act of a sponsor leveraging their association with an event to promote their products or services?
    (a) Activation (b) Promotion (c) Integration (d) Affiliation
17. Which type of event sponsorship allows sponsors to create their own branded activities or zones within the event?
    (a) In-kind sponsorship (b) Experiential sponsorship
    (c) Media sponsorship (d) Logo sponsorship
18. How do sponsors often measure the success of their event sponsorship efforts?
    (a) By the total number of attendees at the event
    (b) By tracking social media engagement and mentions
    (c) By the cost of the sponsorship package
    (d) By the event organizer's profit margin
19. Which type of event sponsorship involves providing products or services instead of direct financial support?
    (a) Cash sponsorship (b) Media sponsorship
    (c) In-kind sponsorship (d) Title sponsorship
20. Which of the following is NOT a common source of event sponsorship?
    (a) Ticket sales (b) Government grants
    (c) Vendor booths (d) Volunteer participation
21. Which of the following is the most correct answer to the question "Why do event sponsors provide financial and in-kind support for an event" ?
    (a) It is their legal obligation to do so
    (b) They are afraid that other companies will do so instead
    (c) They can write off the cost against the tax system
    (d) They anticipate receiving exposure of their brand in a particular market segment

Answers to Multiple-Choice Questions

1. (c)	2. (d)	3. (c)	4. (c)	5. (c)	6. (d)	7. (c)	8. (a)
9. (c)	10. (c)	11. (c)	12. (b)	13. (b)	14. (c)	15. (c)	16. (a)
17. (b)	18. (b)	19. (c)	20. (d)	21. (d)			

Chapter 17

Entrepreneurship in Sports, Leisure and Events

Objectives

After going through this chapter the reader will be able to:

- Know the possibilities to start event/recreational business.
- Understand to meaning, concept, and types of entrepreneurships.
- Work and build entrepreneurial organization.
- Know the importance of sports and leisure in community.

17.1 INTRODUCTION

This chapter deals with the transformative potential of entrepreneurship within the realms of sports, leisure, and events, aiming to drive sustainable growth. It introduces readers to vital tools, strategies, and methodologies that empower sports and leisure organizations to embrace entrepreneurship as a central pillar of their culture. Entrepreneurship embodies the aptitude and willingness to conceive, organize, and manage a business venture, even in the face of uncertainties, with the goal of generating profits. One of the quintessential illustrations of entrepreneurship is the inception of novel enterprises. In the economic context, entrepreneurship, coupled with the judicious utilization of land, labour, natural resources, and capital, can yield financial gains and need to consider return on investment (RoI). Rooted in the spirit of discovery and a willingness to take calculated risks, entrepreneurship plays a pivotal role in bolstering a nation's ability to thrive in an ever-evolving and intensely competitive global arena.

17.2 MEANING OF ENTREPRENEUR

An entrepreneur is an individual endowed with the capability and aspiration to establish, oversee, and steer a start-up enterprise, accompanied by the associated risk, with the intention of reaping financial rewards. A prime exemple of entrepreneurship is the initiation of a fresh business endeavour. Entrepreneurs often serve as fonts of innovative concepts, ushering in new ideas to supplant outdated ones and introducing novel inventions to the market.

The spectrum of entrepreneurship encompasses diverse entities, ranging from small or home-based businesses to multinational corporations. In economics, the profits accrued by entrepreneurs' stem from a blend of land, natural resources, labour, and capital. Pre-event engagement refers to the practice of building relationships with potential attendees and generating buzz before an event. Event entrepreneur creates a unique event identity for proper event branding.

Entrepreneur is a person who start a business staying within the organization. In essence, anyone harbouring the determination to inaugurate a nascent enterprise and confront the inherent risks has the potential to become an entrepreneur.

17.3 TYPES OF ENTREPRENEURSHIPS

17.3.1 Small Business Entrepreneurship

This variant encompasses endeavours such as local hair salons, grocery stores, travel agencies, consultancy firms, artisans, carpenters, plumbers, and electricians. Proprietors of such businesses typically manage their operations and may hire family members or local staff. Their aspiration is often to generate sufficient profit to sustain their families rather than amass vast wealth or dominating an entire industry. Financing for such ventures may arise from personal savings, small business loans, or contributions from friends and family.

17.3.2 Scalable Startup Entrepreneurship

Entrepreneurs adopting this approach embark on ventures with the conviction that their innovative concepts possess the potential to revolutionize the world. They attract investors who share their unconventional outlook and are prepared to think beyond conventional boundaries. Such entrepreneurs prioritize scalable business models and experimental frameworks, seeking out the most talented and forward-thinking personnel. Ventures of this nature necessitate substantial venture capital to fuel and bolster their ambitious projects.

17.3.3 Large Company Entrepreneurship

Prominent corporations traverse distinct life cycles, often fostering growth and sustainability by introducing fresh and inventive products complementing their core offerings. Evolving technology, shifting consumer preferences, emerging competitors, and related factors compel large companies to continually innovate and introduce novel products, thereby addressing new markets. These companies may opt to acquire innovative enterprises or undertake internal product development endeavours in response to the swift pace of technological evolution.

17.3.4 Social Entrepreneurship

This genre of entrepreneurship revolves around the creation of products and services that address societal needs and challenges. The primary objective of social entrepreneurs is to contribute to society's well-being rather than amass profits.

17.4 ENTREPRENEUR

An entrepreneur is an individual who conceives an idea and diligently works to manifest a product or service that garners consumers' interest. Additionally, entrepreneurs establish and nurture the organizational framework required to support their endeavours. Central to entrepreneurship is the willingness to embrace substantial risk and undertake a proactive role in establishing a new business. Entrepreneurs are often lauded as visionaries and innovators, driving forward novel concepts and solutions.

17.4.1 Entrepreneurs Exhibit Diverse Traits, each Contributing to their Dynamic Profiles. Common Attributes Encompass

- Appreciation of autonomy and flexibility.
- Innovativeness and creativity.
- Goal-oriented nature, coupled with ambitious aspirations.
- A propensity for inventive thinking.
- Fearlessness in tackling challenges.
- Proficiency in problem-solving.
- Self-driven initiative.
- Profound grasp of fundamental financial principles.

17.5 PROS AND CONS OF ENTREPRENEURSHIP

While aspiring entrepreneurs stand to reap substantial recognition and financial rewards from the establishment of a thriving enterprise, entrepreneurship is not devoid of challenges. Here is an overview of the pros and cons.

17.5.1 Pros of Entrepreneurship

1. **Work flexibility:** Entrepreneurship affords the liberty of self-employment, empowering individuals to dictate their schedules and choose their work locations.
2. **Passion pursuit:** When an innovative idea aligns with personal passions or hobbies, entrepreneurship allows individuals to convert their interests into viable careers.
3. **Total autonomy:** Entrepreneurs wield complete control over their ventures, enabling swift decision-making and the implementation of their vision.
4. **Creative licence:** Free from the bureaucratic constraints often present in larger corporations, entrepreneurs can adopt creative problem-solving strategies and engage in experimentation.
5. **Unlimited earning potential:** The success of a groundbreaking business concept can catapult entrepreneurs, such as Mark Zuckerberg and Bill Gates, to staggering financial heights.

17.5.2 Cons of Entrepreneurship

1. **Financial risk:** Entrepreneurs assume financial liability for their initiatives. In the event of failure, they must navigate disappointed investors and manage outstanding loans.
2. **Long working hours:** The journey from conceiving novel ideas to securing potential investors and overseeing day-to-day operations entails arduous effort, resulting in prolonged working hours.
3. **Heightened Responsibility:** As leaders of their ventures, entrepreneurs shoulder the expectations of providing vision and direction, often leading to substantial personal stress.
4. **Intense competition:** Novel business ideas are likely to encounter fierce competition, either from established industry players or fellow entrepreneurs striving to outpace one another.
5. **Irregular income:** While triumphant entrepreneurs may ultimately bask in financial rewards, instant gratification is rare. As they channel earnings into business growth, lean times may ensue.

17.6 CHARACTERISTICS OF ENTREPRENEURSHIP

Not all entrepreneurs achieve success; however, specific traits contribute to the triumph of entrepreneurship.

Key attributes include:

1. **Risk-taking aptitude:** Entrepreneurs exhibit the courage to assess and undertake calculated risks, a pivotal facet of entrepreneurial endeavours.
2. **Innovativeness:** Successful entrepreneurship hinges on the generation of novel ideas, initiating startups, and extracting profits. Innovation encompasses the introduction of groundbreaking products or more efficient processes.
3. **Vision and leadership:** Entrepreneurs must harbour a clear vision for their ventures. Leadership acumen is indispensable for translating ideas into reality and guiding employees towards the path of triumph.
4. **Open-mindedness:** Entrepreneurship thrives on harnessing opportunities presented by varied circumstances. Pioneering companies like Paytm capitalized on the dynamics of demonetization, bolstering their presence during the transition.
5. **Adaptability:** Entrepreneurs must readily embrace change as per situational demands. Flexibility facilitates the timely alteration of products and services to suit evolving market requirements.
6. **Product mastery:** Profound comprehension of product offerings and awareness of prevailing market trends are crucial for entrepreneurial success. Entrepreneurs must gauge if existing products satisfy market needs or necessitate modification.

17.7 IMPORTANCE OF ENTREPRENEURSHIP

1. **Creation of employment:** Entrepreneurship engenders employment opportunities, offering entry-level positions vital for skill acquisition and training among the unskilled workforce.
2. **Catalyzing innovation:** Entrepreneurship serves as a catalyst for innovation, yielding novel product lines, technological advancements, enhanced product quality, and heightened living standards.
3. **Societal and community development:** A flourishing entrepreneurial landscape contributes to the advancement of society, fostering diverse employment prospects, improved educational facilities, superior sanitation, reduced slum dwellings, and elevated rates of homeownership. This synergy fortifies community well-being and stability.
4. **Enhancing standard of living:** Entrepreneurial pursuits elevate individual income, directly translating to an improved standard of living characterized by elevated consumption of goods and services.
5. **Research and Development (R&D) support:** Entrepreneurs fuel research and development endeavours by collaborating with research institutions and universities, thereby propelling innovation and economic growth.

Incorporating cutting-edge research, innovation paradigms, and interdisciplinary insights, this chapter introduces fundamental entrepreneurship, innovation, and enterprise concepts. Topics encompass digitalization, research, and development (R&D), diversification, extensibility, and sustainability. The chapter seamlessly interweaves perspectives from industry veterans, addressing day-to-day management dilemmas and underlining the significance of social enterprise and social entrepreneurship amid challenging socio-economic conditions.

Replete with real-world case studies, scenarios, and engaging features that prompt critical contemplation, this chapter is indispensable reading for academic courses delving into entrepreneurship in sports management, leisure, sports studies, recreation, event studies, entertainment management, and tourism. It equally enthrals practitioners seeking to elevate their professional acumen in these domains.

17.8 CREATING A SPORT AND LEISURE ENTREPRENEURSHIP CONCEPT

Originally coined by Schumpeter, entrepreneurship was defined as recognizing the commercial potential within a novel invention and exploiting it to extract added value from the market. This viewpoint emphasizes that entrepreneurial opportunities thrive during market shocks and cycle disruptions, leveraging uncertainty and risk to yield greater rewards. Given that sports entrepreneurship exists as a subset of entrepreneurship, the concept of sport entrepreneurship inherently relies on entrepreneurial theory. Scholars converge on the notion that entrepreneurship within academia centres on the process of identifying, capitalizing on opportunities, and subsequently generating value. This understanding prompted us to bifurcate the process into two phases, enabling a comprehensive exploration of the interaction between sport and entrepreneurship at each juncture.

The concept of entrepreneurial orientation (EO) emerges as a pivotal driver for uncovering opportunities, navigating emerging threats, harnessing existing resources, and crafting innovative processes, products, and services to excel in a competitive market. EO stands as a strategic framework dictating an organization's operations, with entrepreneurial behaviour shaping the organization's characteristics, decisions, activities, processes, and overall performance.

In contrast to other service or entertainment sectors, impermanence and uncertainty emerge as significant attributes within the realm of sports. Sports management is inherently entwined with managing uncertainty, as the outcome of any sporting event remains unpredictable. Unlike choreographed entertainment realms like theatre, the essence of sports hinges on unpredictability, creating suspense, excitement, and a captivating spectator experience.

Risk, distinct from uncertainty, is calculable and predictable. Entrepreneurs set themselves apart by proactively seeking uncertain opportunities for profit. Navigating uncertainty, and capitalizing on its potential benefits, becomes feasible with an entrepreneurial mindset. Organizations adept at formulating strategies to navigate uncertainty outperform those who do not. The willingness to embrace uncertainty defines the entrepreneur, a quality profoundly present in entrepreneurship, including sports where the thrill arises from uncertain outcomes.

An entrepreneurial mindset facilitates evaluating impact of uncertainty on organizational behaviour, fostering heightened value creation and consequent competitive advantage. Persistence in exploring new opportunities remains integral to entrepreneurial success. Risk, often in the form of uncertainty, unveils opportunities. Identifying these opportunities is fundamental to commencing an entrepreneurial venture. Individuals inclined toward greater risk tolerance are more likely to pursue an entrepreneurial career. Entrepreneurship is inherently tied to innovation, driving economic growth by creating and commercializing novel ideas.

17.9 BUILDING AN ENTREPRENEURIAL ORGANIZATION

1. Hiring entrepreneurial individuals

Entrepreneurial DNA characterizes these individuals. Inquisitive and critical of the status quo, they often defy authority and stand out as innovative thinkers. Their propensity for generating a plethora of ideas, albeit eccentric, serves as a driving force for creativity.

2. Learning to manage

Entrepreneurial individuals thrive on meaningful and challenging projects. Routine tasks and autopilot assignments repel them. Managers must navigate their idiosyncrasies, recognize their intrinsic motivation, and harness their strengths.

3. Building entrepreneurial teams

Innovation results from coordinated teamwork, necessitating the assembly of entrepreneurial teams. Synergy within such teams arises from congruent beliefs, complementary skills, and harmonious styles.

4. Creating an entrepreneurial culture

This pivotal aspect empowers every employee to exhibit entrepreneurial behaviour, fostering risk-taking, decision-making autonomy, experimentation, and a culture of exploration. Trust and autonomy are paramount, with employees treated as equals in driving the organization's vision.

In essence, entrepreneurship is a dynamic force propelling progress. It embodies individual innovation, organizational growth, and societal advancement. While entrepreneurship is often linked to new business ventures, its essence transcends this realm. Whether running a business, being self-employed, or being employed by others, individuals can display entrepreneurial orientation and drive innovation. Modern corporations recognize the value of entrepreneurship, infusing innovation into their core strategies to remain agile and competitive. Thus, fostering entrepreneurship requires deliberate cultivation, encompassing hiring the right talent, effective management, team synergy, and the creation of a culture that celebrates risk-taking and innovation.

17.10 STRATEGY IN ENTREPRENEURSHIP, SPORTS, AND LEISURE

Entrepreneurship serves as a transformative process, fostering social change, economic advancement, and novel service/product offerings through the stimulation of creativity and innovative ideas. As a potent catalyst for overcoming economic crises, entrepreneurship fuels robust economic development and generates fresh employment opportunities. Academicians and researchers across disciplines have increasingly gravitated toward entrepreneurship as a realm of discovery and explanation.

Within this expansive landscape, sports entrepreneurship emerges as a dynamic and continually evolving facet of the business and management domain. It encapsulates innovative social endeavours executed in a sports context, aimed at forging new markets, and fostering social inclusion. Sports organizations' managers find entrepreneurial knowledge and skills imperative, especially within the challenging sports industry landscape.

An entrepreneurial perspective in sports offers potential solutions to economic decline and unveils novel opportunities crucial for value creation. This approach, particularly vital in hostile sports environments, propels sports organizations toward professionalism and heightened competitiveness. Sports entrepreneurs, acting as change agents within the sports sector, drive productivity enhancement, elevate user experiences, and stimulate market development.

Theoretical foundations for sports entrepreneurship trace back to Hardy, who proposed a tripartite model delving into the analysis of entrepreneurship within sports. Hardy's model encompasses the sports product, the roles of entrepreneurs and managers in product development, and the creation of diverse organizational forms. Schumpeter's entrepreneurial model aligns well with sports entrepreneurs, as risk-taking, proactivity, innovation, and profit-seeking resonate within both fields. Notably, professional soccer teams epitomize this entrepreneurial spirit, akin to small and medium enterprises in terms of organizational characteristics.

Recent years have witnessed the integration of Hardy's tripartite model by Porter, who emphasized the importance of media in disseminating sports and underlined the entrepreneurial process's role in forming networks, exploiting innovative combinations, and fostering value creation.

While the significance of entrepreneurship in sports is indisputable, limited entrepreneurial activity within the sports sector has prompted an academic focus on nurturing entrepreneurial skills among younger generations, particularly university students and marginalized youth. Sports for Development (SFD) programmes, removing socio-cultural barriers and harnessing the power of sports, stand as tools for inclusive action, enhancing personal development, and increasing avenues for social inclusion.

In this context, this study's objective is to comprehensively analyse empirical research and theoretical advancements in sports entrepreneurship. This endeavour seeks to glean insights into the present research landscape, identify strengths, weaknesses, and potential directions, and lay the foundation for future explorations. Evaluation is the last phase of event entrepreneurship, involving a comprehensive review of the event's success and failures.

17.11 IMPORTANCE OF SPORT AND LEISURE IN COMMUNITY

Sport and leisure play a pivotal role in community well-being and cohesion, driven by several key factors

Emotions

Sport evokes profound emotions, ranging from joy to testing one's patience. The interplay between these emotions imparts valuable life skills, serving as an outlet for emotional release. Positive emotions that promote mutual respect and love for the game contribute to both physical and emotional well-being.

Community involvement

Various sports levels, from amateur to professional, engage with charity organizations, making positive community contributions. Athletes serve as mentors, dedicating time, and expertise to support the community and foster positive change.

Promoting physical activity

In an era where obesity rates are rising, sports serve as a powerful tool to combat sedentary lifestyles. Role models in sports encourage individuals to engage in physical activities, promoting weight control, mental health, and overall well-being.

National unity

Sport serves as a unifying force, rallying individuals to support their country in international events. National pride and unity are amplified during events like the Olympics and World Cups.

Provincial/city pride

Sports foster camaraderie among residents of the same city, united in their support for local teams and clubs.

Job opportunities

The sports industry provides a range of career options beyond athleticism, including health services, sales, marketing, administration, and media. These roles contribute significantly to the industry's growth and well-being.

Economic impact

The sports industry generates substantial revenue, stimulating economic growth through ticket sales, broadcasting rights, and marketing. It also bolsters indirect job opportunities through tourism and related businesses.

Enhancing employability

Sports teach essential life skills, such as resilience, teamwork, and problem-solving. Engaging in sports at a young age cultivates critical skills needed for personal and professional success, especially in an ever-changing world.

Sports ecosystem

A holistic approach to sports encompasses a multi-dimensional ecosystem involving diverse stakeholders, power dynamics, and human rights considerations. This approach positions individuals and their rights at the core of sports, recognizing the interconnectedness and interdependence of various actors and institutions.

Athletes, coaches, administrators, fans, volunteers, and more collectively form the sports ecosystem. This intricate web of relationships can impact individuals and communities, highlighting the importance of safeguarding human rights. Vulnerable groups, including minorities, people with disabilities, and marginalized populations, warrant special attention within this framework.

The sports ecosystem encompasses private, public, and third-sector entities operating at different levels, from local to global. Institutions, including sports bodies, are integral to the ecosystem but are only one facet among many. Each action, decision, and behaviour within this framework can reverberate across the entire ecosystem, affecting trust and legitimacy.

Adopting a human rights lens helps ensure responsible sport, promoting the well-being of athletes and all stakeholders. The centre's inclusive approach fosters engagement with all actors to uphold human rights and create a positive impact.

PROGRESS CHECK

1. Who is the father of entrepreneurship?
2. What are the two main types of entrepreneurships?
3. What are the key concepts of entrepreneurship?
4. What are entrepreneur traits?
5. Write a short note on importance of sports and leisure in community

MULTIPLE-CHOICE QUESTIONS

1. What does ROI stand for in the context of event entrepreneurship?
   (a) Return on investment (b) Reach of influence
   (c) Return of interest (d) Rate of income
2. A person who starts a business staying within the organization
   (a) Intrapreneur (b) Entrepreneur
   (c) Start-up (d) None of these
3. Which stage of event planning involves defining the event's objectives, target audience, and budget?
   (a) Execution (b) Evaluation
   (c) Planning (d) Promotion
4. What term refers to the practice of building relationships with potential attendees and generating buzz before an event?
   (a) Post-event analysis (b) Pre-event engagement
   (c) Event debriefing (d) On-site interaction
5. What does SWOT analysis assess for event entrepreneurship?
   (a) Event venue options
   (b) Social media engagement
   (c) Event ticket pricing
   (d) Strengths, Weaknesses, Opportunities, Threats
6. What is the primary goal of event branding?
   (a) Maximizing vendor profits (b) Minimizing event costs
   (c) Creating a unique event identity (d) Expanding event duration
7. Which form of sponsorship involves a company providing financial support in exchange for prominent logo placement?
   (a) Experiential sponsorship (b) In-kind sponsorship
   (c) Logo sponsorship (d) Cash sponsorship
8. What is the term for a targeted marketing strategy that focuses on creating content relevant to potential attendees?
   (a) Mass marketing (b) Guerrilla marketing
   (c) Content marketing (d) Viral marketing
9. What technology can enhance attendee engagement by allowing them to interact digitally during presentations?
   (a) Virtual reality (VR) (b) Augmented reality (AR)
   (c) Fax machines (d) Cassette tapes
10. What is the last phase of event entrepreneurship, involving a comprehensive review of the event's success and failures?
    (a) Planning (b) Execution
    (c) Debriefing (d) Evaluation

Answers to Multiple-Choice Questions

1. (a) 2. (a) 3. (c) 4. (b) 5. (d) 6. (c) 7. (d) 8. (c)
9. (b) 10. (d)

Glossary

Account: An ordered record of public supports showing receipts, payment, and the equilibrium.

Active recreational activities: Physical pursuits and exercises undertaken during leisure time, such as sports, hiking, or biking, contribute to physical fitness and well-being.

Administrative close down: This side of the close-down will involve filing, completion of accounts and paying bills, and collecting feedback.

Affecting: The vital component of initiative, performed through conveying, direction, and inspiration. A supervisor instructs individuals, while a pioneer rouses individual by making a craving inside them to get things done all alone.

Agenda: A list of speakers, presentations, and associated timings, given conference delegates as part of the pre-registration or on-site registration.

Agon: Competitive play, such as sports or games.

Alea: Chance-based play, such as gambling or lottery.

Amateur sports: Sporting events where participants engage without remuneration.

Ambassador: A brand ambassador is whose employer your organization and communicates as a delegate of the organization. An ambassador can be a salesman, leader, or even a customer service delegate.

Ambient music: Background music that enhances the atmosphere of an event without being the primary focus, usually selected to match the theme or mood.

Asana: It is our go-to tool for keeping track of all the moving components in event planning.

Assistant director: He who helps the Director by taking notes on all moves and different choices and holding them together in one duplicate of the content. In certain organizations this is finished by the Stage Manager, on the grounds that there is no assistant.

Assistant stage manager (ASM): One more name for stage team (as a rule, in the expert theatre, likewise a student for one of the minor jobs who is, thus, additionally understudying a significant job). The most minimal bar on the expert performance centre stepping stool.

Atmosphere: The overall mood and sensory experience that guests feel upon entering an event space, influenced by decorations, lighting, music, and more.

Attendance: The overall number of people at an event.

Audio-Visual: Has both a sound and visual component. Typically, in the form of images and recorded speech or music.

Award ceremony: An event where the performance of individuals and groups in a company or industry are recognized. It is used to honour and motivate key staff.

Awareness: What number of individuals are known about an organization and its items or services? Awareness ought to be checked on a size of poor to incredible, which estimates how well individuals understand what items/services an organization offers and what is truly going on with an organization.

Backup plan: A contingency plan is an essential part of any event's preparations.

Benchmark: A quantifiable exhibition level used to evaluate the degree to which programme targets are being gotten.

Board meetings: Scheduled annual meetings of a corporation's board of directors.

Brand awareness: The extent to which a business or organization is recognized and associated with its products, services, or values.

Brand exposure: The visibility and recognition gained by a brand when it is showcased or advertised to a target audience.

Budget process: The process of deciphering, arranging and programming choices into explicit monetary plans.

Budget: An arrangement of monetary activity exemplifying a gauge of uses for a given period and the proposed method for funding them (income gauges).

Buffet arrangement: The organized setup of food and beverages on a buffet table, often following a specific layout to ensure ease of access for guests.

Business model: The framework that outlines how a business operates, generates revenue, and delivers value to customers, encompassing key elements such as target market, revenue streams, cost structure, and distribution channels.

Capability: Ability is conduct-based and portrays the singular's qualities and character. Skills can likewise be mastered, yet because of their conduct-based nature, it is unimaginable just to instruct or quantify them.

Cash management: The process of overseeing monies for the event to guarantee working cash accessibility and safe venture of inactive cash.

Cisco WebEx: A web conferencing platform used for virtual meetings and events.

Client: The person or party of an event planner and/or various event components required to hold the event.

Communicating: Contains the capacity to communicate one's thoughts in individual and gathering circumstances, either orally or recorded as a hard copy. It includes a shipper communicating a plan to a collector.

Concert: A performance of music in public by singers and/or instrumentalists for the purpose of entertainment. Concerts can take many different forms – paid or unpaid, for profit or charity, indoors or outdoors.

Confectionery: The section within F&B that deals with creating and presenting desserts, sweets, and baked goods, often contributing to the aesthetic appeal of an event.

Conference: Debate or discussion on a narrow topic; often convened by an academic group and following a strict set of guidelines. While educating attendees is certainly one of the conference's aims, it also serves as a venue for participants to share what they have learnt. It is often held in conjunction with a larger gathering such as a congress or symposium.

Conventions: Large events organized by associations to discuss important issues, often lasting several days.

Cooperative play: It involves children collaborating and working together in organized activities with shared goals.

Corporate retreats: Organizational gatherings for team building exercises, training, and strategic planning.

Creative process: The process of engaging in a series of exercises meant to spark original thought.

Creativity: The capacity to create, bring into existence, transform into a new form, produce through imaginative skill, and produce something new.

CRM: Customer relationship management.

Customer service: Everyone from your association is liable for a great encounter for clients. It can represent the moment of truth for your association's brand.

Destination marketing: Using events to build reputation and promote destinations for business and tourism.

Emcee: The master of ceremonies or host of an event, responsible for engaging the audience, introducing acts, and guiding the flow of the event.

Empathy: Ability to understand and share the feelings of others.

Engagement: The level of interaction, involvement, or participation from attendees or participants during a virtual event.

Entertainment: A show or performance designed to amuse an entertaining audience.

Entrepreneurial mindset: A set of attitudes, behaviours, and thinking patterns characterized by a willingness to take risks, seize opportunities, think creatively, and adapt to changing circumstances.

Etiquette: It refers to customary behaviours, manners and social conventions that govern interactions in a specific culture or context, promoting respectful and appropriate conduct in various situations.

Customary code of polite behaviour in society or among the members of a particular profession or group.

Event advertising: Promoting occasions to attract attendees through strategic communication and marketing efforts.

Event communication: It is a non-media communication tool used by organizations to spread the word about an upcoming event, such as a trade show, conference, incentive programme, gala banquet, etc., whether it is intended for internal or external consumption. Like an advertising agency, a specialised firm is responsible for conceptualising and executing this event.

Event design: It is the thoughtful arrangement of elements like décor, lighting and layout to create impactful and memorable event experiences.

Event evaluation: Process of measuring how an event turned out.

Event logistics: Event logistics is the discipline concerned with the planning, control, and management of the flow of resources and the physical and immaterial activities involved in the production of an event.

Event manager: A person in charge of planning, organizing, and executing all types and sizes of events.

Event planner: A person who coordinates all aspects of professional meetings and events.

Event proposal: It is a brief / synopsis of an event.

Event sponsorship: Financially supporting or sponsoring an event to promote a brand in exchange for valuable brand exposure.

Event sponsorship packages: Different levels or options for sponsorship that event organizers offer.

Event staffing: Enough employees are hired to manage the responsibilities necessary for a successful event.

Event staging: Examine the needs for event setup.

Event theme: A central idea or concept that guides the overall design, decor, and atmosphere of an event, often reflecting a particular time, culture, or location.

Exercise: It contributes to the prevention of degradation, biological degeneration, and increases the body's ability to counteract some tensions.

Exhibitions: Events showcasing new goods, services, and knowledge to potential customers.

F&B (Food and Beverage): The department responsible for planning, preparing, and serving food and drinks at events, ensuring high-quality culinary experience.

Facebook live: A feature on Facebook that enables live video streaming.

Fair: A live, public gathering for a variety of commercial or entertainment activities. It could last for a single afternoon or for a few weeks.

Far-reaching development: An event connected with and respecting society in its different structures and viewpoints and considered an important, advancing, and edifying for the public.

Feedback: The process of sharing thoughts and observations – positive or negative.

Gender differences: Disparities in leisure and recreational activities, attitudes, and behaviours between men and women, often influenced by factors such as societal norms, personality attributes, and lifestyle.

Goal: A long-range explanation of wide heading, reason, or purpose, considering the necessities of the event. A specific strategy's intended outcome; frequently used in place of event objective.

Gratitude: It is a feeling of thankfulness for something received or experienced.

Guest experience: The collective interactions and impressions that attendees have during an event, including the decor, entertainment, other services, and overall ambience.

Health and well-being sessions: Virtual sessions focused on fitness, yoga, and mental well-being, offered to support individuals during challenging times.

Housekeeping: The department responsible for maintaining cleanliness and orderliness in the event space, including setting up and cleaning after events.

Human services agencies: Organizations that provide a wide range of services to support individuals and communities, such as group homes, mental health centres, and family services agencies.

Ilinx: It is dizzying or vertiginous play, such as spinning around or riding a roller coaster.

Image: How a brand is seen by its interest group. The way a brand appears to expected customers or clients is vital for the progress of an organization.

Incentive travel: A management strategy rewarding employees, sales representatives, etc., with travel experience as incentives.

Independent direction: The process of arriving at obvious end results, tackling issues, investigating verifiable data, and making fitting moves in view of the ends.

Independent work group: A little free, self-coordinated, and self-controlling gathering in which individuals plan, sort out, decide, and deal with their obligations and activities, as well as carry out numerous other strong roles.

Indoor recreation: Recreational activities that take place within enclosed spaces, such as art, music, dance, or other creative pursuits, provide entertainment and personal growth.

Innovation: The process of introducing new ideas, products, services, or methods that create value and lead to positive changes within an organization or industry.

Input: The progression of data back to the student so that genuine execution can measure up to arranged execution.

Intangible: Brand resources unequipped for being contacted. These all work together to make the substance of the brand. Intangibles incorporate brand names, skill, plans, and so on.

Integrity: The value of honesty and honesty alone should be self-evident.

International conferences: Gatherings involving participants from different countries to share information and discuss matters.

Interpersonal skills: Used for connecting with others, gaining insight from them, and inspiring them to action.

Lead generation: The process of attracting and capturing potential customers' interest in a product or service, often through gathering their contact information.

Leadership: It involves guiding, inspiring and influencing individuals towards shared goals and growth.

Leadership is the capacity to inspire and mobilise others to achieve goal.

Learning agility: Knowing what to do when you do not know something is a sign of learning agility.

Learning: A long-lasting shift in attitude or propensity to act because of some kind of learning or exposure to stimuli.

Leisure management: The practice of planning, organizing, and delivering recreational activities, services, and facilities to meet the needs and interests of individuals and communities for leisure and relaxation.

Leisure: The time available for activities outside of work or essential responsibilities, characterized by freedom and the pursuit of personal interests, hobbies, and relaxation.

Live event: Unlike online or virtual events, live events or in-person events have attendees who are physically present at a specific (physical) location.

Live streaming: Broadcasting live video over the Internet in real time, often used on social media platforms to connect with audiences and promote brands.

Logo: An interesting plan or custom image that goes about as the identifier of a brand. It is a visual portrayal of a company's brand.

Manpower planning: The process of assessing, selecting, and managing human resources within an organization to meet its staffing needs effectively.

Market disruption: The significant and often unexpected changes that occur in a market due to the introduction of a new product, service, or business model, altering the competitive landscape.

Marketing success: Achieving desired outcomes and objectives in marketing efforts is often measured by increased brand awareness and sales.

Mega events: Major and mega events are typically events that have global reach and international appeal.

MICE: Acronym for Meetings, Incentives, Conferences, and Exhibitions, referring to the business-oriented tourism sector.

Microsoft teams: A collaborative platform that includes videoconferencing capabilities, often used for virtual events.

Mimicry: It is imitative play, such as pretending to be a superhero or an animal.

Motivation: The motivating factors that guide the reward system. Employees are incentivized to perform in certain ways by the organization's compensation and benefits system, which is comprised of all the people, processes, rules and procedures, and decision-making activities involved in the distribution of pay and perks to workers.

National Recreation and Park Association (NRPA): A leading advocacy organization focused on public parks, recreation, and conservation, working to improve communities and promote research, education, and policy initiatives.

Negotiate: Confer with others to settle the matter smoothly.

Negotiation: The act of coming to terms between two or more organizations whose members have different needs or goals.

Networking: The intentional process of building and nurturing relationships with individuals, organizations, and stakeholders within and beyond one's field, often leading to collaboration, knowledge sharing, and mutual support.

Online trade shows: Digital exhibitions that replicate the experience of in-person trade events, often featuring webinars and opportunities for attendees to visit virtual booths.

Online workshop: A virtual event providing skill-based training and encouraging audience.

Opportunity recognition: The ability to identify and capitalize on potentially advantageous situations or gaps in the market, leading to the development of innovative solutions and business ventures.

Organization: Relationships of command, control, and feedback between individuals and information systems. Examples: A privately owned business, an administration office.

Organizational structure: The arrangement of roles, responsibilities, and relationships within an organization, including elements like authority, accountability, and reporting mechanisms.

Outdoor recreation: Leisure activities that occur in outdoor settings, including parks, gardens, playgrounds, and sports fields, encourage physical activity and interaction with nature.

Passive recreational activities: Calmer and more relaxed leisure activities, such as reading, listening to music, or watching movies, aimed at mental and emotional relaxation.

Play: Engaging in activities for amusement and enjoyment, often involving physical or mental stimulation. It has various physical and psychological benefits.

Power distance: How resigned those with less authority are to their position of inferiority.

Profession: A specialized occupation that requires formal education and offers disinterested objective counsel and services to others, typically for direct compensation, and is distinct from other business interests.

Professional competence: The mastery of skills, knowledge, and abilities required for effective performance within a specific profession.

Professional development: Activities aimed at enhancing skills, knowledge, and expertise, often through continuing education, research, networking, and other growth-oriented endeavours.

Professional organization: A group or society dedicated to advancing a specific profession's interests, advocating for its practitioners, and promoting the public good within that field.

Props: Something you use as a support for the beautification or match the theme of the event.

Protocol: The word 'protocol' literally translates to 'first glue' in Greek. Protocol is the 'glue' that keeps society's formal institutions functioning smoothly.

Recreation services: Facilities, programmes, and initiatives provided by government agencies, voluntary organizations, and private entities to offer opportunities for leisure, entertainment, and personal development.

Recreation: Activities undertaken for enjoyment, relaxation, or pleasure, aimed at restoring energy and well-being. These activities can be physically, mentally, or emotionally uplifting.

Registration fee: Cost of attending conference. Fees can vary according to the time of registration, level of participation and membership type.

Rehearsal: Practice or mock show before the actual event.

Reliability: The intangible bond considering a genuine commitment; it involves the right requesting of our commitments and responsibilities. Faithfulness requests obligation to the association and is a precondition for trust, collaboration, cooperation, and fellowship.

Resilience: The capacity to bounce back and recover from setbacks, challenges, or failures, demonstrating adaptability and perseverance in the face of adversity.

Restoration: The process of renewing one's energy, mental state, and overall well-being through leisure and recreational activities, often resulting in increased productivity and a sense of balance.

Seminar: A professional conference involving discussions and presentations on specific topics. The seminar is usually organised by a private firm with the goal of teaching and exchanging on a certain subject, and it brings together experts who may or may not be members of the same organizing committee/organization.

Stakeholder: A person with an interest in the objectives and outcome of an event.

An individual or gathering with an interest in the outcome of an association in conveying planned results and keeping up with the suitability of the association's items and administrations.

Stopover/transfer: The term "stopover" is used when a group of travellers stays in one location for more than 24 hours. The traveller is considered a transfer if they do not exit the airport or if their total time in the nation is shorter than 24 hours.

Strategic alliances: Collaborative partnerships formed between organizations to leverage each other's strengths, resources, and expertise, often with the goal of achieving common objectives or entering new markets.

Strategy: A way to deal with involving assets inside the imperatives of the climate to accomplish a bunch of goals. An association figures out a strategy in view of the climate, and states the goals, targets, and the way things will meet the goals through strategies to direct its centre business capabilities.

Strengthening: A condition by which representatives have the position to decide and make a move in their workspaces, occupations, or tasks without earlier endorsement. It permits the representatives the obligation regularly connected with staffs. Models are planning, quality, or buying choices.

Sustainability: The practice of conducting business and operations in a way that preserves and enhances environmental, social, and economic well-being for present and future generations, aiming for long-term viability.

SWOT: Acronym for Strength, Weakness, Opportunity, and Threats.

Tangible: Resources that can touched or felt, like structures, property, items, and bundling.

Target market: The ideal potential customer crowd. The most effective way to figure out who is in your target market includes: making a customer profile of a phony individual who addresses your optimal client.

Targeted audience: The specific group of people or customers that a brand aims to reach and engage with through its marketing.

Technology: Industrial processes are the combination of mechanical and mental steps necessary to get from raw materials to finished goods.

The physical close: Close Taking apart and removing the equipment, etc.

Theme decoration: The process of creating a visually cohesive and immersive atmosphere that aligns with a specific theme or concept for an event.

Timelines: Setting deadlines and committing to action.

Toddlerhood: Children age group of 2-3 years.

Trade Mart: The term 'trade mart' is often used to refer to a large, permanent commercial building that has several retail showrooms showcasing the goods and services of a variety of sectors.

Trade shows: Exhibitions where businesses display products and services to potential buyers.

Travel incentive or incentive: A type of group travel that is paid for by businesses to send their employees or customers on unforgettable trips lasting a few days. Motivating force events are dependably live/in-person events.

Uncertainty: The state of not having enough information to make an informed choice on the likelihood of various events.

Value creation: The act of generating benefits, advantages, or improvements that enhance the worth or desirability of a product, service, or organization, ultimately meeting the needs and preferences of customers.

Value proposition: What your client gets when they pay for your item or service. It for the most part incorporates the significant benefit of picking you over a contender.

Venue manager: The person in charge of allocation or event space.

Venues: The location where something is going to take place. Restaurants, reception halls, and nightclubs are all referred to as 'venues' in the meetings, incentives, conventions, and exhibitions.

Virtual career fairs: Events that facilitate job seekers and employers to interact through one-on-one video chats, job boards, and assessment tools in a virtual environment.

Virtual conference: A multi-day event featuring keynotes, panel discussions, and educational sessions, hosted online to bring together people with a shared interest in a specific industry.

Virtual event: An event that brings people together digitally, using various platforms and tools to create an interactive experience.

Virtual networking: Events that allow individuals to connect with like-minded professionals to discuss and share ideas, typically included as part of conferences or webinars.

Vision: An objective that lies outside the scope of arranging. It depicts on association's most positive future state.

Webinars: Online seminars or presentations can reach a wide audience, allowing attendees to connect without active participation.

Welcome signage: A sign that introduces or welcomes visitors to the venue/event.

Well-being: A state of physical, mental, and emotional health and happiness, often achieved through activities that promote relaxation, personal growth, and positive emotions.

Workshop: Activities in workshops tend to be more interactive and communal. People are required to engage in the seminars because they are extremely engaging.

Zoom: A popular video conferencing platform used for hosting virtual events.

References

Balachandran, S. (2004). Knowing the customer. In: Customer-Driven Services Management (pp. 66-67): Response Books.

Berridge, G. (2006) Events Design and Experience. Oxford: Butterworth-Heinemann.

Bowdin, G. A. J. (2011) Events Management. 3rd Edn., London: Butterworth-Heinemann.

Bechky, B.A., Okhuysen, G.A. (2011) Expecting the unexpected? How SWAT officers and film crews handle surprises. *Academy of Management Journal* 54: 239-261.

Brent Ritchie, J. R. (1984). Assessing the impact of hallmark events: Conceptual and research issues. *Journal of Travel Research,* 23(1), 2-11. https://doi.org/10.1177/004728758402300101.

Columbus, G. and Goldblatt, J. J. (2010) The Complete Guide to Careers in Special Events: Step Toward Success! New York: Wiley.

Commun Hall, C.M., (1992). Hallmark Tourist Events: Impacts, Management and Planning. Belhaven: London.

Cooper, C., Fletcher, J., Fyall, A., Gilbert, D. & Wanhill, S. (2008). Tourism, Principles and Practice. Essex: Pearson-Prentice Hall.

Davidson, R. and Rogers, T. (2006) Marketing Destinations and Venues for Conferences, Conventions and Business Events: A Convention and Event Perspective. Oxford: Butterworth-Heinemann.

Ferdinand, N. and Kitchin, P. (2012) Events Management: An International Approach. Los Angeles, [Calif.]: Sage.

Fenich, G. (2007). Meetings, Expositions, Events & Conventions. New Jersey: Pearson-Prentice Hall.

G. Berridge (2007). Events Design and Experience, Elsevier Ltd. Great Britain 2007.

Getz, D. (2005). Event Management and Event Tourism. 2nd Edn., Cognizant Corporations.

Getz, D. (2007). Event Management and Event Tourism. New York: Cognizant Corporations.

Getz, D. (2016) Event Studies: Theory, Research and Policy for Planned Events. 3rd Edn., London: Routledge.

G. Bowdin, J. Allen, W. O‟Toole, R. Harris, I. McDonnell, (2006). Events Management, Elsevier Ltd., Great Britain, 2006.

Hall, C.M. (1992). Hallmark Tourist Events: Impacts, Management and Planning. London: Belhaven Press.

J. Tum, P. Norton, J. Nevan Wright, (2005). Management of Event Operations, Elsevier Ltd., Great Britain, 2005.

J. Goldblatt, (2002). Special Events, 3rd Edn., John Wiley & Sons, Inc., New York, 2002.

Moyles, J. (Ed.) (2010). The Excellence of Play, 3rd Edn., Maidenhead, UK: Open University Press.

Torkildsen, G. (2012). Leisure and Recreation Management, 5th Edn., Routledge, London and New York.

Trawick-Smith, J. (2010). Drawing back the lens on play: A frame analysis of young children's play in Puerto Rico. *Early Education and Development*, 21(4): 536–567.

Veal, A.J. (2002). Leisure and Tourism Policy and Planning, 2nd Edn., CABI Publishing.

Vygotsky, L. S. (1978). The role of play in development. In: Mind in Society. (pp. 92-104). Cambridge, MA: Harvard University Press.

Whitebread, D., and Jameson, H. (2010). Play beyond the foundation stage: story-telling, creative writing and self-regulation in able 6-7 year olds. In: J. Moyles (Ed.), The Excellence of Play, 3rd Edn. (pp. 95-107). Maidenhead: Open University Press.

https://courses.lumenlearning.com/suny-principlesmanagement/chapter/what-makes-an-effective-leader/

https://smartchurchmanagement.com/church-event-planning/

https://www.slideshare.net/eiramespi07/theories-of-play

protocols-of-event-management-15-638.jpg (638×479) (slidesharecdn.com)

Suggested Readings

Birkland, T. (1998). Focusing events, mobilization, and agenda setting. *Journal of Public Policy* 18: 53-74.

Fyall A, Wanhill GD, (2008). Tourism: Principles and Practice, 2008.

Getz, D., (2008). Event tourism: Definition, evolution, and research. *Tourism Management*, Volume 29.

Goldblatt, J. J. and Goldblatt, J. (2011). Special Events: A New Generation and the Next Frontier. 6th Edn., Hoboken, N.J.: Wiley.

Ladkin A, Weber K (2010). Career aspects of convention and exhibition professionals in Asia. *International Journal of Contemporary Hospitality Managemen,* 2010; 22

Masterman, G. (2009). Strategic Sports Event Management. 2nd Edn., Olympic ed. Amsterdam: Butterworth-Heinemann.

OECD (2009), The Impact of Culture on Tourism.

Quinn, B. (2013). Key Concepts in Event Management. London: Sage.

Raj, R., Walters, P. & Rashid, T. (2013). Events Management: Principles and Practice. 2nd Edn., London: Sage.

Rogers T. (2013). Conferences and Conventions: A Global Industry, Routledge.

Shone, A. and Parry, B. (2013). Successful Event Management: A Practical Handbook. 4th Edn., Andover: Cengage Learning.

Smith, A. (2012) Events and Urban Regeneration: The Strategic Use of Events to Revitalise Cities. London: Routledge.

Taylor, P. and Torkildsen, G. (2011). Torkildsen's Sport and Leisure Management. 6th Edn., London: Routledge.

Veitch, J., Bagley, S., Ball, K. and Salmon, J. (2006). Where do children usually play? A qualitative study of parents' perceptions of influences on children's active free-play. *Health and Place* 12: 383–393.

Watt, D. C. (1998). Event Management in Leisure and Tourism. Harlow: Addison Wesley Longman.

Yeoman, I. (2004). Festival and Events Management: An International Arts and Culture Perspective. Amsterdam: Elsevier Butterworth-Heinemann.

www.incredibleindia.org

Index